AF291871

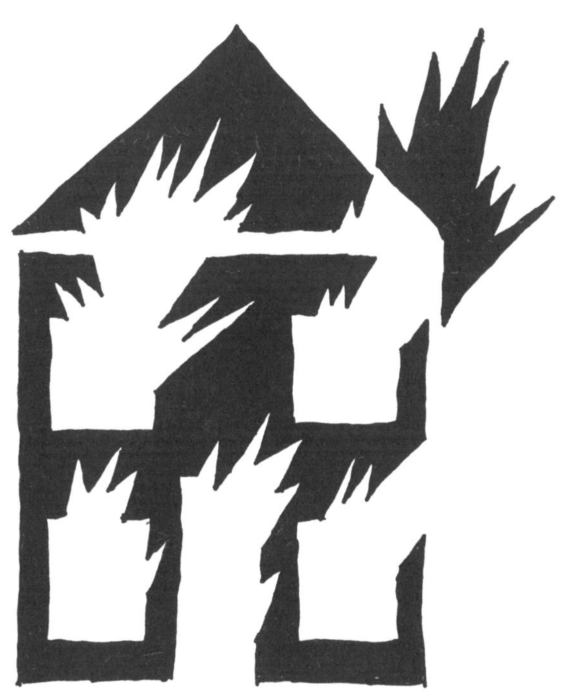

Donald Rodney

A Reader

Foreword

Gilane Tawadros

*Black Art is not just Art produced by Black People.
There is a necessary consciousness that goes with it.*

Donald Rodney first gained visibility as a founding member of the pioneering Blk Art Group: an association of young Black artists, critics and curators formed in Wolverhampton to foreground issues of racism and racial identity through a variety of artistic languages. However, Rodney's wide-ranging practice resists simple categorisation both thematically and through his innovative approach to materials and technical processes. He worked across sculpture, installation, drawing, painting and digital media, experimenting with new materials and technologies throughout his career. Rodney lived with sickle cell anaemia and harnessed his condition to confront the prejudices and injustices surrounding racial identity, Black masculinity, chronic illness and Britain's colonial past. Timed to coincide with 'Donald Rodney: Visceral Canker', a major survey exhibition of his work curated by Robert Leckie and Nicole Yip and presented at Spike Island, Nottingham Contemporary and Whitechapel Gallery, this reader brings together for the first time a selection of texts on the artist covering a period of twenty years, as well as previously unpublished writing by Rodney himself.

In the mid 1990s, Rodney started developing a work called *Autoicon* (pp. 118–119) which, in the event of his death, would continue to make 'original' Donald Rodney artworks. Originally produced as both a website and a CD-ROM, *Autoicon* was not completed until 2000, two years after his death from complications relating to sickle cell disease. 'Consisting of a Java-based AI and neural network', as Richard Birkett describes, 'the platform engages the user in text-based "chat" and provides responses by drawing from a dense body of data related to Rodney, including documentation of artworks, medical records, interviews, images, notes and videos.'[1]

Having been diagnosed with sickle cell at a young age, Rodney lived with the knowledge that he was likely to die prematurely as a result of his condition. His treatment 'involved a relentless cycle of blood transfusions, painkillers and surgery'.[2] Compelled to spend progressively longer spells in hospital, he became increasingly reliant on a group of close friends and artists ironically known as the 'Donald Rodney plc' who assisted him in the fabrication of his artworks and who completed *Autoicon* after his death. Like much of Rodney's work, the piece looks backwards and forwards in time. It harks back to Rodney's days as a student at Slade School Fine Art in the mid 1980s where he studied alongside fellow art student Mike Phillips (who would later work with him on *Autoicon*) and where he would have encountered on a daily basis Jeremy Bentham's Auto-Icon (p. 162), the preserved skeleton of the Victorian philosopher and reformer, dressed in his own clothes, surmounted by a wax head and enclosed in a glass cabinet. It also uncannily anticipates recent developments in AI and machine learning as well as current debates on AI and creativity. *Autoicon* and other late works provide a tantalising glimpse of what might have been Rodney's future trajectory as an artist, continuing his insightful interrogation into questions of race and representation within the wider body politic through bold and pioneering conceptual works.

Rodney's last exhibition, '9 Night in El Dorado' curated by David Thorpe, took place at the South London Gallery in 1997, and was prepared by the artist from his hospital bed in King's College Hospital in south London.

One of the works in the show – *Psalms* (1997, pp. 114–115) – consisted of an unoccupied wheelchair moving around the exhibition space, between the visitors and the artworks, apparently of its own volition. Unable to attend his own exhibition opening, the autonomous wheelchair attended in Rodney's place. This uncanny apparatus would start up, move, stop, turn and start up again, moving in a different direction. In this way, Rodney haunted the exhibition, continuously absent and present.

Determined to defy his own mortality, the artist aspired to have a Donald Rodney wing named in his honour at the Tate Gallery. This has yet to come to fruition but, decades after his untimely death in 1998, Rodney continues to assert his presence through a richly diverse and influential body of work which still inspires successive generations of artists, writers and filmmakers on both sides of the Atlantic.

1   Richard Birkett, *Donald Rodney: Autoicon*, (London: Afterall, 2023). (Excerpt reprinted in this volume, pp. 159–173)

2   Virginia Nimarkoh, 'Image of Pain: Physicality in the Art of Donald Rodney', in *Donald Rodney: Doublethink*, ed. Richard Hylton (London: Autograph, 2003). (Reprinted in this volume, pp. 38–49)

Introduction

Robert Leckie and Nicole Yip

When the idea of a Donald Rodney exhibition first emerged in 2020, we pitched it as a 'dream exhibition' – an exhibition that we, as long-standing admirers of his work, had always wanted to realise, but one that felt sufficiently far-fetched. We had a gut feeling, perhaps due to the conspicuous absence of any kind of museum retrospective at the time, that the practical and conceptual complexities of curating such an exhibition would be significant. An initial conversation with the estate left us no more reassured.

What was abundantly clear from the outset was that the materiality of Rodney's work has always worked both for and against him. From his ingenious approach to materials came pastel paintings on X-rays, sculptures made of human skin, and installations using bodily fluids: a conservator's nightmare. We knew little about what had happened to these works – and the state of the precarious materials from which they were made – in the years that had passed between their production and their placement in various national and regional collections. Equipped with a list of works from the estate, we came to understand that, sadly, much has been lost. We then set out to track down the location, conservation status and availability of all that remains. Fast forward two years of false starts, dead ends, loan requests, negotiations, costings and concessions until, at last, we were adequately confident we could secure enough work to make a survey show worthwhile.

Meanwhile, as we delved deeper into our research on Rodney's life and work, the more convinced we became of the need for a major exhibition that would help cement his place as a vital figure in the history of British art. Here was an artist whose work has been widely acknowledged as influential, but who had not had a significant public presentation since 2008, when Iniva mounted *Donald Rodney: In Retrospect* on the 10-year anniversary of his death. We ourselves are of a generation of artists and curators for whom Rodney occupies a semi-mythical status: we had read about his work in books, heard it cited by peers, seen images on the internet, but had never had that crucial opportunity to experience it firsthand.

The more we discovered, the more we also came to recognise the biases and assumptions that have sometimes distorted how Rodney's work has been contextualised and understood. Though the entanglements of issues of race and representation, illness and medicalisation undoubtedly form an important spine of his practice, these are not the only terms through which his work can be read. It felt equally necessary to invite other routes through his practice, including an appreciation of his philosophical approach to questions of the self and personhood; his anticipation of contemporary discourses around Black technopoetics, artificial intelligence and machine learning; and the ways in which he destabilised singular notions of artist as auteur, to name but a few.

One key aspect for us has been the formal, conceptual and technological innovation to which Rodney was committed throughout his life. Take, for example, the use of medical tubing in *Visceral Canker* (the work after which we titled the show, pp. 62, 90–91). While it is obviously indebted to his experiences of hospitalisation, it is not *about* these experiences per se. It is more a reflection of how, for Rodney, the hospital became the studio, and so the materials of medicalisation became the materials of artmaking.

The fact that the interpretation of his work remains contested today is a sign of its continued potency. It is also a result of the fact that many of the people who have written about Rodney's work knew him intimately and cared for him deeply, as was clear in how they supported and challenged us along the way. In some cases, they even helped him make the work in the first place. This has made navigating the existing scholarship (some of which is reproduced in this book) an insightful, but at times, overwhelming process. It even left us questioning if re-presenting the work today made any sense, and if we were the right people to be leading the task. In the end, it was Diane Symons and Keith Piper from the estate who emboldened us to continue, and we feel profoundly indebted to their trust in us, and support throughout. Our impulse has always been to bring the work together for a new generation of audiences, including ourselves; in hindsight, we are glad to have played a small part in enabling Rodney's work to live a new life, if only temporarily.

Our greatest regret through all of this is that we never got to meet Rodney himself during his lifetime. This is especially true given that everyone who knew him always has such a good story to tell. From a distance, we can only cherish – and continue to grapple with – his surviving work, catching glimpses of his personality along the way, through his notebooks, video interviews and papers. In many cases, all we have are ideas and fragments, some realised and others not, and it's clear to us that they don't tell the whole story, far from it. As Rodney said in response to the question 'are you there yet?' when he was interviewed for *The Voice* the year before his death:

'God, nowhere near! I'll know when you interview me and ask me what it's like to be there. I wonder where 'there' is? It's like Eldorado.'[1]

1   Kewesa Hennessy, 'Sweet as Sculpture: Interview with Donald Rodney', *The Voice* (1 September, 1997) 26.

In Search of El Dorado

Keith Piper

In September 1997, at the South London Gallery, the artist Donald Gladstone Rodney staged an exhibition of what was to be his final body of work. The exhibition was titled '9 Night in Eldorado', referencing the traditional Jamaican period of mourning following the death of a loved one. For the artist, it re-evoked memories of sitting with his father around a flickering television to watch the classic 1966 Western *El Dorado*. The film was a favourite of Donald's father – a man who had boarded a boat from Jamaica to England in 1958 to test the promised embrace of the 'mother country'.

My own father, who had embarked on a similar journey in the early 1950s, would often bemoan the laying to rest of his siblings and peers in what he termed 'the cold soil of England', as if this unrealised El Dorado would leave their souls restless. Donald's father died in 1995, two years before the exhibition opened. Already suffering from the effects of sickle cell anaemia that would increasingly impact his body, Donald had been too ill to attend his father's nine night. His absence from this event shaped his preparations for his 1997 exhibition and are made explicit in two connected, haunting, landmark works that emerged for the first time in that show: *My Mother. My Father. My Sister. My Brother* (1997, p. 103) and *In the House of My Father* (1997, p. 102).

Donald Rodney first came to visibility as a member of the Blk Art Group, a collective of art students of Black Caribbean descent that was active during the first half of the 1980s. The group was originally conceived by Eddie Chambers while a teenager in the West Midlands in the late 1970s, and already in fledgling form when he took up a place on the art foundation course at Lanchester Polytechnic in Coventry in 1979.

I attended the same foundation course there after studying at the Moseley School of Art, a small secondary school specialising in art education, and the closest school to my parents' home in what is now Birmingham's 'Balti Belt'. For a shy young boy who was 'good at drawing', it was an almost comfortable fit. I left this school in 1979, following the political ruptures of the Winter of Discontent, the rise of the far right and the election of Margaret Thatcher. My personal political evolution was ready to recognise Eddie as a fellow traveller, and he would reluctantly come to recognise me as the same.

In Coventry, I became involved in the exhibition that Eddie was organising, an inaugural show for the group titled 'Black Art an' Done' at

Wolverhampton Art Gallery. Opening on 9 June 1981, the show featured work by Dominic Dawes, Ian Palmer, Andrew Hazel, Eddie Chambers and myself. This collective of artists, originally called Wolverhampton Young Black Artists, began to evolve its line-up through a series of follow-on exhibitions and events with artists such as Claudette Johnson and Marlene Smith becoming involved. These provided visibility to a home-grown politicised art practice that became the hallmark of what came to be known as the Blk Art Group.

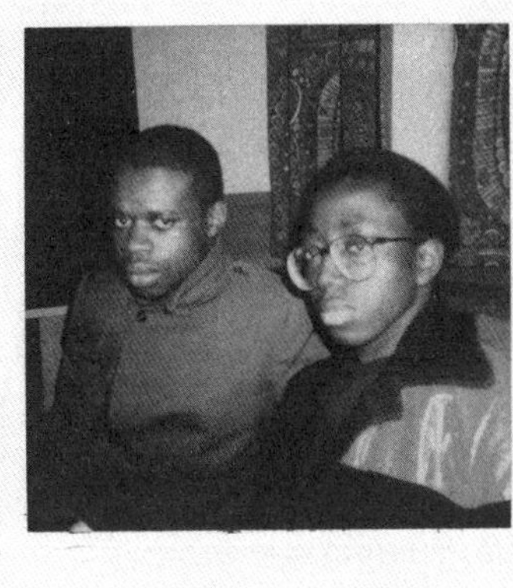

Keith Piper (left) and Donald Rodney (right) in their student days in Nottingham, 1980s

By the time the exhibition was staged, Eddie and I had both left Coventry – he had gone to Sunderland Polytechnic, and I moved to Trent Polytechnic in Nottingham. One of the harsh realities experienced by Black art students in the early 1980s was isolation. Almost invariably, the members of the group were the only artists of colour, or one of a very small number, at their respective institutions. Unusually, Trent recruited four art students of Caribbean descent in their 1981 intake. Already a nagging evangelist for Black artists to accept their 'responsibility' to protest racism and educate Black people, I immediately made myself unpopular among these young Black students, who, for the most part, wanted to be left alone to exercise their freedom to make their art. However, one such student appeared more open to what Chambers and I had to say about art and politics.

In many ways, this artist seemed least likely to welcome our particular 'gospel'. Loud and gregarious, comedic, flirtatious and constantly surrounded by fashionable young women from Knitwear or Theatre Design, he was already cultivating his sartorial style as an artist with trilby hat and baggy clothes. This was the young Donald Rodney.

Already immensely knowledgeable about contemporary art – and for a brief period relatively unimpacted by the debilitating effects of the sickle cell anaemia that had blighted his childhood – Donald launched himself into art-making on an ambitious scale. When he arrived at Nottingham's Trent Polytechnic, he was painting boldly coloured, wax encaustic flowers in the vein of Jean-Michel Basquiat, but, following conversations with Chambers, his content evolved into the more subversively political 'cowboy paintings', such as *How the West was Won* (1982, p. 65). This would mark the start of

Donald's eclectic and innovative use of materials, ranging from hospital sheets and discarded X-rays to plaster casts, robotics, photography and tissue from his own body.

Our formative years in Nottingham impacted our practice in complex ways. We shared a flat in the then-notorious Hyson Green area of Nottingham with Gary Stewart, a BA Electronics student at Trent and old school friend. In this shared flat, awash with the debris one would expect from three young men in their early twenties, multiple creative and political influences collided, overlapped and synthesised. Our home was the postal headquarters and meeting place for the Blk Art Group, and also for peers from across our widening social sphere.

It was from this space, central to every fight and exchange of gossip, that Donald would hold court. He was, however, beginning to suffer from his condition and its corrosive effects on his joints and mobility. His bed was moved to the downstairs living room, and from here he developed his characteristic mode of practice. He worked intensely in sketchbooks to plan ever more ambitious work and developed 'modular' ways of creating art that could be undertaken from bed – using, for instance, individual sheets of X-ray material to build up massive, gridded works such as *Britannia Hospital 3* (1988, pp. 76–77). He also worked with the help and support of others. Nottingham was where Donald connected with fellow Fine Art student Diane Symons, who was to become his life partner and central to his creative support network.

Donald was to continue this way of working after he moved to London to take up a place on the postgraduate course at the Slade School of Fine Art. Through bouts of illness, he increasingly used the fragility of his body as a metaphor for social and political systems in crisis, exploring these themes in a series of exhibitions that were realised via his skilled management of a growing network of fellow artists, enablers and curators.

Beyond this group, humorously referred to as 'Donald Rodney plc', Donald's other supportive network was provided by his expansive family. He was the youngest of twelve siblings who were split between Smethwick in the West Midlands and Jamaica, where many of his older siblings had grown into adulthood. This was a complexly woven family, steeped in the rich traditions and community of Jamaican Pentecostalism with its ties to knowledge, faith, storytelling and generational links. It was also a family sadly familiar with the ravages of sickle cell. Donald's sister was on a cycle of crisis and hospitalisation that mirrored his own, and he spoke of his older siblings born in Jamaica, who, lacking access to the medical interventions available in the UK, had passed away from the illness.

His family's influence is articulated in its greatest clarity and complexity in the two key works of the 1997 '9 Night in Eldorado' exhibition. *My Mother.*

                    In Search of El Dorado

My Father. My Sister. My Brother is an object of incredible fragility, kept in hermetically sealed archival conditions in the vaults of the National Museum of Wales. The human tissue from which it is constructed is the skin that grew over an abscess on the artist's thigh, a protective layer formed over the site of trauma, shed during the act of slow, painful healing. The dressmaker's pins that hold this protective structure together seem to allude, almost with a tinge of violence, to many processes – religious, ritualist and the numerous medical interventions to which Donald's body was subjected to ward off collapse. Could this complex, multi-layered work, this assemblage of protective tissue allowing the traumatised flesh beneath it to regenerate, mirror the role of the family: the protective mechanism of the mother, father, sister and brother, who, while themselves appearing flimsy and transitory, still offer protection at the most intimate of levels?

If this reading is carried into the accompanying photographic work, taken by photographer Andra Nelki while Donald was in King's College Hospital, we can begin to weave a host of interpretive narrations around the work. In the photograph, the tiny protective skin house is balanced delicately in the artist's outstretched hand. Interestingly, this photo was originally intended as one of a pair. The other would have seen the small structure balanced on the artist's tongue, an image that speaks directly to the Christian ritual of communion with which Donald would have been familiar.

I would speculate that Donald's understanding of this metaphor of Christ's body, as fragmented but also protective and redemptive, is key to the reading of this work. The skin house represents the protective mechanism of the family and the support for healing that it provides. Like the bread broken in the act of Communion, it may look small, embattled and fragile, but is symbolic of a larger series of bonds.

Within this metaphor, the title *In the House of My Father* can resonate in a range of directions. It might reference the nostalgia of a lost moment when this protective mechanism – the mother, the father, the sister and the brother – could be engaged with (or cradled delicately in recognition of its fragility) within the domestic space, under the traditional patriarchal leadership of his father. The title could also refer to the words attributed to Jesus in the Gospel of John: 'In my Father's house there are many mansions ... I go to prepare a place for you'. This is a promise of a protective space, a promised land, an El Dorado, within the 'house of the father'. The fact that for Donald Rodney, this promised mansion, this site of reward, protection and replenishment, was constructed from the ephemeral stuff of his own body, is indicative of the immense symbolic, poetic and political power of his work.

First published in *Tate Etc.*, issue 57, (Spring 2023) 104–107.

Enter at Your Own Risk: Artist-as-Trickster-as-Prophet-as-Historian-as-Witness-as-Freedom-Fighter-as-Artist: Donald Rodney

Celeste-Marie Bernier

'From the National Front throwing petrol bombs into people's homes, to the arbitrary police intrusions into homes like Cherry Groce's and Cynthia Jarrett's [. . .] to the deaths of John Shorthouse, Winston Brown and Colin Roach, all of whom died as a result of contact with the police, we are experiencing an infringement of our civil liberties and we ought to be concerned about our welfare.'[1]

So reads Donald Rodney's 1989 summary of the state of Black British life in a white racist UK. A joint artist statement issued by Keith Piper and Donald Rodney further reveals: 'Clinton McCurbin, Cynthia Jarret, Cherry Groce are just a few of the names that come readily to hand when creating a list of recent State atrocities. There is an African proverb that says "An injury to one is an injury to all," there is also, dear reader, another African proverb that reads NO "NEXT" TIME NO "NEXT" TIME.'[2] Warring against the spectre of any 'NEXT TIME', Rodney's and Piper's denunciation of discriminatory police activities applies equally to acts of atrocity that continue to be perpetrated in Britain and to the traumatising situation in the United States, where ongoing protests against the mass torture and death of Black women, children and men at the hands of government officials have inspired the Black Lives Matter movement and a multitude of contemporary civil rights struggles.

A leading member of the Blk Art Group in the UK, Rodney described the importance of image-making as a catalyst for social and political change:

> 'The Black Art Movement tackles the general collapse of the black spirit of self and tries to rebuild that consciousness and pride, and to produce something of immense value to the black psyche. [. . .] We must now build a new and positive self-image. [. . .] Racism in the American and British context has progressed into the very fabric of their individual societies.'

According to his diagnosis, 'Within the Black British perspective we can see certain parallels between the search for the black aesthetic in America.' Yet while he theorised points of social, political and cultural 'parallel' by endorsing a working transatlantic definition of a 'black aesthetic', he ultimately focused on a UK context: 'Black militancy within the art world can be seen as a constructive and powerful weapon against the vicious institutionalised racism endemic in British cultural identity.'[3]

'I'm using my own personal experience as a means of relating other experiences whether they are historic or current.' Rodney placed a premium on autobiographical experiences as conjoined with historical and political content: 'The specific message is just bringing home issues which are already there but I'm trying to look beneath the surface of a lot of things.[4] He pioneered an alternative visual and textual lexicon to 'bring issues home', doing justice to his realisation that 'our flesh become our worth, dehumanised, burned & chained. Forced to breed & work, building empire lands that foam at the mouth with greed & evil.'[5] He was constantly imaginatively excavating 'beneath the surface' of African diasporic social, political, ideological and art historical realities to dramatise Black bodies 'dehumanised, burned & chained.' The handful of critics who have produced pioneering scholarship on Rodney include John Akomfrah, Jane Bilton, Eddie Chambers, Stuart Hall, Lubaina Himid, Richard Hylton, Virginia Nimarkoh, Keith Piper, Adeola Solanke, Maud Sulter and Diane Symons. We confront very real gaps in the art historical archive as we are dealing for the most part with reproductions of works that no longer survive. As Piper notes, 'Much of Rodney's early work has been lost, fragmented or destroyed, existing now only as photographic documentation.'[6]

'Black History is forever haunted by the insidious evel [*sic*] of the European Trade in Slaves,' Rodney wrote in *Sketchbook No. 12* (1986). He laboured to denounce this 'insidious evel' across his bodies of work, including in one notable site-specific installation, *Visceral Canker* (1990, pp. 62, 90–91), a two-part work he mounted on plywood and erected in the Battery at Mount Edgecombe in Plymouth, UK. The work names and shames British monarchical culpability for the slave trade by displaying, only to debunk, the mythological pretensions of the 'heraldic Coats of Arms of Sir John Hawkins, a Plymouth-based buccaneer and slave-trader, and of his patron Elizabeth I.' Writing in *Sketchbook No. 34* (1990), he confirmed the inspiration undergirding this work:

> 'HAWKINS / FIRST COMMERCIAL SLAVER / GIVEN AWARDS AND COMMISSIONS FROM ELIZABETH 1ST / COAT OF ARMS FEATURED SLAVES / COAT OF ARMS REMOVED FROM TOWN HALL YEARS LATER/ ELIZABETH I / COMMISSIONED HAWKINS / EXPANDED THE BRITISH EMPIRE / WITH HER NAVY / MADE THE FIRST LEGISLATION / LIMITING BLACK EMMIGRATION [*sic*] / INTO BRITAIN.'

In his handwritten funding application for the work, he sheds light on his experimental aesthetics and radical political vision: 'MY WORK WOULD BE AN ATTEMPT AT PEELING AWAY THE SKIN OF THE CULTURE OF 'PROTECTION AND DEFENCE,' TO EXPOSE ITS REALITY, ITS GUTS ITS BONES AND RAW NERVES, IN ATTEMPT TO REVEAL THE NAKED TRUTH IN ALL ITS COMPLEXITY.'[7]

Playing out his self-appointed roles as artist, historian, witness, archivist, activist, and even *ad hoc* forensic pathologist, Rodney in *Visceral Canker* (1990) performs an autopsy on the immorality of a defunct nation in order to diagnose the 'naked truth' regarding slavery as a centuries-long crime against humanity. Not only Rodney's art-making and research skills are on show here, but also those of his partner, Diane Symons, and her mother. Inspired by their extensive research in local archives, Rodney reworked Elizabeth I's coat of arms by writing the Latin inscription 'SEMPER EADEM' in black lettering on a white backdrop. In this, he testifies not to monarchical honour but a dishonour that is 'always the same' due to the historical reality of the transatlantic slave trade as a British-originated, British-maintained and British-perpetuated institution. He also revives the historical designs for John Hawkins' coat of arms by replacing the hand-drawn figure of a physically bound enslaved Black man with an individual rendered in minimal outline, in full colour and with a heightened musculature. In a bold departure from the original sixteenth-century design as created by a white artist, he includes the heads and upper torsos of not one but four shackled figures; the three additional Black subjects wearing neck restraints render Hawkins' moral guilt obvious:

'I suddenly discovered his coat of arms which is a quite horrendous piece of heraldry with slaves enchained in neck braces and held on with manacles. [. . .] I read more about it and found that he was actually granted the right to change his heraldry from Queen Elizabeth the 1st.'[8]

He expresses his horror that Hawkins' 'exploits within slavery' not only gained the royal seal of approval but were commemorated in official iconography. Not content with buying and selling Black women, men and children, white British aristocrats unapologetically paraded enslaved Black subjects as trophies in mainstream iconography as well.

As Rodney outlined in his initial proposal for *Visceral Canker*, 'THE MOST IMPORTANT PART OF THE INSTALLATION WOULD BE A TUBULAR REWORKING OF JOHN HAWKINS'S COAT OF ARMS WITH ITS IMAGES OF SLAVES WITH NECK MANICLES [*sic*]. [. . .] THE COAT OF ARMS WOULD BE A CIRCUIT OF TUBES OPERATED BY A PUMP PUMPING BLOOD THROUGH THE COMPLETE IMAGE. [. . .] THE PIECE WOULD HAVE TO BE [IN] A SEALED REFRIDGERATED [*sic*] UNIT CONTAINING FOUR UNITS OF MY OWN BLOOD, OBTAINED FROM MY MONTHLY EXCHANGE TRANSFUSIONS.'[9] To render his symbolic and iconographic denunciation of white British slaveholding practices viscerally palpable, he emphasised that his 'own blood' would be 'pumped round the coat of arms, held in plastic and completely out of reach of the public' – a boldly autobiographical 'tangible connection between me and that sort of history.'[10] But it was not to be. The 'people from the council [. . .] started to get squeamish.' The 'people who run Mount Edgecombe decided there was a risk and I have had to use red dye instead.' He soon realised that 'if I decided to have blood in I would be out of the project entirely.' As one reporter wrote, Rodney 'almost decided to pull out of the project because he felt he was being censored.'[11] For Rodney, the inclusion of his own blood was fundamental to his political, social, historical, and cultural statement regarding the very literal ways in which a chronic medical condition was a direct consequence of the transatlantic slave trade. Insisting on the right 'to use my own blood in this pumping system', Rodney understood that he inspired 'squeamishness' in government officials in part because 'I suffer from sickle cell anaemia, a blood condition almost exclusive to Afro-Caribbean people', a 'condition [that] renders the defence systems of the body inadequate, and necessitates a regular change of blood.' His conception of *Visceral Canker* 'was developed in response to my perception of the uselessness of the fort, which was built as part of a defence system along the south coast of Britain in the mid-19th century.'[12] For the 'uselessness of the fort' read the mortality of his own body. 'The only time I thought about dying' came as a result, he says, of 'constantly being told how difficult' one particular 'operation was going to be and how much blood they were going to need.'[13] The fact that the 'Plymouth City Council ruled against the use of my own blood in this work because they claimed it might cause unnecessary offence to public sensibility' meant that 'fake blood, as used in medical demonstrations, was therefore substituted.'[14] Resisting white racist ignorance surrounding 'sickle cell anemia [which] is not well understood among the majority of doctors in Britain,' his emotional trauma was a platform for his political dissidence: 'I'm using the metaphor of illness as a catalyst for other issues.'[15] To ensure that 'the body politic and disease imagery can be read against social order, economics, political concerns,' he imagined his 'own blood' as securing 'A COMPLEX ELOQUENT EXPLORATION IN THE BODY CULTURE OF THE BRITISH STATE AND BLACK HISTORY.'[16] He sought to pioneer a new 'lexicon of liberation' in order to establish 'a visual discourse that would produce meaning without mimicking Western Art tradition.'[17] In his war against the stranglehold exerted by 'Our Master's Voice,' he fought to do justice to 'Our Slave's history.' In other works, over the decades, he incorporated divergent fine art and found materials, from paint to X-rays, electronic parts, disused objects, recycled mainstream iconography, and even his own flesh and blood. In so doing, he experienced an epiphany: 'I no longer had to use the language given to me by western art traditions.'[18]

'I cannot let my brush be weak and each time I paint visions of my ancestors flood my mind of my stolen history', Rodney testifies in *Sketchbook No. 2* (1982–83). A few years later, he assumed the role of radically revisionist Black historian in *Sketchbook No. 19* (1987): 'Anyway dear reader forming in the womb of middle England were children of uncontrollable energy and black fury. Being born in flames. Being born in poverty Being born into a moral[1]y bankrupt system and society and physical and emotional slavery.' Nowhere is Rodney's testament to Britain as a 'a morally bankrupt system and society' in which his denunciation of Black people's exposure to 'physical and emotional slavery' more palpable than in his epic-size works *Britannia Hospital 2* and *Britannia Hospital 3* (both 1988, pp. 75–77) made from oil pastel on X-rays. *Britannia Hospital 2* frankly depicts a Black woman's pain – she seems to be suffering unbearable grief or loss – via a careful delineation of her emotionally contorted physiognomy, and an orange red flame burning in the palm of her right hand. As Rodney explains regarding this use of spiritual symbolism, 'flames coming from the hands' bear witness to 'the soul burning' and 'wanting to testify'. He prophesied that 'salvation will blaze a flame burning so Red.'[19] To clearly render associations of Black female bodies with martyrdom, and of Black-generated artworks with marginalisation, he typically pieced together fragmented sections. Here he attached each of

　　　　　　　　　　　Enter at Your Own Risk

his X-rays with strands of cellophane tape that are now peeling away. The gesture confirms the extent to which it was not only his subject matter but his artworks themselves that would remain under threat in a white racist UK.

'Scenes from Britannia Hospital', Rodney notes in *Sketchbook No. 23*, summarising his painterly vision as an: 'Imaginary portrait of the artist after being transfer[r]ed from a cell in Stoke Newington Police station to a high security intensive care ward on Britannia Hospital.' He begins but does not complete his thought that 'any similarity between these poisoned circumstances and those of young black man is entire[l]y.' He makes viscerally, emotionally and politically clear his own potential 'similarities' with men mortally wounded in police custody. Writing of Colin Roach, who died in 'Stoke Newington Police station' following a 'blasted scull [*sic*]' caused by a 'gunshot' wound, he scoffs at the police officer's testimony suggesting that 'Colin committed suiside [*sic*]': 'The surg[e]ons found no finger prints of blood on the gun.' In *Britannia Hospital 3* (1998, pp. 76–77), Rodney confirms his determination to represent a 'portrait of the Artist in a cell in Stoke Newington Police Station Watched by empty silluetes [*sic*].'[20] He also shows his indebtedness to Frida Kahlo in his search for a new visual language in which to dramatise bodily pain and physical disability. At the far left of this work, he reproduces one of her self-portraits in which she represented her nude body as imprisoned within a steel support, referring to her injuries, which resulted not from white murderous actions but from a terrible accident. He shores up his protest against Black suffering at the hands of white racists by refusing to represent her exposure to pain in isolation – next to her wounded body is a figure of a Black man lying prostrate in a hospital bed. 'Watched by empty silluetes [*sic*]', he is exposed to the murderous actions of a spectral uniformed officer of the SPG, the now-defunct Special Patrol Group, still infamous among Black British communities. This force was based in London and consisted of racially prejudiced officers who routinely engaged in 'stop and search' acts of violent suppression against revolutionary dissidence. His eyeless sockets and deathlike pallor suggest he is no living human figure. He reaches toward the Black man's face with a hand clutching a metal implement, as he is about to impart a mortal injury.

We are denied access to Rodney's Black subject's face, as he delineates the eyes, nose and mouth according to generalised features that suggest that he is symbolic – not an individual but a representative type. For Rodney, the Black male figure functioned less as an individual in his own right and more as a catalyst for a denunciation of white depredations and abuses terrorising Black lives. He also chose to delineate his figure's enlarged hands in a gesture of self-protection – a visual confirmation of his determination to resist white destruction. A Black female nurse also reaches out her hand to suggest she

is giving life rather than acting as an emissary of death. Offering hope in the
face of despair, she attempts to provide succour and support to her patient.
Writing of *Britannia Hospital 3*, Rodney cryptically admitted to 'Never having
being cloaked with a desire to create or sucomb to the complex contradictory
allure wich shrouds the stance of militant black male protest. [*sic*]'[21] To do
justice to scenes not only of 'militant black male' but militant female 'protest',
as Lubaina Himid emphasises, Rodney took 'the audience by the scruff of
the neck and spectacularly revealed a truth. [...] His X-ray pictures, eerie in
their secret visual codes, overlayed with bright sharp strong realism, are the
perfect metaphor of Britain as a sick nation.'[22] For Maud Sulter, 'The potency
of the X-ray as a metaphor evokes death, fragility, exposure, insight.' Sulter
theorised the onus Rodney placed on the personal as political: 'The layering of
image and X-ray, the complementary use of oil pastel as a part of the surface,
all evoke the body. A body politic. A site of struggle. The location of the
transformation of power to action.'[23]

'If anything was evil my skin was', Rodney declares in *Sketchbook No. 5*
(1983–84). He admits to 'a strange loathing and distaste for the flesh of
my flesh'. He confronts his body as a site of suffering due to the damaging
psychological toll exerted by white racist ideologies that resulted in
internalised self-hatred. As a result, he redefined the genre of self-portraiture
toward the end of his life. He dispensed with his use of the X-ray to penetrate
beneath 'the surface of a lot of things' by switching to an 'an electron
microscope' to create his photographic triptych *Flesh of My Flesh* (1996,
pp. 100–101). In this piece he juxtaposes his examination of 'two human hairs',
one belonging to himself and the other to the white British artist Rose Finn-
Kelcey, with an intimate close-up of his skin as roughly sewn up by a white
surgeon following one of his many operations. As Virginia Nimarkoh writes
of Rodney's intimate view of his 'scarred thigh', even a cursory examination
reveals that 'by medical standards, the scar was exceptionally poor in the sense
that it was evidence of malpractice: over-stitching by a reckless surgeon who
apparently felt that Black skin required more work since it was "tougher" than
White skin.'[24] Rodney gives the lie to white racist claims regarding immutable
differences between Black and white bodies by juxtaposing his own and
Finn-Kelcey's hair strands to show that they are identical under microscopic
examination. He betrays the illusory foundations of a socially constructed
surface that denies an anatomical reality as characterised by biological
sameness rather than immutable differences. He refuses to shy away from his
own body as a site of wounding by relying on the photographic detailing of the
serrated edges of his enlarged scar. Here he testifies to entrenched hierarchical
systems based on white supremacist categorisations that continue to objectify,
dehumanise and mortally endanger Black bodies.

 Enter at Your Own Risk

Another artwork in which Rodney used his own hair is the no longer surviving *Memory Jar* (n.d.), in which he combined strands of his hair with milk – ensuring that the piece would organically change over time – as a meditation on human mortality and fragility. At the same time, it evokes the African diasporic tradition of 'memory jar' making. Over the centuries, African, African Caribbean and African American women and men, enslaved and free, made 'memory jars' full of personally owned and/or salvaged objects as substitute grave markers, incisive testaments to individual lives as lived beyond the pale of official record keeping. Memory jars function as surrogate records, alternative histories and substitute archives by honouring ancestors whose bodies were denied access to an official resting place due to legal, economic and social systems of racist exclusion.

In a related work, *Land of Milk and Honey II* (1997, p. 109) the artist mixed milk, honey and British coins in a monumental tank resembling the door of a house – a reference to slavery, specifically the 'doors of no return' of the Middle Passage and African diasporic migration. As Sonia Boyce explains, *Land of Milk and Honey II* is a mythological descriptor of Britain as a nation of possibility and 'resonates for a generation of West Indians who settled in Britain during the 1950s and 1960s.' For Boyce, the evocative phrase 'Land of Milk and Honey' 'brims over with promise. The comfort of the mother's body. Luxuriating in the labours of the land.'

But this utopian promise is ultimately revealed as a dystopian threat with a racist underbelly. 'Exposed to the light of day', observes Boyce, 'the promise turns sour. Under a magnifying glass the melting pot reveals unsettled layers,

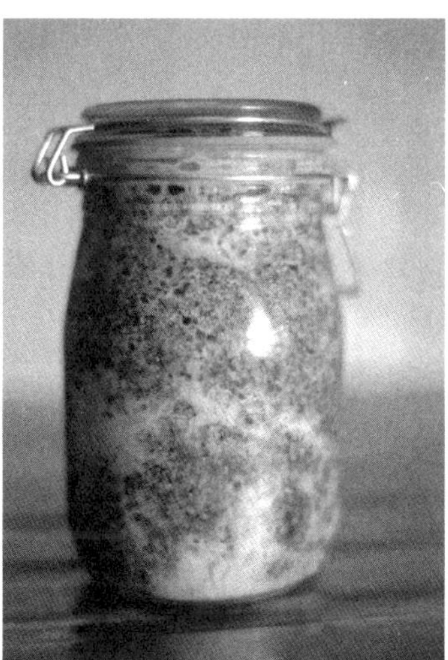

Memory Jar, n.d.
Milk, hair and glass jar mixed media assemblage
Approx. 25 × 13 × 13 cm, no longer extant

sometimes tinged with quiet beauty and inconsistencies.[25] As Rodney himself clarified: 'What happened in this work was that it was sealed bet after a while the milk and honey started to go off and started to change and it became more and more corrupt.' It became, indeed, a testament to the loss of hope among migrant African diasporic communities: 'To see the piece slowly changing and becoming more and more horrible as time went on', by 'changing from this beautiful white of the milk to this greens and blues' made it 'a symbolic piece' – politically and socially – about his family's life in Britain. Of his mother and father, Rodney insisted, 'they were only economic exiles. They just wanted to be here to earn some money, making things better for themselves and their family, then go back to Jamaica or do whatever, and they didn't intend to stay.'[26]

'MY MORTALITY IS SMILING AND MY ART IS CRYING', Rodney declared in *Sketchbook No. 30* (1989), about a decade before his death. And in *Sketchbook No. 9* (1986) he wrote, 'I haven't worked for the past couple of days. It's hard to produce the words that capture the moment of pain.' He noted elsewhere regarding the rationale for his bodies of work: 'I'm trying to portray physical pain, the kind of pain that I have experienced.'[27] He consistently sought out an alternative visual language in which to debunk racist mythologies: 'In its quest for knowledge, science tends to identify and categorise other races.' His determination to expose as fallacious the widely held 'conception' that 'the pain threshold' is 'different for black and white people' remained urgent.[28] In 1997, just months before he died, Rodney turned away from X-rays, oil pastel and photography to create two artworks from his own skin, *My Mother. My Father. My Sister. My Brother* (p. 103) and *In The House of My Father* (p. 102). The first of these is a diminutive form of a family home, delicately held together with pins and mounted on a glass shelf. The second artwork is a photograph showing the same 'skin house' lying in the palm of the artist's hand, which is resting on a white hospital bed sheet. He explained, 'It's about the fragility of the human body [. . .] and of the human ego.' His own skin became his canvas in his desire to show how 'bodies can be suddenly broken down by just a few cells working the wrong way.'[29] He included the following poetic fragment in *Sketchbook: No. 48* (1997–98), his last surviving sketch-book: 'Sugar cube castle / Skin house / Suit of armour / Protection / Wounded.' As Diane Symons confirms, Rodney's 'skin house' bore witness to the biological legacies of transatlantic slavery, the traumatising realisation that 'contained within the bloodlines of inheritance are the genes responsible for the artist's illness sickle cell anaemia and the memories of the slave trade.' As she writes, and as Rodney believed, '[h]ouses and wealth are built out of bodies and souls of his ancestors and this skin house is also presented as a personal memorial, the result of personal and historical trauma.'[30]

                    Enter at Your Own Risk

'Perhaps I should stop making art that is so loaded with critical political weight. Perhaps I should try to look at the ordinary the mundane and challenge the human aspects in all of us. Beauty love. Fear hates colour and joy mistakes and life as we live it with all its complexities and contradictions Art and its day to day relationships its umbelical conection to our existance [sic]'. So reads the last declaration Rodney included In *Sketchbook No. 48*. He engages in soul-searching self-critique: 'I spend too much time searching for a fresh vein on our day-to-day relationships, looking at the blank wall and then attempting to fill it with new work'. Rather, he tells himself, 'I should look at the universal, searching the areas and subjects that art and artists have explored through time. Subjects as wide and full of scope as life, beauty, love, hate and fear and loathing.' And yet 'hate and fear and loathing' were a definitive part of his aesthetic practice. This includes an artwork he was denied the opportunity to create due to his premature death. 'I'll be working on a model of the Tate Gallery made from sugar cubes next year', he informed a newspaper reporter. 'They made their money from sugar from the Commonwealth and by patenting the sugar cube. It's based on slave trade history and since it's the gallery's centenary next year they should exhibit the piece.' Of their strategies of white racist exclusion, he noted: 'They have to give a darkie a go at putting something in the gallery, it's usually White boys from Goldsmiths.'[31] In *Sketchbook No. 12* (1986) he writes of 'Culture Shock / . . . . / Tate Gallery with its [. . .] parifiinallia that dipict [*sic*] it as the store house of national endeavour in imperialism and colonialism'. Elsewhere he confirmed:

> 'I've always found the Tate Gallery full of contradictions and ironies [. . .]. When you go there, there's hardly any work on show by a Black artist but the majority of the security guards are black men sitting next to works of art of great value and outside we sort of wander the streets whatever of no value at all.'

Hoping to galvanise white mainstream recognition of missing histories of enslaved Black labour, Rodney noted, '[t]he history of the Tate is that of the slave trade and sugar and sugar plantations and I wanted to make a scale model of the Tate gallery around 5 to 6 feet tall out of sugar cubes and around it I would place the security guards and they would be my tribute to the Tate and its history.'[32] While Rodney's death prevented him from creating this work, his theorisation of the Tate Gallery's – now Tate Britain's – racist myopia is not lost on numerous other Black British artists. Lubaina Himid observes, 'Tate does not do enough to reflect the substantial and significant work being made by artists from the black diaspora.'[33] Eddie Chambers argues:

'No single institution represented the perceived ongoing alienation of Black artists and large number of Black people in general from the mainstream more than the Tate.'[34] As a national repository arguably still favouring 'white boys from Goldsmiths' – award and nomination of Lubaina Himid and Hurvin Anderson for the 2017 Turner Prize notwithstanding – there is no little irony in the fact that the Tate Archive now hold the entirety of the Donald Rodney papers, which were generously bequeathed by his estate.[35]

'I am the last Painter because / With this brush drenched in the Blood Red of my peoples pain, with this brush glowing gold, with my peoples aspirations with this brush harvest green of my peoples land I herald a new spirit of rebellion and capitolist [*sic*] imperialist walls shall come tumbling down there is only ever one way out Death or Victory', Rodney declared in *Sketchbook No. 2* (1982–83). Working to do justice to a 'new spirit of rebellion', he confirmed in *Sketchbook No. 8* (1985): 'I see the need to create or participate in a type of Black Art that clearly and eloquently defines the course or courses to be taken to establish a new self pride.' And in *Sketchbook No. 9* (1986), 'Once upon a time they used to own slaves Nowadays they Just Rent us. [. . .] 400 years had put the fear of the slave master in me I've been been beaten into submission whilst fear and loathing in the heart of the beast drips blood from my ghetto. Call me victim number one. This wreckage I call me is desised sick and laseration with self inflicted wounds [*sic*]'. Rodney's pioneering 'Black lexicons of liberation' bear artful witness to the 'wreckage I call me'. Black bodies take centre stage as sights and sites of scarring and trauma, reflecting Rodney's realisation that survival is no measure of success: 'Oppression is worse than the grave / Better to die for a noble cause than to live and die a slave.'[36]

First published in *Stick to the Skin: African-American and Black British Art, 1965–2015* (Berkely: University of California Press, 2019) 122–28.

                    Enter at Your Own Risk

1   Unless otherwise noted, all Rodney sketchbooks cited in this chapter are located in the Donald Rodney Papers, Tate Britain. Because they are not paginated, in the interest of saving space, I will refrain from citing them as sources here in the notes when the pertinent information is all in the chapter text.

Adeola Solanke, 'Donald Rodney', *Art Monthly* 124 (1989) 13–14. The epigraph for this section of the chapter comes from Donald Rodney, *Sketchbook No. 12* (1986) n.p.

2   Keith Piper & Donald Rodney, *Devil's Feast*, n.p., Donald Rodney Papers.

3   Donald Rodney, 'Black Independent Film as Part of the Black Art Movement BA. Hons. Fine Art' (March 1985) 6, 8, 30, 17, Donald Rodney Papers.

4   [Author unknown], 'Explosive Crisis at Chisenhale', n.d., n.p., Donald Rodney Papers.

5   [Author unknown], 'The Black Art Group', Artrage, Autumn 2006, 29.

6   Keith Piper & Sebastien Lopez, *Donald Rodney in Retrospect* (London: Institute for International Visual Arts, 2008) 4.

7   Donald Rodney, 'Untitled Manuscript', Diane Symons Archive, Donald Rodney Estate, London.

8   Donald Rodney, 'TSWA Project: Interview', n.d., n.p., Donald Rodney Papers.

9   Donald Rodney, 'Untitled Manuscript', Diane Symons Archive, Donald Rodney Estate.

10 Donald Rodney, 'TSWA Project: Interview', n.p.

11 [Author unknown], 'Blood Ban for Artist', n.d., n.p., Donald Rodney Papers.

12 Tony Foster & Jonathan Harvey (eds.), *New Work for Different Places: TSWA Four Cities Project* (Bristol, UK: TSWA, 1990) n.p.

13 Edward George & Trevor Matthison, *Three Songs on Pain, Light and Time,* Black Audio Film Collective, 1996.

14 Tony Foster & Jonathan Harvey, *New Work for Different Places*, n.p.

15 [Author unknown], 'Explosive Crisis at Chisenhale.'

16 Donald Rodney, 'Untitled Manuscript', Diane Symons Archive, Donald Rodney Estate.

17 Donald Rodney, *Crisis* press release, n.d., Donald Rodney Papers.

18 Donald Rodney, 'Trent Polytechnic Final Art Degree Show 1985', n.d., n.p., Donald Rodney Papers.

19 Donald Rodney, *Sketchbook No. 2* (1982/83) n.p.

20 Ibid.

21 Ibid.

22 Lubania Himid & Maud Sulter, Donald Rodney: *Critical*, 1 (Reprinted in this volume, pp. 189–191).

23 Ibid., 12

24 David Thorp, 'Flesh of My Flesh', in *Body Visual*, eds. Helen Chadwick, Letiza Galli and Donald Rodney (London: Arts Catalyst, 1996) 29, 30.

25 Donald Rodney & Carl Freedman, *9 Night in Eldorado* (exh. cat.) (London: South London Gallery, 1997) n.p.

26 'Donald Rodney in Conversation with Carol Shapman', BBC Radio recording, 26 October 1997, Donald Rodney Papers.

27 Ruth Kelly, 'The Blk Art Group in Historical and Cultural Context,' 357.

28 Lena Corner, 'A Body of Work: Donald Rodney,' n.d., n.p., London.

29 Cedric Porter, 'In Sickness and in Health,' n.d., n.p., Donald Rodney Papers.

30 Diane Symons, 'In the House of My Father: Fragments of Body and Time', *PAPER*, issue 1, October 2012, n.p. (Reprinted in this volume, pp. 151–158).

31 Donald Rodney, 'Answer the Question: Sweet as Sculpture', [publication unknown], 1 September 1997, n.p., Donald Rodney Papers.

32 George & Matthison, *Three Songs on Pain, Light and Time.*

33 Jane Beckett, 'Diasporic Unwrappings: Lubaina Himid in Conversation,' in *Women, the Arts, and Globalization,* eds. Marsha Meskimmon & Dorothy C. Rowe (Manchester: Manchester University Press, 2015) 206.

34 Eddie Chambers, *Things Done Change: The Cultural Politics of Recent Black Artists in Britain* (New York: Rodopi, 2011) 179.

35 Donald Rodney, 'Answer the Question', n.p.

36 Donald Rodney, *Sketchbook No. 11* (1986) n.p.

Making Myself Visible: Self-Portraiture and Representations of Blackness in the Work of Donald Rodney

Alice Correia

In her landmark postcolonial essay 'Can the Subaltern Speak', Gayatri Chakravorty Spivak posited the notion of 'epistemic violence.'[1] Described as 'the heterogeneous project to construe the colonial subject as other', whereby the ideological perspectives of the coloniser are established as normative, epistemic violence may be enacted both explicitly and insidiously, whether experienced as political discourse or everyday racism.[2] Applied to a late-twentieth-century British context, epistemic violence may be understood as a pervasive systemic racism that sought to estrange Black British subjectivities from dominant – white –national and cultural narratives. As Kobena Mercer noted in 1994, 'for Black Britain, the 1980s were lived as a relentless vertigo of displacement'.[3]

Donald Rodney (1961–98) forged his artistic career within this milieu of state-sanctioned epistemic violence and its counter force of radical Black, antiracist politics. A leading figure in the Blk Art Group of the early 1980s, alongside Eddie Chambers, Claudette Johnson, Keith Piper and Marlene Smith, he produced politically inflected, challenging artworks that addressed what he called 'the vicious institutionalised racism endemic in British cultural identity'.[4] Using mixed media, collage, found mass-media imagery and often working beyond the confines of medium-specificity in what Mercer has called a 'hybridised aesthetic', Rodney's work engaged with the prejudices faced by Britain's Black youth, while simultaneously addressing colonial histories of slavery, derogatory anthropological classifications of the Black body and the discrimination faced by postwar Caribbean migrants in Britain.[5] For Rodney, his artistic practice encompassed 'the fears of Black life', which included not just public displays of physical or verbal attack, but the ways in which discriminatory and dehumanising narratives of Blackness were disseminated within the print and broadcast media.[6] Stereotypes of young Black men as dangerous, if not explicitly criminal, were commonplace, particularly in the wake of civil unrest, or riots, which occurred in multiple British cities in 1980, 1981 and 1985. As bell hooks noted in 1992, '[o]pening a magazine or book, turning on the television set, watching a film, or looking at photographs in public spaces, we are most likely to see images of Black people that reinforce and reinscribe white supremacy.'[7] Through his use of self-portraiture (loosely defined), Rodney's work reflexively investigated his own position within this discriminatory visual culture. He stated, 'Black masculinity intrigues me because of being a black man and constantly being told that I am a threat.'[8] This article will consider how Rodney appropriated and critiqued these mediated perceptions of Black masculinity through a series of self-portraits that both ventured beyond portraiture's limits and challenged the homogenising effect of epistemic violence.

For a younger generation of artists entering the British art scene in the early 1980s, artist Rasheed Araeen's politically motivated strategic interventions into the visual discourse of a dominant (white) imperialist culture became 'benchmark'.[9] In his artworks such as *How Could One Paint a Self Portrait!* (1978–79), Araeen presented his 'colonized self': a rendition of the self in which a discriminatory discourse of cultural imperialism has not only had a depersonalising effect, but has been internalised by the subject.[10] Araeen's portrait, with its brow-beaten, downcast gaze, is obliterated with racist graffiti, including the phrases 'Paki Go Home', 'Blacks Out' and 'NF Rule OK' sprayed in red and blue.[11] In addition to these overtly aggressive and exclusionary slogans, Araeen also included small typed statements, collaged to the surface of the canvas. Among these statements is the rejection of his submission to an open exhibition, suggesting that alongside the visceral forms of racism endured, oppression, defined by Iris Young as the experience of 'exploitation, marginalisation, powerlessness, cultural imperialism and violence', persisted within the apparently egalitarian art world and expressed itself through insidious and seemingly generic vocabularies.[12] Cumulatively, Araeen's self-portraits articulated a 'double consciousness' – the compulsion to always see oneself through the lens of the dominant culture – asserting that Black artists were denied the luxury of narcissistic individualism afforded to white artists and were, consequently, destined to create self-portraits that were not representative of the self but rather reflected a series of historically formulated stereotypes that cast the Black body as primitive and degenerate.[13]

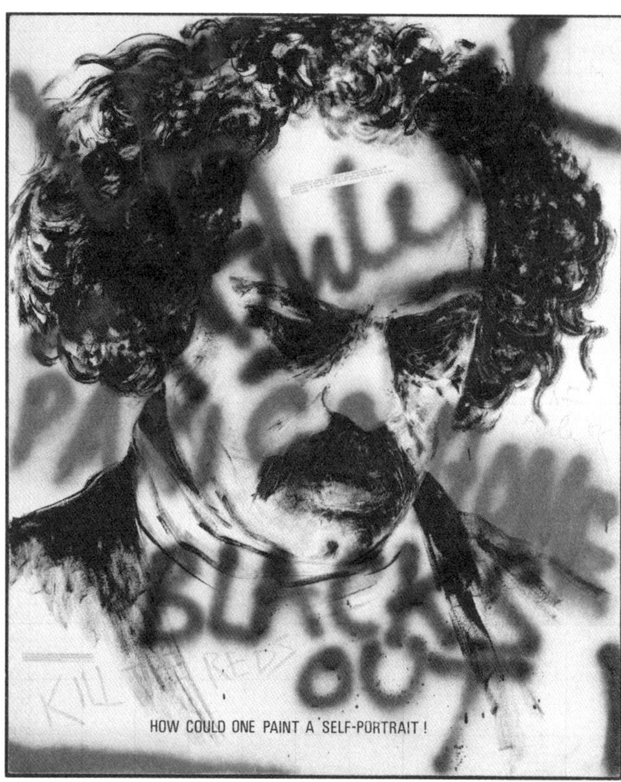

Rasheed Araeen, *How Could One Paint a Self-Portrait*, 1978–1979
Sharjah Art Foundation Collection. Photo: Danko Stjepanovic

This proposition had a lasting impact on young Black artists, including Donald Rodney, who, like Araeen, sought solutions to the question: How is it possible to create a self-portrait under the enduring conditions of colonial oppression?

In 1991, Rodney reflected that 'the attempt to produce a self-portrait when all black images have been appropriated and put under clearly defined areas of political and anthropological control has been a growing pre-occupation.'[14] His solution regarding Black self-portraiture was to approach the genre metaphorically, testing the limits of its parameters, and in doing so, challenging the framing space of representation. In making these self-portraits, Chambers notes, '[Rodney] was strenuously careful *not* to present himself within his work'.[15] Approaching the genre with the understanding that his identity as a Black man automatically positioned him within the purview of distinct inferiorising and dehumanising stereotypes, Rodney eschewed the presentation of what Stuart Hall described as the 'counter-

 Making Myself Visible

position of a "positive" black imagery', as a strategy of contestation.[16] Rather, in his self-portraits Rodney self-consciously took on the guise of those stereotypes in order to highlight and critique the ways in which all Black men are essentialised as homogenous threat. As Homi Bhabha argued, the only way of displacing the stereotyped image is 'by engaging with its *effectivity*'.[17] Thus, in the project of decolonising the visual representations of Black people, one of the central strategies used by Rodney was to appropriate preexisting imagery in order to highlight the ideological intent of media images that circulated in daily life.

In a small drawing, *Portrait of the Artist Taking a Political Initiative* (1989–90, p. 126), Rodney utilised a widely published media image of a young Black man holding a homemade petrol bomb during the so-called Handsworth riots of 9–10 September 1985.[18] However, rather than reproduce the photograph, Rodney presents the figure as a Black silhouette. Emphatically present but devoid of his identifying features, the figure literally becomes an unidentified Black man, both visible and invisible; Rodney's blacked-out body erases the identifiable 'I' and plays with the notion of an unidentified Black threat; the shadow cast could be filled by any body. Nevertheless, if any young Black male is a threat, Rodney's presentation of the silhouette as a self-portrait, as claimed in the accompanying caption, dynamically mimics that proposition to subversive affect.

Rodney had previously utilised this press image of the Black man striding purposefully with his petrol bomb in the collage *Framed Youth* (1986). When he created the work, the photograph had been published on the front cover of the British tabloid newspaper *The Sun* and reproduced in broadsheet newspapers including *The Observer*, and the unnamed subject was vilified as typifying the mindless, violent tendencies of Britain's Black youth. *The Sun* reported, 'A black thug stalks a Birmingham street with hate in his eyes and a petrol bomb in his hand.'[19] Like the majority of Britain's Black population, Rodney himself did not participate in militant or violent acts, and the work questions how the actions

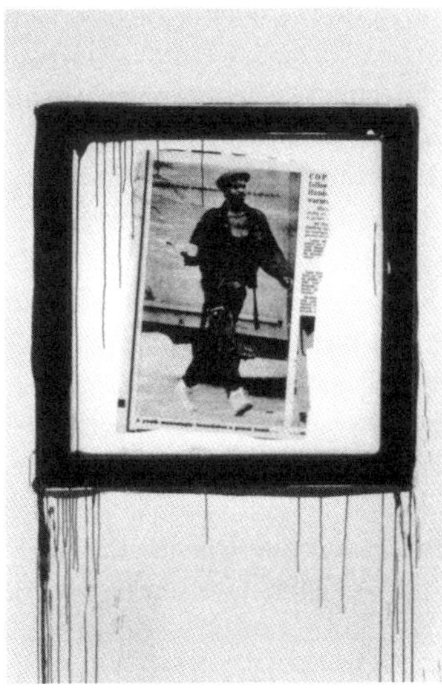

Framed Youth, 1986
Print on constructed wall, Approx. 61 × 61 cm

of a single figure may be upheld as typifying the attitudes and actions of a diverse group of people. *Framed Youth* suggests that the type of sensationalist reporting of the Handsworth riots was a continuum of the ways in which Blackness and criminality had historically been interwoven within British consciousness by the media; in 1974, Paul Hartmann and Charles Husband charted how the British print and broadcast media's construction of the Black male as a source of fear and site of discriminatory reporting had a long and deep history.[20] Similarly, in the seminal 1978 publication *Policing the Crisis: Mugging, the State, and Law and Order*, Stuart Hall and others discussed the ways in which Black male youths were scapegoated by the police and local and national media in order to explain a rise in criminal activity.[21] *Policing the Crisis* concluded that the presentation of crime as a 'Black problem' established the stereotype of the Black criminal in public consciousness, while diverting attention away from the social inequalities and injustices faced by large numbers of Black people.

Building on these publications, in 1987 Paul Gilroy argued in *There Ain't No Black in the Union Jack: The Cultural Politics of Race and Nation* that Black crime, like Black immigration, came to be seen in Britain as disrupting the national status quo, in which unlawful outsiders were a threat to a law-abiding white population. Gilroy outlined how Black violence became for the media 'evidence of [black people's] alien character and their distance from the substantive, historical forms of Britishness which are the property of white people.'[22] As such, the presentation of Black youth as criminal was regarded as evidence that Black Britons – cumulatively – were a threat to national security. Rodney's *Framed Youth* acutely demonstrates how those negative correlations between Blackness and criminality permeated through British society; caught within an enclosing square, the youth is surrounded, captured, and becomes proof of the Black threat to civil society.

Rodney's depiction of the bomber in *Framed Youth* and *Portrait of the Artist Taking a Political Initiative*, however, is double-edged. Understanding the effectivity of stereotyped imagery, while also aware of the debates surrounding the role of violence in the processes of racial and political struggle against a more powerful oppressor, Rodney saw the petrol bomber as a type of 'avenging angel'.[23] In this regard, his choice of imagery, and his presentation of the figure as a self-portrait, suggests an empathy with the complaints and aims of the minority of young Black people engaged in direct action, and it is possible to discern Rodney's appreciation of Frantz Fanon's discourse on violent anticolonial struggle. For Fanon, '[t]he development of violence among the colonised people will be proportionate to the violence exercised by the threatened colonial regime'.[24] Fighting fire with fire, the uprisings of the 1980s could be explained as proportionate

     Making Myself Visible

responses to prolonged and sustained oppression. As such, Rodney does not sentimentalise or seek to downplay the militant intent of the black urban warrior, but rather champions him as an expression of 'revolutionary consciousness'; here, the Black man is depicted as being proactive in shaping his destiny.[25] Rodney's framed appropriation of the image in *Framed Youth* could also reflect a populist championing, wherein pictures of heroes are framed. Rodney's problematisation of the frame thus anticipates Bhabha's assertion that 'in the postcolonial text the problem of identity returns as a persistent questioning of the frame, the space of representation', wherein there is the potential that different audiences may construe different meanings from the same image.[26]

Rodney returned to the dialectic of the artist as militant in 1992 and in a sketchbook outlined his ideas for an ultimately unrealised project:

> 'The self portraits 10, 11, 12 would contain a milk crate filled with bottles of paraffin and plugged with rags . . . on the wall a thick glass frontage held in place by bolts. I would sandblast sayings about myself that become my identity, my self portrait, a chronicle of positive and negative, or happy and sad, a complexity of reading that place me as . . .
> 1: typical black male
> 2: individual
> 3: stereotypical figure of fear'[27]

Together with *Framed Youth* and *Portrait of the Artist Taking a Political Initiative,* Rodney's unrealised self-portraits, combining inflammatory sculpture and inscribed text, can be understood as a challenge to recognise that colonial stereotyping has far-reaching consequences. Bringing (or at least proposing to bring) the militancy of the street into the space of the liberal white-cube gallery, Rodney sought to challenge (white) audiences with regard to their own prejudices. Here is the possibility that an educated artist might fulfil an incendiary political role; it is a proposition that is threatening, not simply because it proposes a violent act, but because it undermines the notion that violent action undertaken by Black people is always, and simply, mindless.

Although some of his work remained unrealised or no longer survives, Rodney's photographic light-box, *Self-Portrait: Black Men Public Enemy* (1990, p. 92) perhaps encapsulates his approach to self-portraiture. Through his use of the metaphoric, Rodney confronted the elision of the young Black male and threat, reflexively investigating his own position within a discriminatory visual culture. Discussing this work, he explained:

'I wanted to make a self-portrait. I didn't want to produce a picture with an image of myself in it. It would be far too heroic considering the subject matter. I wanted generic black men, a group of faces that represented in a stereotypical way black man as "the other," black man as the enemy within the body politic.'[28]

Venturing beyond portraiture's established objective of showing a true, physical likeness of the individual sitter and/or giving insight into his essential character, Rodney engaged with the ways in which his personal identity became subsumed within a normative schema of generic stereotypes.[29] *Self-Portrait: Black Men Public Enemy* comprises five lightbox panels, each containing a face, arranged to form a capital T shape.[30] On the vertical section is a half-length image of the young boy and, below, an identikit reconstruction of a Black male face, while the upper horizontal section includes two mug shot images of the same man. Although titled a self-portrait, none of the panels depict Rodney himself, and the images are reproductions of those found in British newspapers *The Sunday Times* and the *Evening Standard*, and a book on blood diseases.[31] Cumulatively, however, if we include Rodney's reference to himself in the title, the work illustrates four different and distinct individuals and simultaneously presents and problematises the categorisation of undifferentiated Black men as a 'public enemy'. Rodney's distillation of multiple Black men into a single enemy demonstrates Bhabha's assertion that a stereotype 'is a simplification because it is an arrested, fixated form of representation . . . [which denies] the play of difference.'[32] The Black man is fixed within the framing discourse of imperialism, and despite the existence of multiple subjects, and therefore subjectivities, all are reduced to a single character by virtue of their common skin colour. In the simple identifying coda, *Black Men, Public Enemy,* threat is not only determined according to skin colour, but skin colour become evidence of a threat, and, as such, Rodney's work articulates Fanon's lament that 'I am overdetermined from without.'[33]

In his transgressive appropriation of publicly available imagery of Black men, Rodney demonstrates how distinct individuals are regressively distilled to become representative of enmity. For example, the inclusion of a composite photofit image highlights the ways in which the Black body is scrutinised and criminalised within a surveillance society. The constructed nature of the Black face, in addition to its pixilation due to Rodney's enlargement of his newspaper source material, creates a grotesque image that presents the male as subhuman. Physical malformation becomes, here, evidence of moral turpitude. However, it is also noteworthy that this rendition of criminality is literally made up; in contrast to the other faces represented, the identikit image is not real but rather rendered from memory that may or may not be

     Making Myself Visible

accurate. Thus, the Black face is a construct and subject to the inaccuracies of memory recall brought on by prejudicial fear. Arguably, in the moment of enacting a controlling gaze, the actions intended to control and contain the Black body instead produce fear: 'The white man's eyes break up the black man's body and in that act of epistemic violence its own frame of reference is transgressed, its field of vision disturbed.'[34] Similarly, the diseased or contaminated body, as presented in the images of the young boy sourced from a medical text, like the grotesque identikit face, is regarded as a threat and ostracised from society because of its perceived otherness. Identifying that his image of the boy originated from a book on blood diseases, Rodney highlights not only the epidermalisation of racism, but also the historic, medical designation of Blackness as biologically impure and inferior. It is worth noting that Rodney made this work during a period of intense media paranoia with regard to the spread of blood diseases. The clinical identification of, and subsequent public panic (fuelled by deliberately frightening government-sponsored public-health announcements) about HIV/AIDS during the 1980s resulted in a fear of any and all blood diseases. As such, the Black boy in Rodney's work is identified as biologically contaminated and potentially contaminating, regardless of whether his illness is contagious. In this infected state, the Black figure is classified as a threat to public safety and has parity with the Black criminal. Given that Rodney himself suffered from what is often seen as a racially specific blood disease (sickle cell anaemia), *Self-Portrait: Black Men Public Enemy* becomes a provocation to audiences: do we regard Rodney as a public enemy thrice over because of his skin colour, gender and medical diagnosis?

That Rodney chose to use two versions of a mug shot in the horizontal part of *Self-Portrait: Black Men Public Enemy* is also significant. According to John Tagg, the mug shot is a 'standardised image' that 'is more than a picture of a supposed criminal'.[35] Tagg asserts that the mug shot is representative of the views held by the dominating power structures and a product of a disciplinary society that demands the classification of those who do not conform to its particularities. In light of this controlling visual system, Rodney's use of the frontal and profile mug shots is confrontational. He makes visible the ways in which discriminatory power is exerted and forces audiences to recognise the ways in which the Black subject is held under surveillance while simultaneously denied the right to assert his identity. The denial or absenting of subjectivity from the two mug shots is achieved not simply by the disciplining framing of the portraits, but also through the presence of the Black rectangle over the man's eyes. This use of the Black rectangle, or censor bar, is a reference to the newspaper practice, common in Britain during the 1980s, of obscuring the suspect's face in order to protect their identity, or to comply with legal requirements when the identity of a suspect cannot be released to the general public. Despite the supposed protection that this rectangle provides, when applied to the Black face it instead becomes a mark of improbity. The young Black man is placed within a self-fulfilling cycle in which he becomes the stereotype that he is branded with because of a suppressive act of branding. If the censor bar acts as a signifier of criminality, it also serves as a blindfold prohibiting vision. Using the vocabulary of purportedly benevolent control, Rodney invites audiences to actively look at the ways in which the individual Black subject is denied agency through the denial of sight. Repeating the Black bar over four of the portraits, the opportunity to return the discriminating look is refused, recalling Bhabha's comment that the blindfold is used as a strategy for neutering 'the threatened return of the look', particularly when the returning gaze, or look from the margins, is an act of resistance and assertion of resilience.[36] Although the men depicted in Rodney's work are unable to look for themselves, cumulatively, the artwork as self-portrait becomes the embodiment of the returning gaze of the artist. Rodney thus creates in *Self-Portrait: Black Men Public Enemy* a vertiginous artwork: audiences are invited to regard each figure and acknowledge both their individual particularities and the denial of those characteristics. The epistemic violence done to (representations of) the Black body is highlighted, while Rodney simultaneously challenges the ideological grounding of that violence.

In 1991, Rodney elaborated on the visual strangeness of the photofit image in his exhibition 'Cataract' at Camerawork gallery, London. The exhibition press release suggests that the show, as a totality, was conceived as a self-portrait, while sketches and notes held in his archive at Tate reveal Rodney's initial plans (p. 128).[37]

> 'Within the complex make up of the City, video cameras serve the same purpose as the microscope or the X-ray; to spot or detect disorder. Video cameras will appear at various points as part of "war on crime" specifically they are there for traffic control, but are used to monitor political demonstrations. The black male has been criminalised within the popular psyche, the image of the video surveillance cameras serves as a code for this criminalisation. Fifty or more surveillance cameras will be installed across the walls of the exhibiting space, confronting the viewer. Between these cameras a photo-fit face will be projected, reminiscent of the artist's impression of black criminals, different facial features belonging to different people will create a composite image.'[38]

Although the eventual exhibition did not include the surveillance cameras,

                                    Making Myself Visible

large photofit portraits were projected (p. 93). Rodney produced a series of hand-coloured photo-collages that were rephotographed to make 35mm slides for a slide tape projection (p. 197). The images mimicked the employment of composite photographic facial images during the 1970s and 1980s by the police and the atomisation of the Black (male) body by that particular agent of sociopolitical power, while simultaneously referring to the medium specificity of photo-montage to suggest subversive intent.[39] Recalling the history of collage and assemblage as rooted in a politics of dissent, Rodney's use of photographic fragments challenges the nature of the photograph as indexical record by questioning the implicit assertion that a photofit could be an accurate recall of a real, individual person.[40] Making no attempt to obscure the suture lines between the different facial fragments, the collation and coexistence of different features belonging to different people in 'Cataract' creates a composite that retains its visual tension and multiplicity. Rather than seeking to present a single subject, as in the photofit used in *Self-Portrait: Black Men Public Enemy*, Rodney's composite portraits present a community of faces. In this regard, 'Cataract' prefigures Mercer's assertion that rather than see the hybrid as a grotesque that is at odds with a modernist sense of the holistic individual, 'composite beings who exist in a state of incompletion are by definition open to future possibilities of growth and further transformation.'[41] As such, Rodney's portraits gesture towards potentiality: of multiple Black subjects coming into being.[42]

In the early 1990s, British filmmaker Pratibha Parmar noted that 'the deeply ideological nature of [portrait] imagery determines not only how other people think about us but how we think about ourselves.'[43] Throughout his career, Rodney probed and challenged the explicit presentation of the negative figuration of Blackness as an enemy to the status quo within British society. Engaging with the ways epistemic violence, in the form of media imagery, worked to stereotype and homogenise, Rodney created a series of provocative self-portraits that challenged and undermined normative inferiorising discourses. Aligning himself within the purview of militant or threatening Blackness (whether that threat was real or not), Rodney put pressure upon the ease with which that stereotype may be applied to heterogeneous Black constituents. As such, through his appropriation and unpicking of Britain's institutionalised discriminatory visual culture, his self-portraits may be regarded as not only attempts to decolonise the self, but provocations regarding the very nature of Black identities.

First published in *Nka Journal of Contemporary African Art*, issue 45, (November 2019) 74–86.

1   Versions of this paper were presented at the Association of Art Historians annual conference, Belfast, 2007, and *Understanding British Portraits* annual seminar, National Portrait Gallery, London, 2015. My thanks to the organisers and participants of those events, and to Eddie Chambers, for their feedback on this research.

    Gayatri Chakravorty Spivak, 'Can the Subaltern Speak?', in *The Post-Colonial Studies Reader*, eds. Bill Ashcroft, Gareth Griffiths, and Helen Tiffin (New York: Routledge, 1995) 24–28, 24–25.

2   Spivak, 'Can the Subaltern Speak?', 24–25.

3   Kobena Mercer, *Welcome to the Jungle: New Positions in Black Cultural Studies* (New York: Routledge, 1994) 2.

4   Donald Rodney, 'Black Independent Film as Part of the Black Art Movement' (BFA diss., Nottingham Trent University, 1985), Donald Rodney Collection, Tate Archives, London, TGA/200321/2/1.

5   Kobena Mercer, 'Then and Now: Black Artists and Modernism', keynote address presented at the conference 'Now & Then … Here and Now, Black Artists and Modernism', Chelsea College of Art, London, October 6, 2016. Published art-historical scholarship on Rodney's work remains scarce, see, however, Richard Hylton, (ed.) *Donald Rodney: Doublethink* (London: Autograph, 2003), which includes essays by Eddie Chambers, Stuart Hall and Virginia Nimarkoh; Eddie Chambers, 'His Catechism: The Art of Donald Rodney,' *Third Text* 12, no. 44 (1998) 43–54; and Celeste-Marie Bernier, '"X is for X Ray, X Slave, X Colony": A "Lexicon of Liberation" Versus "My Slave History" in the Paintings, Installations, and Sketchbooks of Donald Rodney', in *Visualising Slavery: Art Across the African Diaspora*, eds. Celeste-Marie Bernier & Hannah Durkin (Liverpool: Liverpool University Press, 2016) 218–47, for insightful analysis.

6   Donald Rodney, 'Artist's Statement' in *The Image Employed*, eds. Keith Piper & Marlene Smith (exh. cat.) (Manchester: Cornerhouse, 1987) 11.

7   bell hooks was discussing a US context, but her point is applicable to the United Kingdom. bell hooks, *Black Looks: Race and Representation* (Boston, MA: South End Press, 1992) 1.

8   Quoted in Virginia Nimarkoh, 'Image of Pain: Physicality in the Art of Donald Rodney', in *Donald Rodney: Doublethink*, 83.

9   Eddie Chambers, 'The Art of Donald Rodney' (paper presented at Tate Britain, London, October 2004).

10 Rasheed Araeen, 'In Conversation: Nick Aikens and Rasheed Araeen,' in *Rasheed Araeen: A Retrospective*, ed. Nick Aikens (Zurich: JRP/Ringier, 2017) 204. The title of my article is indebted to Araeen's monograph, *Making Myself Visible* (London: Kala, 1984).

11 'NF' here is shorthand for the National Front, a violent far-right group.

12 Iris Marion Young, *Justice and the Politics of Difference* (Princeton, NJ: Princeton University Press, 1990) 9.

13 The phrase is taken from W. E. B. Du Bois, *The Souls of Black Folk* (1903; repr. Oxford: Oxford University Press, 2007) 8, and is the principle theme of Paul Gilroy's *The Black Atlantic: Modernity and Double Consciousness* (London: Verso, 1993).

14 News release for Donald Rodney exhibition 'Cataract', Camera Work gallery, London, 13 February 13 – 6 March 1991, Donald Rodney Collection, Tate Archives, London, TGA/200321/1/7.

15 Eddie Chambers, 'The Art of Donald Rodney', in *Donald Rodney: Doublethink*, 34. My italics.

16 Stuart Hall, 'New Ethnicities,' (1989), in *The Post-Colonial Studies Reader,* eds. Bill Ashcroft, Gareth Griffiths and Helen Tiffin, 224.

17 Homi K. Bhabha, *The Location of Culture* (New York: Routledge, 1994) 67.

18 See Les Back & John Solomos, *Race, Politics, and Social Change* (New York: Routledge, 1995) 83.

19 *The Sun*, 11 September, 1985, cited in Back & Solomos, *Race*, 82. The man was later identified as James Hazell, aged 32; he was subsequently jailed for five years by Birmingham Crown Court. For original press image, see https://www.gettyimages.co.uk/detail/news-photo/youth-carrying-a-fire-bomb-on-the-second-day-of-the-news-photo/848234836?%20-%20youth-carrying-a-firebomb-on-the-second-day-of-the-handsworth-riots-picture-id848234836. The photograph was used on the cover of *The Sun* on 11 September 1985. In contrast to this negative framing, Hazell was championed as a working-class warrior by the direct-action anarchist publication *Class War*, October 1985; see 'Working Class (Oct 1985),' UK Class War Front Covers 1984–87,

   Making Myself Visible

(www.wussu.com/zines/clas.htm). For further discussion of this image, see Eddie Chambers, 'Through the Wire: Black British People and the Riot,' in *Nka: Journal of Contemporary African Art* 36 (2015) 6–15.

20 Paul Hartmann & Charles Husband, *Racism and the Mass Media: A Study of the Role of the Mass Media in the Formation of White Beliefs and Attitudes in Britain* (London: Davis-Poynter, 1974).

21 Stuart Hall, et al., *Policing the Crisis: Mugging, the State, and Law and Order* (London: Macmilllan, 1978).

22 Paul Gilroy, *There Ain't No Black in the Union Jack: The Cultural Politics of Race and Nation,* 2nd ed. (New York: Routledge Classics, 2002) 141. See also Hartmann & Husband, *Racism and the Mass Media*, 159, for news-worthiness of criminal acts.

23 Chambers, 'The Art of Donald Rodney', in *Donald Rodney: Doublethink*, 22.

24 Frantz Fanon, *The Wretched of the Earth* (1963; repr. London: Penguin, 1967) 69.

25 Chambers, 'The Art of Donald Rodney', in *Donald Rodney: Doublethink*, 25.

26 Bhabha, *The Location of Culture*, 46.

27 Donald Rodney, *Sketchbook 38*, 1992, 23, Donald Rodney Collection, Tate Archives, London, TGA/200321/3/38/23.

28 Donald Rodney, 'Artist's Statement', in *Shocks to the System: Social and Political Issues in Recent British Art from the Arts Council Collection,* eds. Isobel Johnstone & Roger Malbert (exh. cat.) (London: South Bank Centre, 1991) 66.

29 See Shearer West, *Portraiture* (Oxford: Oxford University Press, 2004) 9–20; and Ernst van Alphen, 'The Portrait's Dispersal: Concepts of Representation and Subjectivity in Contemporary Portraiture', in *Portraiture: Facing the Subject*, ed. Joanna Woodall (Manchester: Manchester University Press, 1997) 239–56.

30 For Chambers, Rodney's use of the T shape resembled 'the appearance of a Christian cross, with all its resonance of sacrifice and martyrdom.' Space does not permit a detailed exploration of Rodney's use of religious symbolism here, but I agree that it is a significant point of investigation for discussions of *Self-Portrait: Black Men Public Enemy*. See Chambers, 'The Art of Donald Rodney', in *Donald Rodney: Doublethink*, 34.

31 See Johnstone & Malbert, *Shocks to the System*, 66. The identikit/photofit image was used on a 'wanted' poster produced by the *Evening Standard* newspaper; the poster is reproduced in Kobena Mercer & Isaac Julien, 'True Confessions: A Discourse on Images of Black Male Sexuality', *Ten.8*, vol. 2, no. 3 (Spring 1992) 40–50, 46.

32 See Bhabha, *The Location of Culture*, 74.

33 Frantz Fanon, *Black Skin, White Masks,* trans. Richard Philcox (New York: Grove, 2008) 87.

34 Bhabha, *The Location of Culture*, 42.

35 John Tagg, *The Burden of Representation: Essays on Photographies and Histories* (New York: Palgrave Macmillan, 1988) 76.

36 Bhabha, *The Location of Culture*, 81.

37 news release for Donald Rodney exhibition 'Cataract', Camerawork gallery, London, 13 February – 6 March 1991, the Donald Rodney Collection, Tate Archives, TGA/200321/7/3.

38 news release for Donald Rodney exhibition 'Cataract', Camerawork gallery, London, 13 February – 6 March 1991, the Donald Rodney Collection, Tate Archives, TGA/200321/1/7.

39 During the 1990s, the use of the photographic composite declined and was generally superseded by digital systems, in which likenesses evolved holistically through witness recognition rather than being dependent upon the recall of specific internal facial features. See Graham M. Davies, Lisa J. Morrison and Paul van der Willik, 'Facial Composite Production: A Comparison of Mechanical and Computer-Driven Systems', *Journal of Applied Psychology* 85, no. 1 (2000) 119–24. As such, Rodney's use of the photofit was historically specific and, arguably, a commentary on the representation of Black men from his generation.

40 See Brandon Taylor, *Collage: The Making of Modern Art* (London: Thames and Hudson, 2004).

41 Mercer, 'Then and Now', (see note 5).

42 At the time of writing access to the work *Cataract* was extremely limited, but I was pleased to commission a digitised version of the slide tape for the exhibition, 'A Tall Order: Rochdale Art Gallery in the 1980s', Touchstones Rochdale, 2022.

43 Pratibha Parmar, 'Black Feminism: The Politics of Articulation', in *Identity: Community, Culture, Difference*, ed. Jonathan Rutherford (London: Lawrence & Wishart, 1990) 116.

Image of Pain:
Physicality in the Art
of Donald Rodney

Virginia Nimarkoh

Flesh of My Flesh is a large-scale colour photographic triptych. It is approximately 5.5 × 1.2m in total size, with each panel measuring some 183 × 122cm. The first panel depicts the image of a knot taken under electron microscope. The knot is made of human hair. The same knot, photographed from a different angle, is shown in the third panel in a kind of asymmetrical repetition. The centerpiece of the triptych is a close-up photograph of the artist's thigh. Stretching across the thigh is a scar – the result of what was, at the time, his most recent hip operation. The scar is not only wide, but also thick.

Ladder-like stitch-marks run down either side, reiterating its size. In each respective panel, the object/subject (hair/scar) spans the width of the image, forming a shallow, fragmented arc (of hair, scar and hair again) which links the three panels. The piece could be described as a monochrome, the sepia tones of the microscopic hairs complementing the hue of the artist's Black skin.

1.

Flesh of My Flesh (1996, pp. 100–101), described above, is the first of a small number of photographic works produced by Donald Rodney in the eighteen months before his death. Through works like *Flesh of My Flesh* and *In the House of My Father* (1997, p. 102), we are offered the briefest of glimpses at, what was for Donald, a new type of engagement with photography.[1] Particular to these photographs is a distinctly intimate use by the artist of his own body. I want to consider, specifically in relation to *Flesh of My Flesh*, how Donald Rodney constructed an image of pain, both physical and psychological, based on his own physicality as a metaphor to critique Black masculinity, which in turn impacts on what we term 'the body'.

But, first, to put these late photographic works into some kind of context. Combining self-portraiture with photo-based imagery had been a constant thread running through Donald Rodney's multifarious practice for some time in works such as his signature X-ray pieces of the 1980s – *Self-Portrait as Clinton McCurbin* (1988, p. 79)[2] – through to the appropriated photography in lightbox works like *Self-Portrait: Black Men Public Enemy* (1990, p. 92). In his early self-portraits Donald often assumed other personas, real and imagined: posing as the eponymous McCurbin, a young Black man who had died in police custody in 1987 and as a suspect of crime in *Self-Portrait: Black Men Public Enemy*. Donald Rodney presents a heterogeneous notion of 'self' through these two self-portraits. Both works are on attempt to subvert the pernicious stereotyping of the Black male that was extensive within the British press and media in the decade following the Brixton riots of 1981 and those in Tottenham of 1985. In doing so, it became part of Donald Rodney's strategy to appropriate those very stereotypical images – culled from TV, newspapers and magazines.[3] Implicit within this strategy, of assuming roles that had been mediated by the press and media, was a certain reflexivity. Donald implicated himself, the artist, in what was (and, to a degree, still is) the precarious position of the Black male within British society. As Donald Rodney himself put it:

'More and more of my work is dealing with Black sexuality, Black masculinity, because it's there all the time. Black masculinity intrigues me because of being a Black man and constantly being told that I am a threat. Being constantly told I am this and I'm that makes me wonder about it a great deal.'[4]

Inevitably, the works *Self-Portrait as Clinton McCurbin* and *Self-Portrait: Black Men Public Enemy* highlight the relentless malleability of Black male stereotyping as it flips back and forth between perpetuating images of Black victim and Black aggressor. In the period between his early photo-based self-portraits and those of the late nineties, the terms and conditions under which Donald Rodney practised his art underwent some significant shifts. During the mid to late 1990s, Donald's work enjoyed something of a renaissance. His work was being recontextualised under the umbrella of projects emerging at that time which sought to examine the relationship between art and science. Exhibitions including 'Care and Control' (1995), 'The Invisible and the Visible' (1996) and 'Body Visual' (1996) – in all of which Donald Rodney participated – sought to create a physical dialogue between the medical institution and the artist by being staged in hospitals, medical research centres and the like. Concurrent with this recontextualisation of his work, Donald's mobility was becoming increasingly limited and the periods he spent in hospital increasingly lengthy. Ever pragmatic, Donald came to rely more and more upon an informal network that included his partner, Diane Symons, plus various friends and contacts, to help orchestrate his projects when he was confined to hospital and had exhibition deadlines to meet. To my mind, the combination of these factors – the re-evaluation of his work in the 'art and science' context, the insularity of his existence in hospital and his worsening health – had a very specific effect on Donald's practice. They provoked a level of introspection that is reflected in works like *Flesh of My Flesh* and *In the House of My Father* that distinguishes them from his earlier photo-based self-portraiture.

So, to return to my initial proposal – to examine the image of pain, based on his own physicality, that Donald Rodney presents as a metaphor to critique Black masculinity and also what we term 'the body'. What was the nature of the pain that provided the catalyst for a work like *Flesh of My Flesh*?

2.

Inherent to Donald Rodney's medical condition, sickle cell anaemia, was that he lived with intense and chronic pain. Donald's situation was complex. To paraphrase Eddie Chambers' review of the documentary on Donald Rodney, *Three Songs on Pain, Light and Time,*[5] sickle cell anaemia is, by its very nature, a condition that affects only Black people, and as such, has come to signify Blackness. The issues surrounding the condition – the lack of government funding into research; the limitations in treatment for sickle cell patients; the use of the highly addictive painkiller Pethidine in that treatment – are highly political, and ultimately racialised.[6]

Donald's medical treatment involved a relentless cycle of blood transfusions, painkillers and surgery. Paradoxically, the disabling effects of sickle cell – the necrosis of his bones – rather than galvanising Donald's relationship with the Black community, were in fact to provoke in him a profound sense of isolation from that community. For example, here Donald Rodney recounts an incident that happened to him as a child, which was to ostracise him from his predominantly Black Pentecostal church:

'So even though I'd been going to Sunday school, sometimes I couldn't go because I'd been ill: or I'd have trouble walking and couldn't sit down due to having trouble with my joints [. . .] Eventually when I got disease of the hip, I had to wear this really bizarre contraption for several years – it was a huge leather thing and I had to walk with crutches. I was taking up a lot of room in the church van that came to collect the people to take them to church [. . .] They eventually explained to my mum that I was taking up too much room and suggested she didn't bring me. I thought this was very unchristian of them [. . .]'[7]

                                   Image of Pain

Basically, Donald Rodney's experience was that the Black community is no more accommodating to illness than any other, regardless of whether that illness affects only Black people. During the period around the mid-nineties, Donald had to renegotiate his identity in relation to his worsening medical condition. The decision was whether to define and register himself as disabled. Donald had lived with the effects of sickle cell all his life. But his level of mobility was such that, up to this point, registering as disabled had been an option. It now meant confronting head-on the degree to which his health had deteriorated. Despite more positive attitudes in Britain towards illness and disability between the 1960s and 1990s, Donald confirmed in 1996 that 'within the Black community and within the art world as well, you become partially invisible because of having a disability'.[8] This decision impacted in various ways. For example, Donald applied for the first time to the Digital Arts and Disabled People Scheme set up by the Arts Council of England in 1997. His successful application was, of course, a bittersweet experience – confirming for Donald a status that he was still coming to terms with. Consequently, for Donald Rodney, the issue of his own identity, and specifically his own self-determination – whether as a Black male, an artist, Black artist, disabled or otherwise – could never be taken for granted, and was very much hard won.

So if, as Eddie Chambers suggests, sickle cell anaemia has come to be recognised as something of a negative signifier of Blackness, how does Donald Rodney attempt to transform that signifier? As I outlined earlier, the central panel of the triptych *Flesh of My Flesh* depicts an image of Donald Rodney's scarred thigh. The artist presents a close-up, tightly cropped, view of his skin, pores, scar and hair. The body is fragmented, almost to the point of abstraction – clues to the subject's identity are given only in the work's titling. These formal aspects – the framing, cropping and lighting of the scar – contribute to the intimate, yet highly aestheticised, almost fetishised image of his own pain that Donald Rodney presents us with. The photograph of Donald's scar is visually potent, beautiful even. What is indeed striking about *Flesh of My Flesh* is the beauty of its imagery, despite its grim subject matter. The use of beauty, of sensuality, serves to subvert the stereotypes of the Black body in crisis – be it the AIDS sufferer, the drug addict, the schizophrenic or the famine victim. Moreover, *Flesh of My Flesh* negates the equally oppressive stereotype of Black body perfection as promoted by multinational sportswear companies and also within the Black music industry.[9] But Donald Rodney's use of beauty is not for its own sake – in fact, it is the tension between the viewer's experience of visual pleasure and the artist's successful imaging of physical pain that activates critique. The late Jo Spence, in her pioneering photographic work into the politics of her own illnesses – cancer and, finally,

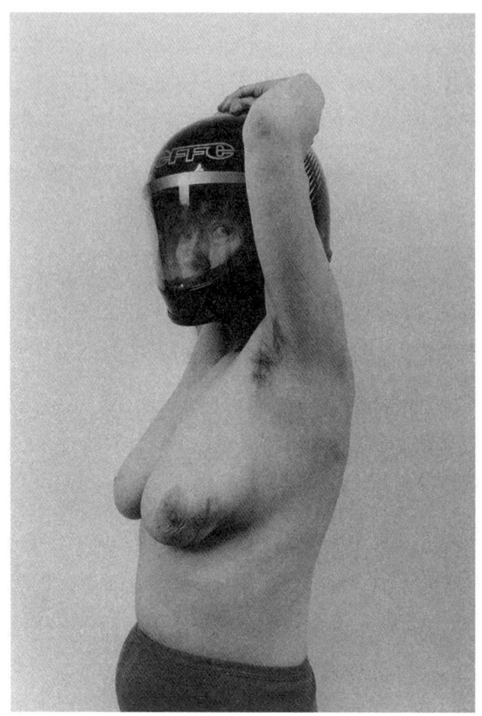

Jo Spence in collaboration with Terry Dennett, [Jo Spence wearing a helmet], 1982, from *The Picture of Health?*, 1982–86, chromogenic colour print

leukaemia – set as a condition of success for her work that it convey 'critical visual pleasure' to the viewer.[10] Whilst operating in a very different manner to the work of Spence, *Flesh of My Flesh* could equally be considered as having made such an achievement. For me, most disturbing is how *Flesh of My Flesh* declares itself as an image of pain. The declaration is neither sensationalist nor emotional, but almost deadpan in the manner it confronts the viewer. It does not present an open wound as the site of trauma. It does, however, show us healing having taken place – the body intact, but clearly altered. When we are sick, we naturally speak of getting 'better', the inference being that recovery may erase any trace, visual or otherwise, of what we have experienced. Of course, despite successful treatment, 'better' may also mean 'changed'; our self-image may also need some adjusting. *Flesh of My Flesh* acknowledges that the trauma, which Donald's body underwent was (in this instance) over. The scar is evidence of that trauma and of its finiteness. But the scar is equally and inexorably a living memory of that trauma.

Also, the subtext to this central panel should not be forgotten. The photograph of Donald's scar, though visually striking, is proof of a disturbing event. By medical standards, the scar was exceptionally poor in the sense

                                                 Image of Pain

that it was evidence of malpractice: over-stitching by a reckless surgeon who apparently felt that Black skin required more work since it was 'tougher' than White skin.[11] What *Flesh of My Flesh* comes to represent then is an assault on the body as much from without as from within. Inevitably, *Flesh of My Flesh* becomes a critique of the very medical institutions that Donald inhabited both as an artist and patient and serves as testament to the politics surrounding sickle cell anaemia.

The two remaining panels of the *Flesh of My Flesh* triptych depict a knot made up of two hairs photographed under an electron microscope. Again, the image conveys a sensuality – the smooth contours of the hairs emerging from a rich, deep brown background. Of the two hairs, one belonged to Donald Rodney, the other to the artist Rose Finn-Kelcey. The photograph was the bittersweet remnant of a troubled collaboration between the two artists.[12] Donald had wanted to use the hairs as signifiers of identity.[13] His plan had been to expose stereotypical notions of the Black male (crude, thick, rough, dark) versus those of the White female (delicate, smooth, fine, blonde), by photographing the hairs under an electron microscope. What the experiment revealed was that at such close proximity, visual difference is indistinguishable. The image showed complete parity between the two hairs. The irony of these findings was not lost on Donald Rodney.

The juxtaposition of the photographs of the hairs with that of the scar provides a paradoxical take on racial difference. The notion of 'difference' so boldly displayed in the image of Donald's scarred thigh is complexified, perhaps even contradicted, by the visual difference between the two hairs that has been eradicated by the electron microscope. The images offer up conflicting, but nonetheless valid, notions of photographic truth – one confirming racial difference, the other denying it. (I will return to the issue of photographic truth later in this text.)

3.

So, as I have outlined, through 'art and science' type exhibitions of the mid 1990s Donald Rodney found himself in the realm of what is benignly referred to as 'body art'. Indeed, he certainly identified with a diverse range of artists working with notions of 'the body' – from Franko B, Zarina Bhimji and Helen Chadwick to Mona Hatoum and Andres Serrano. Body art has come to be an all-encompassing term that covers any number of artworks that relate to the human figure, parts thereof, or indeed, its absence. Consider, for example, Zarina Bhimji's disturbing photographic lightbox *Vulnerable and Sticky* (1995) – a still life depicting six freshly dissected brains neatly arranged on a surface of black rubber sheeting. Or Franko B's potent performances such as *I Miss You* (1999) and *Oh Lover Boy* (2000), where the artist bleeds before his audience. Or

Mona Hatoum's now famous video, *Corps étranger* (*Foreign Bodies*, 1994), where the viewer is taken on a journey through the artist's body via the assistance of an endoscopic camera. In Mark Sladen's examination of the abundance of work that nowadays might be termed 'body art', he argues that 'the artists who can be grouped under the term are so diverse that they can hardly be said to be part of a movement'. He continues that 'body art can become part of a reductive discourse in which the body is simply a totem – standing in for supposedly universal truths about the "human condition".'[14] The specificity of Donald Rodney's situation – his medical condition, the politics surrounding it and his dual existence as artist and patient – prevent his work from ever straying into the generic. Equally, his situation set him apart from many of the artists with whom he identified. This is not to make an essentialist argument for a type of experience-based practice validated on levels of suffering. The issue I do want to raise, however, is that the presentation of the artist's damaged body by the artist who has suffered that damage, as a result of illness or injury, ultimately complexifies what we might term 'body art'. As Jo Spence succinctly described her attempts to find a way to represent her cancer, 'This isn't just an art work. This is an actual body that someone inhabits.'[15] This very specific making public of what is intensely private takes such work into a realm of its own. Of course, it can still be termed 'body art' but, having its own distinct set of motivations and points of reference that respond to the politics of illness, such work does challenge our understanding of what we term 'body art', and ultimately, what we term 'the body'.

It seems pertinent here to raise the issue of agency in relation to Donald Rodney's presentation of the damaged body. The imperative that drove his later practice was more than aesthetic, conceptual or even political. As I have outlined above, the period in which *Flesh of My Flesh* was produced coincided with a deterioration in Donald's health – months rather than weeks were being spent in hospital and the surgery undertaken was increasingly radical. For the artist living with the prospect of his or her own death, and making work that responds to that experience, the question 'What is at stake for the artist in the making of their work?' can surely only be answered, 'Everything'. *Flesh of My Flesh* is an intensely introspective look at the body by Donald Rodney, its fragility and mortality, or more specifically, *his* body, *his* fragility and *his* mortality. For Donald Rodney, his art was indeed a testament to his having survived thus far. It was also a tool of self-empowerment – a means of retaining an identity, a survival strategy.[16]

Donald Rodney shared with Jo Spence the need to communicate physical pain as a visual experience. In an interview with Ruth Kelly in 1994 outlining his plan for what was to be a new project, Donald articulated the isolating nature of pain:

Image of Pain

'How can you evoke pain within an image? You can be sitting next to me and say you feel pain, but how do I know [. . .] whether you are feeling pain or not, or if your pain is anything like my pain [. . .] I'm trying to portray physical pain; the kind of pain that I have experienced.'[17]

Donald Rodney and Jo Spence, in their own quite distinct ways, attempted to convey the incommunicable, the invisible – the experience of physical pain, that which is hermetically sealed within the body of the sufferer. In Spence's renowned image from the series *The Picture of Health?* (1984), she poses naked from the waist up, her arms folded above her head, wearing a crash helmet and confronting the viewer with the physical damage to her body – the result of invasive treatment for her breast cancer. The pose is reminiscent of a Page Three 'glamour' model, provocative and uncompromising in its display of the female body. Yet, the damage to her breast renders the artist vulnerable. The crash helmet seems to try to serve as much as a protection against the viewer's gaze that Spence subjects herself to, as against the prospect of aggressive surgery. Despite the differences between these two practitioners' work – Jo Spence's background within photo-therapy and Donald Rodney's within fine art – both were drawn to the indexical nature of photography as a means of verifying their respective illnesses. And, importantly, both utilised the scar as the image of physical pain made visible.

4·

So, to return to the issue of photographic truth. In her essay, 'Notes on the Index', Rosalind Krauss outlines the nature of what might be termed photographic truth via the index or 'trace':

'It is the order of the natural world that imprints itself on the photographic emulsion and subsequently on the photographic print. This quality of transfer or trace gives to the photograph its documentary status, its undeniable veracity [. . .]'[18]

Of course, the notion of photography as 'truth' cannot be taken as a given, as the work of both Spence and Rodney often sought to prove. The various methods of altering photographic reality – whether chemically, digitally or manually – for aims that are personal, political or aesthetic, are intrinsic to the development of photography itself. Yet, despite the increasingly sophisticated artifice of photography, the basic premise of the photographic index remains intact – for what is captured by the camera still remains a direct trace of the object before it. Krauss goes on to propose that within contemporary society, 'truth is understood as a matter of evidence'. If we accept Krauss's proposal, then the photographic representation of the scar – in Donald Rodney's *Flesh of My Flesh* and also in Jo Spence's *The Picture of Health?* – serves as a double articulation of truth as evidence. Firstly, in the photograph as trace of the body's physicality and, secondly, in the scar as the physical trace of injury.

Truth, as is manifested through Donald Rodney's utilisation of the index (or trace), is key to the potency of *Flesh of My Flesh*. The photograph of his thigh is proof of the impact of sickle cell upon his body; the photographs of the hairs are evidence of the unreliability of what is visible to the naked eye. But it is surely the work's self-reflexivity, that operates in tandem with the index, that gives Donald Rodney's *Flesh of My Flesh* its real critical efficacy. In order to subvert the construct of the Black victim, Donald turns to the source of his own pain – his body. In my view, this symbiosis of self-reflexivity and indexicality takes Donald Rodney's work into the realm of the transgressive. Aptly, it is Jo Spence who quotes James Baldwin:

> 'The victim who is able to articulate the situation of the victim has ceased to be a victim; he, or she, has now become a threat.'[19]

To examine this idea of transgression in relation to the damaged body, I want to look at two separate incidents that occurred around the staging of two artworks, *Visceral Canker* (1990, pp. 62, 90–91) and *Flesh of My Flesh*, by Donald Rodney.

5.

In 1990, Donald Rodney exhibited *Visceral Canker*, a sculpture involving the reconstruction of the heraldic shield of Sir John Hawkins, an Elizabethan slave owner whose shield incorporated an image of shackled slaves.[20] Donald's intervention in the object was a network of transparent plastic tubes that were intended to pump a quantity of his own blood around this basic circulatory system. As I have mentioned, the blood transfusion was a fundamental part of Donald's treatment for sickle cell. The relationship between the blood shed by Hawkins' slaves, the 'disease' of colonialism and Donald's own blood is overt. Just prior to the show's opening, the local city council ruled that in order to meet health and safety regulations, and not offend public taste, the real blood needed to be substituted with a theatrical variety. A similar incident occurred when *Flesh of My Flesh* was first shown in 1996.[21] The piece had successfully been shown at London's Barbican Centre and was to tour to hospitals and medical institutions nationally. At St Bartholomew's Hospital, London, *Flesh of My Flesh*, unlike the rest of the work in the exhibition, was shown in a non-public area, out of public sight. The reason given was that the image of the artist's scar might offend patients and visitors.

In *Visceral Canker*, the earlier of the two works, Donald Rodney had attempted to materially confront his audience with the physicality of his body, the work being made in part from his own blood. Yet in the triptych, *Flesh of My Flesh*, Donald exhibited photographic representations of his body. No threat to public health here, not even a trace of blood, but evidently still a threat to public taste.

These two incidents, one involving the removal of a crucial material, and the second, restricting the work's viewing, undoubtedly compromised both the aesthetic and conceptual premises of these respective works. Of course, context may play a part in these works' troubled reception. *Visceral Canker* and *Flesh of My Flesh* were both shown outside conventional gallery spaces and were unfortunate victims of the type of bureaucratic negotiations often involved in staging projects outside of the gallery. Equally, one might say that the 1990 incident harks back to a different time when the media was particularly obsessed with AIDS and its transmission. Evidently, the idea of exhibiting 'damaged' blood in a publicly funded venue was not considered worth the risk of bad press, despite sickle cell anaemia being a congenital blood disorder rather than a disease transmissible via the exchange of bodily fluids. For *Flesh of My Flesh* to be censored on the grounds of 'taste' is even more troubling.

The reception of *Visceral Canker* and *Flesh of My Flesh*, in these instances, reveals some of the problems of showing art that challenges what might generally be considered as an 'acceptable' notion of the body. Both works are, in quite different ways, uncompromising and personal takes on the body in pain. Interestingly, where Donald Rodney faced physical censorship of his work, Jo Spence spoke of silence – another form of censorship, less invasive, but equally demoralising – as the response to her works on her cancer. She said at the time, 'I put up these photographs of my illness and progress and I got no feedback from anyone. I felt as though I were in a madhouse.'[22] For these respective bodies of work by Donald Rodney and Jo Spence to have provoked such negative responses is perhaps telling of their ability to counter normative ideas of the body. This is not to suggest purely altruistic motives on the part of either Rodney or Spence. Both were undoubtedly aware of the shock value of the images they produced. But surely any shock experienced by the viewer is simply a reiteration of that experienced by the artist witnessing and recording the tangible signs of their own prospective deaths.

At a lecture in London in March 2001, performance artist Carolee Schneeman was asked whether she thought the body was still a viable site for a transgressive type of art practice.[23] She answered that, given the proliferation of the body – particularly the naked body – as a commodity within the media and advertising and its over-use in sensationalist types of 'body art', it could no longer be used as a basis for transgressive art. To an extent, I am in agreement with Schneeman. But when I think of Jo Spence's photograph from *The Picture of Health?* series or Donald Rodney's *Flesh of My Flesh*, such works surely exist within the realm of the transgressive. To my mind, a distinction can be drawn in terms of the health of the body being depicted and by whom that depiction is carried out. Within a society obsessed with body perfection, the artist presenting a public image of their unhealthy body transgresses dominant notions of perfection. The reasons raised by Schneeman for why 'the body' in general may no longer be regarded as transgressive are indeed the very reasons why the damaged body offers up the possibility of transgression. For, in this instance, the damaged body:

> 'resists being taken up by mainstream consumer culture, because of its imperfection.
>
> subverts a normative idea of the naked body by revealing the site of disease.
>
> challenges sensationalism in 'body art' since the injuries depicted are the result of disease and are not self-inflicted, as has been the case in some 'endurance' art that seeks to test the limits of the body.'

Despite external attempts to stifle his work, in *Flesh of My Flesh* Donald Rodney succeeds in renegotiating the terms on which the damaged body is presented. He activates the photographic index politically as a means of articulating the issues surrounding sickle cell anaemia specifically and Black masculinity in general. Donald Rodney's image of pain rejects a notion of 'the body' as biologically, politically and socially neutral. And in doing so, he eschews any notion of victimhood that knowledge of his condition might provoke in the viewer by his defiant aestheticisation of his damaged body. In fact, 'the threat' represented by the Black male that Donald Rodney saw propagated in the media, and which he sought to critique in earlier works, has been transformed through works like *Flesh of My Flesh*. In the work of Donald Rodney, the damaged body becomes the threat.

To conclude, I will return to the words of James Baldwin:

> 'The victim who is able to articulate the situation of the victim has ceased to be a victim: he, or she, has now become a threat.'

First published in Richard Hylton (ed.), *Donald Rodney: Doublethink*, (London: Autograph ABP, 2003) 82–91

1   These late photographic works include *In the House at My Father* and other works in progress at the time of Donald Rodney's death. Since 1998, these works – *In the House of My Father* in particular – have come to represent something of a signature for Donald Rodney's later practice. This is perhaps rather misleading since Donald continued to work in a variety of mediums including sculpture, Super-8 film and collage. *In the House of My Father* has been shown extensively in the UK and also internationally. Exhibitions include: 'The British Art Show 5' which toured to Edinburgh, Southampton, Cardiff and Birmingham (2000–01); 'Give and Take: works presented to museums by the Contemporary Art Society', London (2000); 'Homes for the Soul: Micro-Architecture in Mediaeval and Contemporary Art', Henry Moore Institute, Leeds (2001); 'Retuge', Henie Onstad Kunstsenter, Norway (2002).

2   McCurbin died during an attempted arrest by police at a Wolverhampton shopping centre in 1987. As such it is termed a 'death in police custody'. See, the Liberty web site: www.liberty-human-rights.org.uk. Also the Institute of Race Relations: www.irr.org.uk.

3   *Self-Portrait as Clinton McCurbin* also goes under the title of *Self Portrait: Policing the Black Community, Death in the City: Mr Winston Rose, Mr Stephen Bogle and Mr Clinton McCurbin – A Postmodern Postmortem* (p. 79).

4   For an overview of British press coverage of the turbulent race relations in Britain around this period see Paul Gilroy, 'Urban Social Movements, "Race" and Community' in *There Ain't No Black in the Union Jack* (London: Hutchinson, 1987) 223–48.

5   See the documentary video by Edward George and Trevor Matthison, *Three Songs on Pain, Light and Time,* Black Audio Film Collective, 1996.

6   Eddie Chambers, 'Three Songs on Pain, Light and Time', *Art Monthly*, No. 200 (October 1996) 65–66.

7   Interview with Ruth Kelly, Landon, 11 March 1994. See www.iniva.org/auto-icon/DR/interv2.htm.

8   George and Matthison, *Three Songs on Pain, Light and Time.*

9   In earlier works such as *John Barnes* (1991, p. 93) and *Doublethink* (1992, p. 96–97), Donald Rodney sought to examine the paradoxical relationship between Black people and sport.

10 Jo Spence, *Cultural Sniping: The Art at Transgression* (London and New York: Routledge, 1995) 86.

11 See the interview with Donald Rodney in *Three Songs on Pain, Light and Time* (see note 5). Also, David Thorp, 'Flesh of My Flesh' *Body Visual* (exh. cat.) (London: Arts Catalyst, 1996).

12 The collaboration resulted in the exhibition 'Truth, Dare, Double Dare' at the Ikon Gallery, 1994. It is also discussed by Michael Archer in his article 'Collaborators', *Art Monthly*, No. 178 (July/Aug 1994) 3–5.

13 The scarred thigh – with all its erotic connotations – combined with the entwined hairs that signify Black male and White female identity, provide a subtext of latent sexuality.

14 Mark Sladen, 'The Body in Question', *Art Monthly*, No. 191 (November 1995) 3–5.

15 Spence, *Cultural Sniping*, 214.

16 Artists such as Hannah Wilke and Bob Flanagan employed similar strategies of self-documentation in response to their respective terminal illnesses. For example, in Wilke's *Brushstrokes: January 19, 1992*, three locks of the artist's hair are kept and displayed as the result of chemotherapy treatment. And in Bob Flanagan's *Pain Journal* (1995), he acerbically records his final months before succumbing to cystic fibrosis.

17 Interview with Ruth Kelly, London, 11 March 1994. See www.iniva.org/auto-icon/DR/interv2.htm.

18 Rosalind E. Krauss, 'Notes on the Index: Port 2', *The Avant-Garde and Other Modernist Myths* (Cambridge, MA: MIT Press, 1985) 211.

19 Spence, *Cultural Sniping*, 163.

20 *Visceral Canker* was shown as part of the 'TSWA: Four Cities Project', Mount Edgcumbe Park, Plymouth, 6 September–28 October, 1990.

21 *Flesh of My Flesh* was first shown at the Barbican Centre, London, and touring, as part of the 'Body Visual: Artists Examine the Essence of Medical Research', 2–27 May, 1996.

22 Spence, *Cultural Sniping*, 213.

23 Lecture by Carolee Schneeman, Goldsmiths College, London, 15 March 2001.

Virginia Nimarkoh

Who'd a Thought It?: Exploring the Interplay Between the Work of Frida Kahlo and Donald Rodney

Eddie Chambers

Following Frida Kahlo's meteoric rise to posthumous fame and celebrity that occurred during the 1980s and 1990s, many people are now aware of the multiplicity of ways in which she dealt with, and painted, the issue of pain. Kahlo suffered, and endured, several types of pain, which have been increasingly fetishised and are particularly celebrated (I use the word advisedly) aspects of her work.[1] There were the after-effects of her childhood polio, the horrific accident she suffered as a teenager and the never-ending assortment of physical complications. There was the emotional pain of her husband Diego Rivera's affairs and the consequent separation from him as well as the pain of loss, both physical and emotional, when Kahlo lost the baby she was carrying.[2] Notwithstanding the canonisation of Kahlo, her work has been of immense value in terms of its vivid attempts to depict and visualise physical and emotional pain. Pain is, for the most part, something unseen and, therefore, fiendishly difficult for artists to portray. Furthermore, there exists the difficulty of an artist seeking to visualise graphically that which friends, relatives and audiences may well have grown immune or accustomed to. Therefore, ongoing or long-suffering pain carried with it even greater challenges in Kahlo's attempts to represent it in her art.

Frida Kahlo's work is seldom discussed in terms of the explicit influences it had on artists who came after her. Rather, writers have tended to discuss her work in introspective terms and have focused primarily on casting Kahlo as an inspirational figure and a role model for feminists and other women of the

          Who'd a Thought It?

late-twentieth and early twenty-first centuries. This has had the unfortunate consequence of ignoring the ways in which Kahlo's work can be located in a much wider variety of contexts. As publications on Kahlo grew ever more grandiose in scale, and legion in quantity, the texts rarely exceeded the crafted readings of the earliest material on Kahlo. Donald Rodney, a British-born African-Caribbean male, drew inspiration from the corpus of this mid-twentieth-century female Mexican artist, as much as he did from European masters of modernism such as Pablo Picasso. It is a grave deficiency that the work of Donald Rodney has been disregarded when he should rightly be discussed alongside Kahlo, as a compelling example of her influence.

Donald Rodney was born in 1961[3] in Smethwick, Birmingham, UK. One of the most consistently innovative and intelligent artists of his generation, he battled sickle cell anaemia until he died from the condition in March 1998. Rodney's work, from his earliest days as an art student at Trent Polytechnic in Nottingham through to his final one-man show at the South London Gallery six months before he died, had distinctive qualities that marked him out as a practitioner of unique ability and sensitivity. Over time, Rodney became incapacitated by the effects of his illness and spent ever-longer periods in hospital. The episodes of hospitalisation were followed by post-operative convalescence, when he was confined to his London home. As his condition worsened, Rodney drew inspiration from a number of figures from art history, including Kahlo and Pablo Picasso.

Rodney sampled one of Picasso's most celebrated paintings, *Guernica* (1937), to create his work *Soweto/Guernica* (1988, p. 81) which was hugely successful. Picasso's monumental commentary on a particularly violent episode from the Spanish Civil War was used by Rodney to illustrate a more recent episode of equal barbarity; the suppression by the South African state of Black South Africans demonstrating against Apartheid. The demonstrations were sparked by schoolchildren protesting against being taught in Afrikaans, a language they perceived to be that of their oppressors. Rodney's *Soweto/Guernica* was, in essence, a composite of Picasso's painting and an equally iconic photograph by Sam Nzima, a South African photographer. Nzima's image was of the dead schoolboy, Hector Pieterson, the first casualty of a series of clashes in Soweto that began in June 1976 between Black youths and the South African authorities. In this solitary frame, the photograph quickly came to symbolise the brutality of the Apartheid system and its destruction of Black lives, particularly those of young people. The Soweto uprising at that time represented the latest episode in the anti-Apartheid struggle. Over several months more than five hundred people died, though it was the killing of Hector Pieterson on the first day of the uprising that eclipsed all others in the imagination of the world outside that fractured country. Nzima's photograph

showed the twelve-year-old Pieterson being carried by a young man, with
Pieterson's distressed sister running alongside. The image was in many ways
surreal – showing the force of one of Africa's most sophisticated militaries
being unleashed on protesting schoolchildren. No other single image
provoked as much outrage and garnered as much sympathy as Nzima's picture.

Guernica was one of Pablo Picasso's most famous paintings and was
created in response to the bombing of the town of Guernica in the Spanish
Basque Country in April 1937 by German and Italian warplanes, at the
instigation of the Spanish Nationalist forces during the Spanish Civil War.
The painting drew attention to this brutal act against innocent people and
was first exhibited later that year. Thereafter, it came to represent not only
the callousness of the Spanish Nationalist forces, but also the wider tragedies
of war and the suffering it inflicted – increasingly so during the course of the
twentieth century – upon civilians caught up in conflicts not of their making
or choosing. *Guernica* is widely regarded as a commentary against war and
helped bring the Spanish Civil War to the world's attention. In the same
way, Nzima's photograph helped draw the world's attention to the brutality
of Apartheid. Rodney's work *Soweto/Guernica* represented an arresting and
innovative fusion of these two powerful pictures, from different spaces and
times, in a compelling late-twentieth-century work.

Rodney's work was fresh as well as politically and socially relevant; and it
was characterised by a distinctive use of image and text, and a keen awareness
of modern art trends such as Pop Art, mixed media and assemblage sculpture.
His mid-1980s pieces revealed the influence of major figures of mid-twentieth-
century American art such as Robert Rauschenberg. In a television interview
of the late 1980s, Rodney highlights the extent of his knowledge of art history:

> 'When I went to Trent [Polytechnic] I'd been brought up in the tradition
> of painting. I knew how to paint. I knew the history of painting. I knew
> my Picassos, my everything.[4]

Rodney sought not so much to make work that stood outside of this history;
instead, he made work that critiqued that history (in terms of its partiality
and bias), whilst simultaneously demanding for himself a credible place
within a more equitable and textured history of art.

In the mid-to-late 1980s, Rodney was spending greater periods of time in
hospital. From the confines of his bed, he cast around for material with which
he could make art. He seized on discarded X-rays as the perfect material.
Costing nothing, Rodney was able to access large quantities of X-rays,
(once identifying markers such as names had been removed to protect the
confidentiality of patients), and he began making considered and considerable

 Who'd a Thought It?

use of them within his work. Rodney's technique, though simple, was innovative and hugely effective. Seeking to produce large, expansive pieces of work, he would first create smaller outline versions in his sketchbook. These outlines would then be divided by means of a grid of uniform squares laid over the image. Each of these squares, no more than an inch or two, represented, in miniature, a discarded X-ray of equal shape but much larger size. Thus, once each of the larger panels on which he had drawn or painted (and in some instances cut into with the aid of a scalpel) were pieced together, Rodney was able to faithfully and accurately scale up his drawings, to produce work on a majestic scale. Having developed this way of working, he employed it in contexts beyond his hospital bed. It was this technique and this use of discarded hospital X-rays that Rodney employed in the making of *Soweto/Guernica*.

Many of Rodney's X-ray pieces were brought together for his exhibition 'Crisis' at Chisenhale Gallery, London in 1989. The body of work, comprising ten pieces, had largely been made when Rodney was artist-in-residence at a community centre in Sheffield, a project that had been organised with the Graves Art Gallery. The press release for the 'Crisis' exhibition describes Rodney's use of the X-ray medium:

> 'Rodney has in the past, as now, used X-rays as the ground or base material for much of his work, either drawing on their surface or using them as screens to obscure other images . . . The potency of the X-ray as a metaphor is extensive – referring to death, fragility, what lies beneath the surface, menace, insight etc. Rodney develops new ways of exploiting this unusual medium, and has recently started drawing in oil pastels upon their surface, as well as using layers of images and X-rays.'[5]

Rodney's use of X-rays was multifaceted, and indicated both the artist's perceptiveness and his resourcefulness. In the first instance, he had found a way to make work – frequently on a monumental scale – that did not necessarily rely on access to a studio and could, to a large extent, be conceived and, in some instances, executed from his hospital bed or the confines of his London flat. As Mark Currah observed:

> 'using a series of the uniformly-sized panels in a picture's construction enables him to work up a painting in sections. The grand scale of these works was achieved without a studio.'[6]

Secondly, as Adeola Solanke points out, Rodney used X-rays to 'offer a diagnostic reading of Britain today, with particular reference to the condition of black people'.[7]

Solanke quoted Rodney as saying:

> '[W]ith X-rays you're looking beneath the surface to see what the structures of things really are. That's what I wanted to do: to look beneath the surface of our lives, see how we are, and how the structure of society has made us what we are.'[8]

Thirdly, Rodney seized upon X-rays because very few artists had considered the creative and metaphoric possibilities of this unusual medium. Using X-rays was different.

Emmanuel Cooper summarised Rodney's technique thus: 'Using X-ray plates as a ground, he either draws or paints on them to screen out other images'.[9] Elaborating on his approach, Solanke described Rodney as:

> 'using a surgeon's scalpel to carve out apocalyptic statements on the surface of the X-rays which, against the white chipboard on which they are mounted, glow with an eerie, blueish pallor.'[10]

By their nature, Rodney's X-ray pieces tended to be executed on a monumental scale, making them singularly dynamic in both scale and content. Working on one section of X-ray at a time often meant that when the pieces were assembled – in something of a cross between a jigsaw puzzle and a mosaic – the panels would sometimes join seamlessly, and other times the alignment would be a centimetre or so out of sync. This process had the extraordinary effect of creating panoramas or pictures that were often infused with a kind of Frankenstein aesthetic, in which the grotesque aspects of Rodney's subjects were decidedly amplified.

While Rodney could not escape his illness, he refused to declare himself a victim. In Frida Kahlo he saw another artist who battled with pain and illness to produce extraordinary work and over a decade or so he produced astonishing work that demonstrated Kahlo's influence on him. Yet, unlike Kahlo's focus on her individual pain, his use of X-rays was not to draw attention to his own sickness; instead, they were used as a metaphor to represent the 'societal disease' of Apartheid, police brutality and racism. Thus, it is in Rodney's work about social issues that he most samples Frida Kahlo. Rodney wanted to extend the metaphors of sickness and ill health beyond one person into readings of history, as well as contemporary events and contexts. For example, even before his X-ray pieces, Rodney had produced a series of large hangings around the theme of slavery and the slave trade, rendered on discarded hospital sheets. Evocative of illness and hospitalisation, the threadbare or otherwise frayed and tatty white cotton

                                        Who'd a Thought It?

bed sheets were the perfect surface on which to visualise the imagery and symbolism of slavery and its legacies.

In paintings such as *Henry Ford Hospital* (1932) *The Broken Column* (1944), Kahlo represents her body as if it has, literally, been opened up for the world to see. In *The Broken Column* the viewer looks into Kahlo's rib cage, which reveals a fractured architectural column. In *Henry Ford Hospital*, which illustrates the trauma of her miscarriage, two of the six objects tied to her by means of umbilical cords feature exposed parts of her anatomy. One is the skeletal rendering of a fractured pelvis, wholly dysfunctional when it came to the task of carrying a foetus to full term and safely and healthily giving birth. The other of these two objects takes the form of what appears to be a model of a woman's reproductive and other internal organs, such as those one might find in a biology class. With these works, Kahlo demonstrated a willingness to look inside the human body as a way of portraying the physical damage which would otherwise remain unseen. In this way, Kahlo enables the viewer to see what a surgeon can during an operation. As one of Kahlo's many essayists noted, 'Kahlo made use of medical analogies and metaphors, often picturing – outside the body – hearts, glands, and other organs or displaying a kind of X-ray knowledge of veins and ducts'.[11]

For Rodney, the X-ray was his means of presenting the opening up of the societal body. He posited the idea that, just as a surgeon could see disease and decay in a body through the use of X-rays, similarly – through a

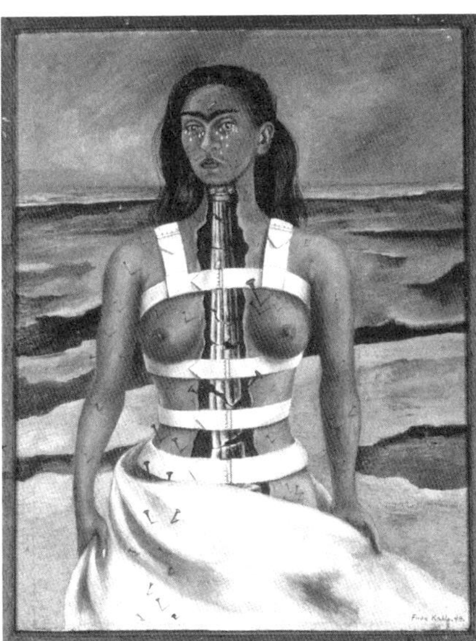

Frida Kahlo, The Broken Column, 1944
Oil on canvas, 39.8 × 30.6 cm
Fundacion Dolores Olmedo, Mexico City, Mexico

potent combination of historical and ongoing societal experiences – Black people saw societal disease that white people refused or were unable to see. Developing his compelling analogy of societal racism = illness, police brutality = illness, and apartheid = illness, Rodney likened Britain to a terminally ill hospital patient, admitted to 'Britannia Hospital'.

The original *Britannia Hospital* was a film released in 1982, directed by Lindsay Anderson. It was created at a time when the prime minister, Margaret Thatcher, was perceived by her supporters to be taking the UK by the scruff of the neck and dragging the country into an age of deregulation, the free market and ultra-conservative values. In the run-up to her election victory, Thatcher was aided by a palpable sense, indulged by dominant sections of the media, that Britain was being threatened by anarchy-minded trade unionists who were effectively holding the country to ransom. So intense was the media-stoked feeling that wanton industrial action was one of the main threats to the UK, that one particular period of industrial and public sector unrest was dubbed a contemporary version of Shakespeare's *Winter of Discontent*. It was this sense that Britain was out of control, without proper order and discipline, that was parodied in the film *Britannia Hospital*. The hospital where the film was set was a large centuries-old facility, in which megalomaniac doctors flexed an equivalent amount of power to the striking manual workers, prioritising their right to strike over the needs of patients who had the misfortune of being admitted to the infirmary. Anderson's film in many ways parodied press and media fixations of sinister labour unrest and, to this end, the crumbling, deeply dysfunctional public institution was a perfect allegory for the supposed decline of Britain.

For Rodney, *Britannia Hospital* was a compelling allegory that he was able to appropriate and expand into his own series. Rodney extended the metaphor of a broken and dysfunctional UK and, in his work, *Britannia Hospital* is represented as a terminally ill patient, riddled with a variety of societal diseases. What made Rodney's *Britannia Hospital* series (1988, pp. 75–77) so compelling was his framing of the patient as believing himself to be in the very best of health. A patient who did not recognise the extent of his own sickness was, in so many ways, more ill than a patient rigged up to a life-support machine, whose life was fading. Many people look at the society around them and perceive it to be in overall good shape. For Rodney, this meant not seeing, or being blind to, the diseases of racism, police brutality and surveillance, privilege and so on.

One of Rodney's most monumental pieces in his *Britannia Hospital* series was *Britannia Hospital 3* (1988, pp. 76–77), which acted as a grim composite assessment of modern Britain. The central aspect of the work is the prone, hospitalised figure of a man, body wracked with pain, being attended by a Black nurse. The Black nurse referenced the historic realities of so many women

                                    Who'd a Thought It?

coming from Africa, South Asia and the Caribbean to fill vacancies in the UK's healthcare sector in the decades following the end of the Second World War. With immigrants vilified by British politicians and the press, Rodney felt that it was important to acknowledge the contribution of Britain's Black nurses.

Behind the patient in Rodney's *Britannia Hospital 3* looms the figure of a police officer from the notorious Special Patrol Group (SPG), the riot-ready unit of the London Metropolitan Police tasked with suppressing urban 'disorder'. This ominous figure could not have been a more striking antithesis of the genteel, benevolent image of television's *Dixon of Dock Green* bobby-on-the-beat.[12] The figure of the police officer symbolised the militarisation of the police and the ways in which the 1980s Conservative government had increased the police's powers to quell civil 'unrest'. In this sense the British police resembled, at times, more an occupying paramilitary force than a public service ready to serve diverse communities of British people. The battle lines between the police and a perceived group of rebellious Black youths had been drawn for decades. The SPG gained notoriety after it killed the anti-racism campaigner Blair Peach during turbulent events surrounding a counter-demonstration against the far-right National Front in April 1979. Several years later, the image of the police as an out-of-control paramilitary body appeared again during the miners' strikes of the mid-1980s. Rodney's battle-ready SPG apparition in *Britannia Hospital 3* looms large over the sick man, and readily symbolises the country's societal problems.

In the left section of the composition is the curious figure of a naked Black woman, shown from the waist up. Around her body is a metal harness, resembling an instrument of torture. The woman's body is open, revealing a broken architectural pillar. Thus, Rodney sampled Kahlo's iconic painting, *Broken Column* (1944). In the painting, Kahlo is described as appearing:

> 'against the fissured earth of an empty volcanic landscape. She looks straight ahead of her, as if challenging the viewer to confront her suffering, and exposes her wounds like a martyr.'[13]

Elsewhere, another Kahlo biographer wrote that the painting:

> 'commonly is considered to relate directly the accident [Kahlo had in her teens in which she was horrifically injured in a collision involving a tram in which she was riding], though it was produced nineteen years later. This association is perpetuated by the fact that the accident is the basis for explaining her chronic pain. Kahlo's body, punctured by countless nails and torn open to reveal a crumbling architectural column as a metaphor for her own spinal column, is held together by an orthopedic brace.'[14]

Kahlo employed the metaphor of the broken column to visualise physical trauma which might otherwise remain unseen, even to sympathetic relatives and close friends. Intrigued by the image, Rodney invoked Kahlo's *Broken Column* as a means of animating the multiple traumas suffered by Black people through history and up to present-day Britain, and the various ways they seemed almost hopelessly unable to avoid or prevent harm being done to them by institutional racism.

Whilst Kahlo's substantial number of self-portraits (a significant aspect of her body of work) tended to portray her emotional and physical pain, as well as her multiple identities as a miscarriage sufferer, a wife, a lover, a woman and so on, Rodney tended to undertake self-portraits for other reasons. Rodney was anxious to avoid the idea that his self-portraits related to himself personally and should primarily be seen in such a context. Though much of Rodney's work was about the oppression and misrepresentation of the Black male, he was strenuously careful not to present himself within his work as some sort of personal Black martyr representatively shouldering the burden of collective oppression. Illustrative of is attitude were Rodney's works such as *The House That Jack Built* (1987, p. 74), *Self-Portrait: Policing the Black Community*, *Death in the City: Mr Winston Rose, Mr Stephen Bogle and Mr Clinton McCurbin – A Postmodern Postmortem* (1988, p. 79) and *Self-Portrait: Black Men Public Enemy* (1990, p. 92). Rodney gave clues to the extent of this ambivalence of placing himself at the centre of his self-portraits in a statement for a catalogue relating to an exhibition in which his work was included:

> 'I've been working for some time on a series . . . about the black male image, both in the media and black self-perception. I wanted to make a self-portrait.
>
> [Though] I didn't want to produce an image with myself in it. It would be far too heroic considering the subject matter. I wanted generic black men, a group of faces that represented in a stereotypical way black man as 'the other', black man as the enemy within the body politic. The pictures come from *The Sunday Times* and a book on blood diseases and the final black and white picture as an identikit picture from *The Evening Standard*.'[15]

Both Kahlo and Rodney, albeit in dramatically different spaces and times, were intrigued by news stories presented in the media. Kahlo had a singular ability to render in visual form stories from the news, such as in *A Few Little Pricks* (1935), and from other events of human tragedy, including in *The Suicide of Dorothy Hale* (1938–39). A profound sense of empathy lay at the heart of both artists' responses to media depictions of certain individuals or types of individuals.

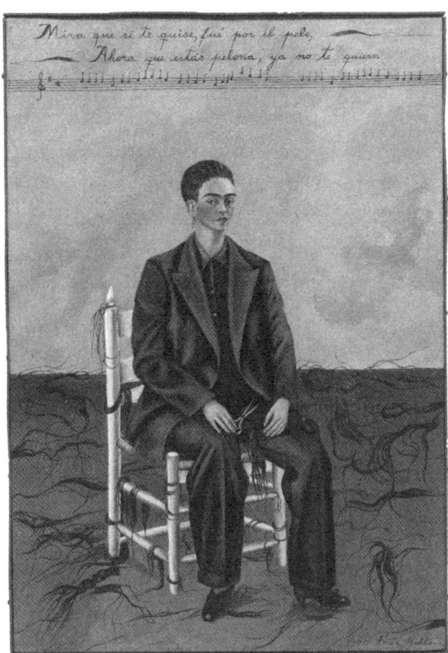

Frida Kahlo, *Self-Portrait with Cropped Hair*, 1940
Oil on canvas, 40 × 27.9 cm

Another work by Kahlo that profoundly influenced Rodney was *Self-portrait with Cropped Hair* from 1940. In the painting:

> 'she appears with her scissors in her hand, dressed in a suit (her ex-husband's?), so enormous it swamps her, and sitting on a rush-seat chair in the middle of a floor stewn with strands of hair. Whether the scene represents female castration or reconquered liberty, or both, is unclear.'[16]

Elsewhere, the same writer describes the painting as one in which:

> 'the viewer witnesses a scene unfolding in private . . . Alone in her chair like a prisoner in her cell, the artist has taken her decision: she has cut her hair and with it her ties to Diego . . . Frida looks at us provocatively, still holding the scissors in her hand, forcing us to witness her act of self-destruction.'[17]

Rodney took several features from the painting *Self-portrait with Cropped Hair* – the figure, seated in the chair, the chair itself and, of huge significance, the scissors – and used them in his self-portrait, *The House That Jack Built*

(1987, p. 74). The work consisted of a two-dimensional house made up of X-rays, out of which had been cut numerous outlines of scissors and similarly embellished with text that consisted of passionate prose, ending with 'I can hear the drums beat out SOS Save our Shit, Save our Souls, Save our Struggle'. In front of the house, on a low-level plinth, sits a scarecrow figure on a chair, in the manner of Kahlo in her *Self-portrait with Cropped Hair*. Also reminiscent of Kahlo's painting *Broken Column,* Rodney's figure has a tree growing through its body and sprouting in place of a head, signifying perhaps the violent pain that so often racked his body. Kahlo's scissors, the outlines of which are liberally scattered across the façade of the house, resonate with the symbolism of destruction, ruination and disfigurement, rather than the more positive and creative uses to which scissors can be put.

In the painting *The Two Fridas* (1939), which predated *Self-portrait with Cropped Hair*, Kahlo depicted herself as two bodies, two entities. One of the bodies, dressed splashed by a severed artery leading from her heart, holds a pair of scissors that have either cut the artery or act as pinchers to stem

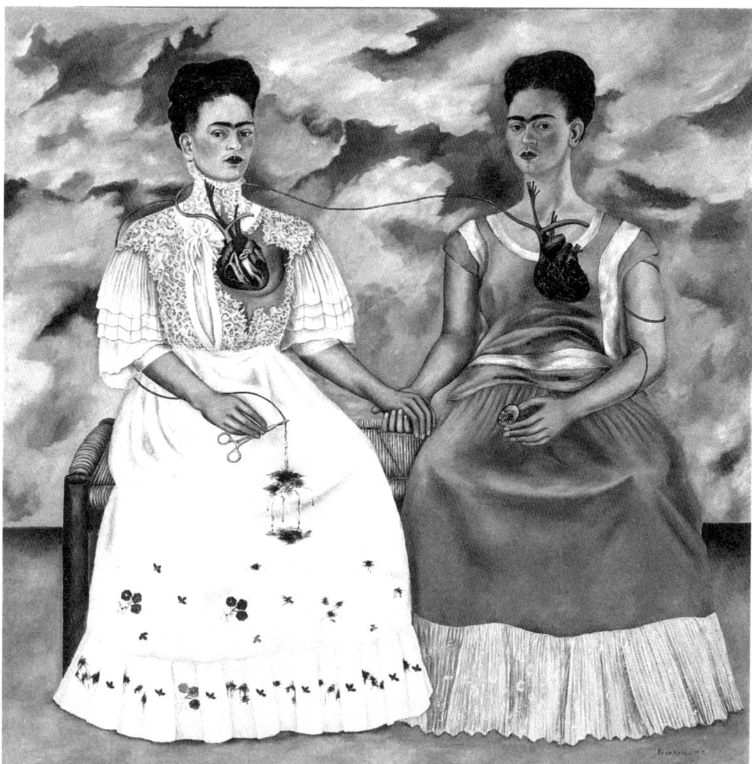

Frida Kahlo, *The Two Fridas*, 1939
Oil on canvas, 171.9 × 171.9 cm

Who'd a Thought It?

the flow of blood. The work, widely and exhaustively discussed in books on Kahlo, features two exposed and interconnected hearts. Thus, circulatory systems of the flow of blood, from one heart to the other, from one body to the other, from one being to the other, lie at the core (some might say, the heart) of the painting. A similar investigation of circulatory systems, from one entity to another and back again, lay at the heart of Rodney's commission for TSWA Four Cities Project, Plymouth, *Visceral Canker* (1990, pp. 62, 90–91). In its original context, *Visceral Canker* was installed in the nocturnal bowels of Drake's Island Battery off the coast of Plymouth, a maritime city in South West England with a pronounced association with seafaring, trade and exploration. Also known as Garden Battery, Mount Edgecumbe or the Palmerston gun-battery (after the nineteenth-century British prime minister, Lord Palmerston, under whose watch the battery was commissioned), this was one of a series of fortifications built around Plymouth Sound during the 1860s as part of a programme of defensive enhancements to Britain's naval bases. Drake's Island Battery had a long history right up until the Second World War as a fortified site, for the purposes of defending the realm and the strategically important city of Plymouth. As an installation, *Visceral Canker* was perhaps a persuasive and telling undertaking, responding as it did to the formal and associated aspects of the space and environment in which it was located. Drake's Island Battery was in some ways a stark metaphor for Rodney and his own ailing body. As a fortified site of defence, Drake's Island Battery was perhaps not the most effective bastion. Likewise Rodney's body, though skin, flesh and bone like other bodies, was increasingly unable to defend itself against the debilitating effects of diseases of the blood such as sickle cell anaemia.[18] When aspects of the work were re-presented in a gallery context some time later, the work was described as using 'the coats of arms of Sir John Hawkins and Queen Elizabeth I, bound together by a tube of the artist's blood, to explore ideas of heredity and slavery'. *Visceral Canker* was a bold attempt to animate several issues relating to Britain's involvement with the Atlantic slave trade. The coats of arms related to John Hawkins, the first English slave trader, sanctioned and supported in his endeavour by Queen Elizabeth I. Hawkins' coat of arms made unashamed references to the source of his wealth and one of the principal aspects of his work that of being a slaver. His coat of arms, bound by means of a circulatory system that pumped blood-like fluid to the coat of arms of Queen Elizabeth I featured, amongst other things, three black men shackled with slave collars.

Another example from Rodney's critical body of work which could be said to betray the influence of Kahlo was *Psalms* (1997, pp. 114–115). In Julie Taymor's biopic *Frida* (2002) (which acted as a fillip to the ever-increasing canonisation of Kahlo), a mawkish scene of triumphalism is played out

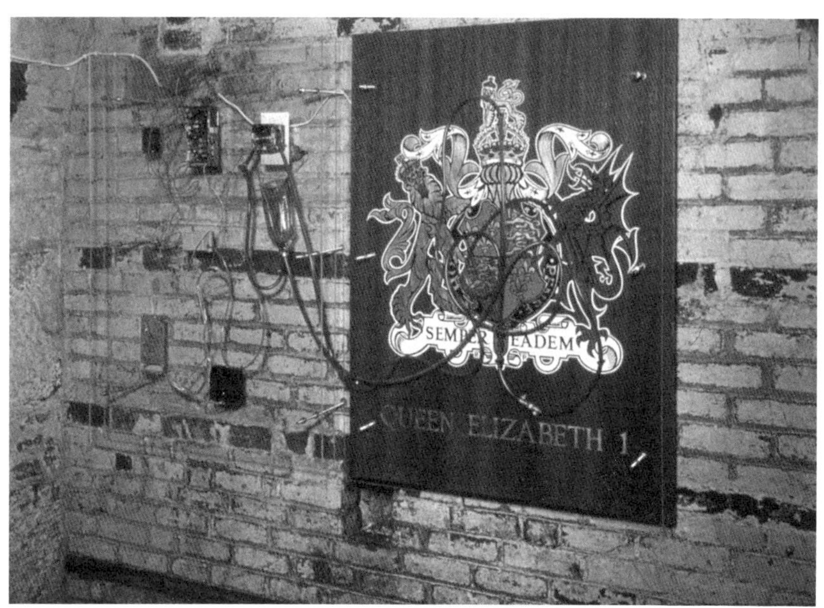

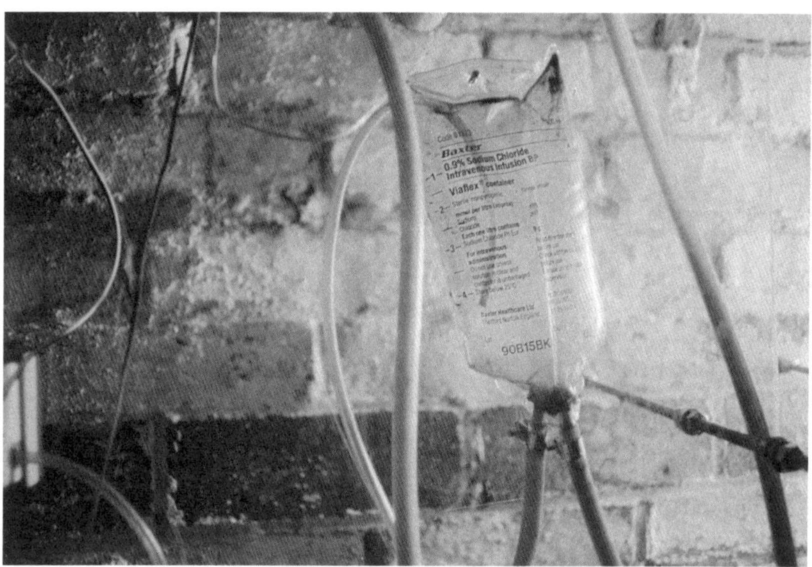

Visceral Canker, installation views, TSWA, Plymouth, 1990
Photographs by Eddie Chambers

 Who'd a Thought It?

towards the end of the film. Kahlo, understandably intent on attending the opening view of what was to be one of the only substantial exhibitions of her work during her lifetime, is ordered by doctors not to leave her hospital bed, as such exertion would likely be catastrophic. Ingeniously, Kahlo subverts the medical advice by having her bed, complete with its regal-like patient, triumphantly transported to the opening. Rodney's *Psalms* had earlier evoked a plaintive framing of an artist's enforced – by virtue of medical debilitation – absence from his own exhibition. In Rodney's case, it was his magnificent '9 Night in Eldorado' exhibition held in the autumn of 1997. The central element of *Psalms* was an unoccupied motorised wheelchair. Kahlo had herself prominently featured her own wheelchair in her painting *Self-Portrait with the Portrait of Doctor Farill* (1951). In the painting, Kahlo sits in her wheelchair, having rendered an affectionate portrait of her doctor. At the time of the painting, Kahlo was increasingly forced to rely on her wheelchair for mobility, a dependency which increased: 'After her gangrenous leg was amputated below the knee in 1953, she relied on a wheelchair for mobility until her death in 1954'.[19]

Psalms was one of the most profound works in what turned out to be Rodney's final solo exhibition before his death. It featured the said motorised wheelchair, equipped with sensors, computer-programmed to navigate continually and near-silently the floor space of the sizeable gallery, avoiding collision with gallery visitors and his wall-based and floor-based art objects. Publicity for the piece described it as '[t]he empty wheelchair courses through its various trajectories on a sad and lonely journey of life, a journey to nowhere. Its movements repeat, like an ever-recurring memory . . .'.[20] Whilst it was of course possible to read narratives of deep pathos into the work, *Psalms* had additional readings of even greater poignancy and symbolism. The wheelchair symbolised Rodney's near-tactile omnipresence within the gallery, whilst simultaneously reminding gallery visitors, in the most understated way, of the artist's enforced absence from his own exhibition. Frida Kahlo would have been impressed.

First published in *Wasafiri*, vol. 27, no. 23, (September 2012) 22–33.

1 The large body of material on Frida Kahlo includes Christina Burrus, *Frida Kahlo: Painting Her Own Reality* (New York: Abrams, 2008); Margaret A. Lindauer, *Devouring Frida: The Art History and Popular Celebrity of Frida Kahlo* (Hanover, NH: Wesleyan UP, 1999); and Hayden Herrera, *Frida: A Biography of Frida Kahlo* (New York: Harper and Row Publishers, Perennial Library, 1983).

2 Since Kahlo's work was introduced to international audiences from the late 1970s onwards, it has been the subject of numerous exhibitions and publications. A critically acclaimed biopic was made along with other biographies of the artist.

3 For information and material on Donald Rodney, see essays by Eddie Chambers and Virginia Nimarkoh in Richard Hylton (ed.), *Donald Rodney: Doublethink* (London: Autograph, 2003).

4 Lubaina Himid, 'Donald Rodney in Conversation' *State of the Art*, Channel 4, 1987.

5 Chisenhale Gallery Press Release for 'Crisis'. London, 18 January – 18 February 1989.

6 Mark Currah, 'Donald Rodney, "Crisis", Chisenhale Gallery' *City Limits*, 17 February 1989, 55

7 Adeola Solanke, 'Donald Rodney, "Crisis", Chisenhale Gallery', *Art Monthly*, no. 124 (March 1989) 13, 14.

8 Ibid.

9 Emmanuel Cooper, 'On Black Art', *Time Out* 1–8 February 1989, 39.

10 Adeola Solanke, 'Donald Rodney, "Crisis"', 13, 14.

11 Sarah M. Lowe, *Frida Kahlo* (New York: Universe, 1991) 18

12 *Dixon of Dock Green* was a genteel drama series that ran on British television for two decades from the mid-1950s. The central character, Police Constable Dixon, was portrayed as reassuring and ready to mildly rebuke wrongdoers but, more importantly perhaps, he showed them the error of their ways. Dixon's paternal nature created a sense of policing as a benign service, the cornerstone of all stable, God-fearing British communities. The popular memory of *Dixon of Dock Green* is in essence a comforting throwback to how television used to be, how life used to be, how society used to be, before all of these things became ever more mixed up and frenetic as the century wore on.

13 Christina Burrus, *Frida Kahlo: Painting Her Own Reality* (New York: Abrams, 2007), 83.

14 Margaret A. Lindauer, 'Frida of the Blood-Covered Paint Brush', 56.

15 Neal Ascherson, 'Shocks to the System: Social and Political Issues in Recent British Art from the Arts Council Collection' (exh. cat.) (Southbank Centre, 1991) 66.

16 Burrus, *Frida Kahlo: Painting Her Own Reality*, 72–73.

17 Ibid., 73.

18 A review of TSWA Four Cities Project appeared in *Art Monthly*, October 1990. Written by John Furse, the review provided a useful introduction to *Visceral Canker*. It read: '[…] the Palmerston gun-battery, part of a complex fortress system built to defend the City of Plymouth against foreign intruders […] Rodney's two-part piece is a terse comment on the parts played by Elizabeth I and her naval commander Sir John Hawkins, a Devon man, in the development of the slave-trade. Coats of arms (there is an image of a hanged Moor in Hawkins's) are linked by transparent tubing to a simple pumping system that acts as a metaphor for the human heart and in turn, as Rodney sees it, the hearts of the nation.'

19 Lindauer, 'Frida of the Blood-Covered Paint Brush', 56.

20 Jane Bilton, 'Introduction', *9 Night in Eldorado* (exh. cat.) (South London Gallery, 1997) n.p.

Who'd a Thought It?

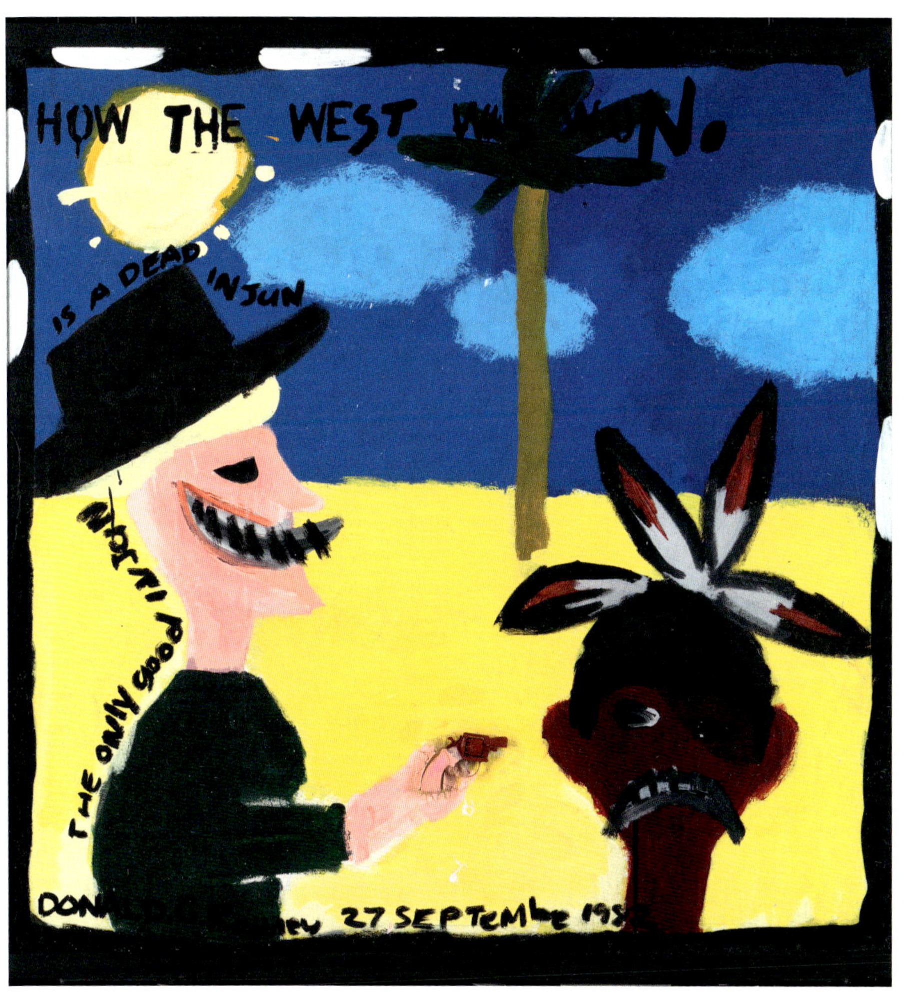

How the West was Won, 1982
Acrylic paint on canvas, 120 × 121.5 cm

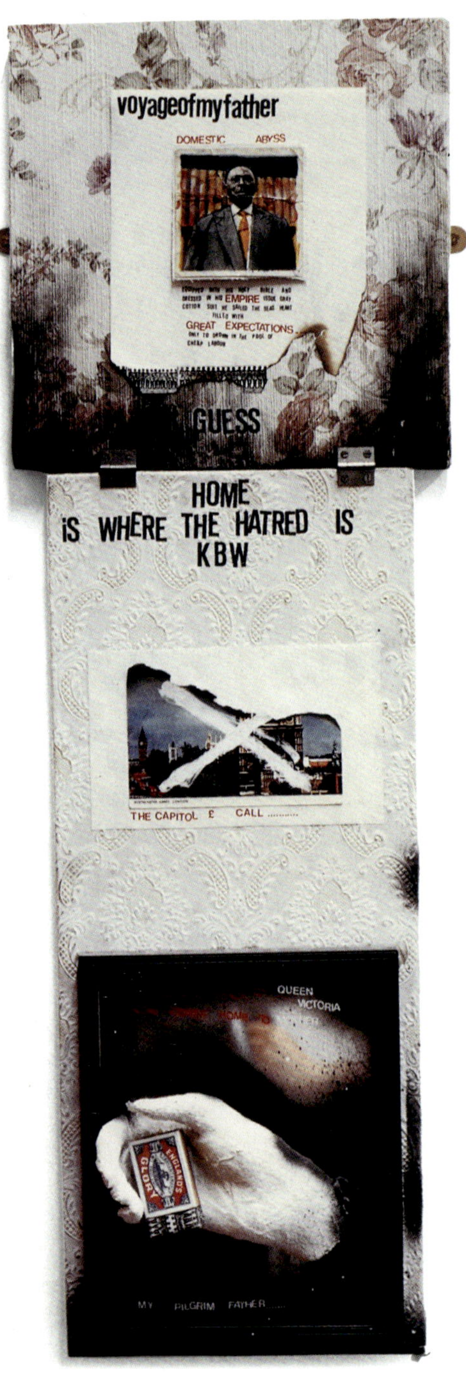

Voyage of My Father, 1985
Mixed media, 122 × 50 cm

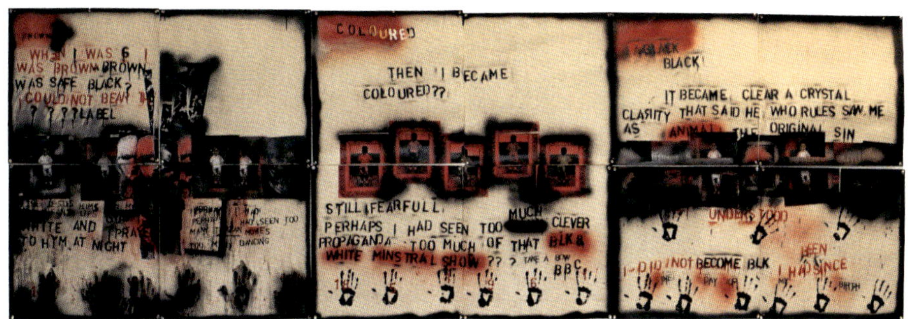

Brown Coloured Black, 1983
Paint, photocopy, spray paint and stencil on graph paper, 122 × 335 cm

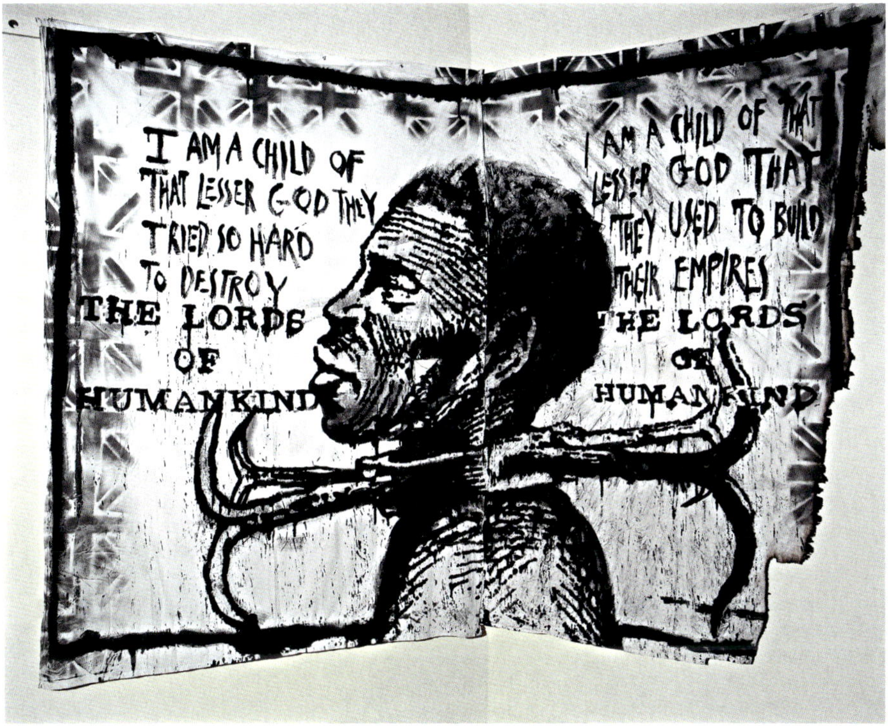

The Lords of Humankind (detail), 1986
Overall installation: 24 metres long
Painting on suspended and burnt hospital sheets

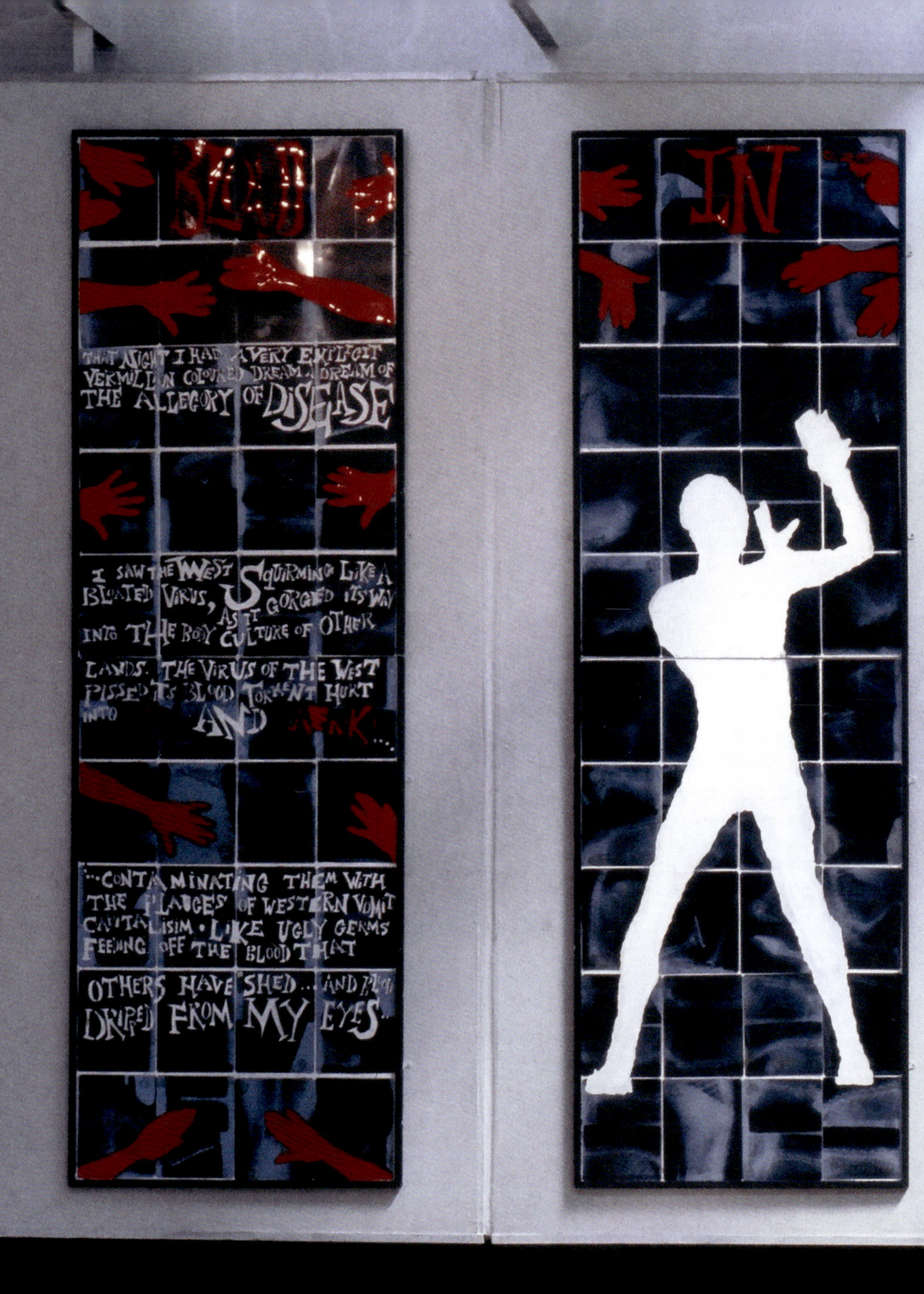

BLOOD
IN
THAT NIGHT I HAD A VERY EXPLICIT VERMILLON COLOURED DREAM A DREAM OF THE ALLEGORY OF DISEASE
I SAW THE WEST SQUIRMING LIKE A BLOATED VIRUS, AS IT GORGED ITS WAY INTO THE BODY CULTURE OF OTHER LANDS. THE VIRUS OF THE WEST PISSED ITS BLOOD TORMENT HURT INTO AND FREAK...
...CONTAMINATING THEM WITH THE PLAGUES OF WESTERN VOMIT CAPITALISIM . LIKE UGLY GERMS FEEDING OFF THE BLOOD THAT OTHERS HAVE SHED... AND BLOOD DRIPPED FROM MY EYES.

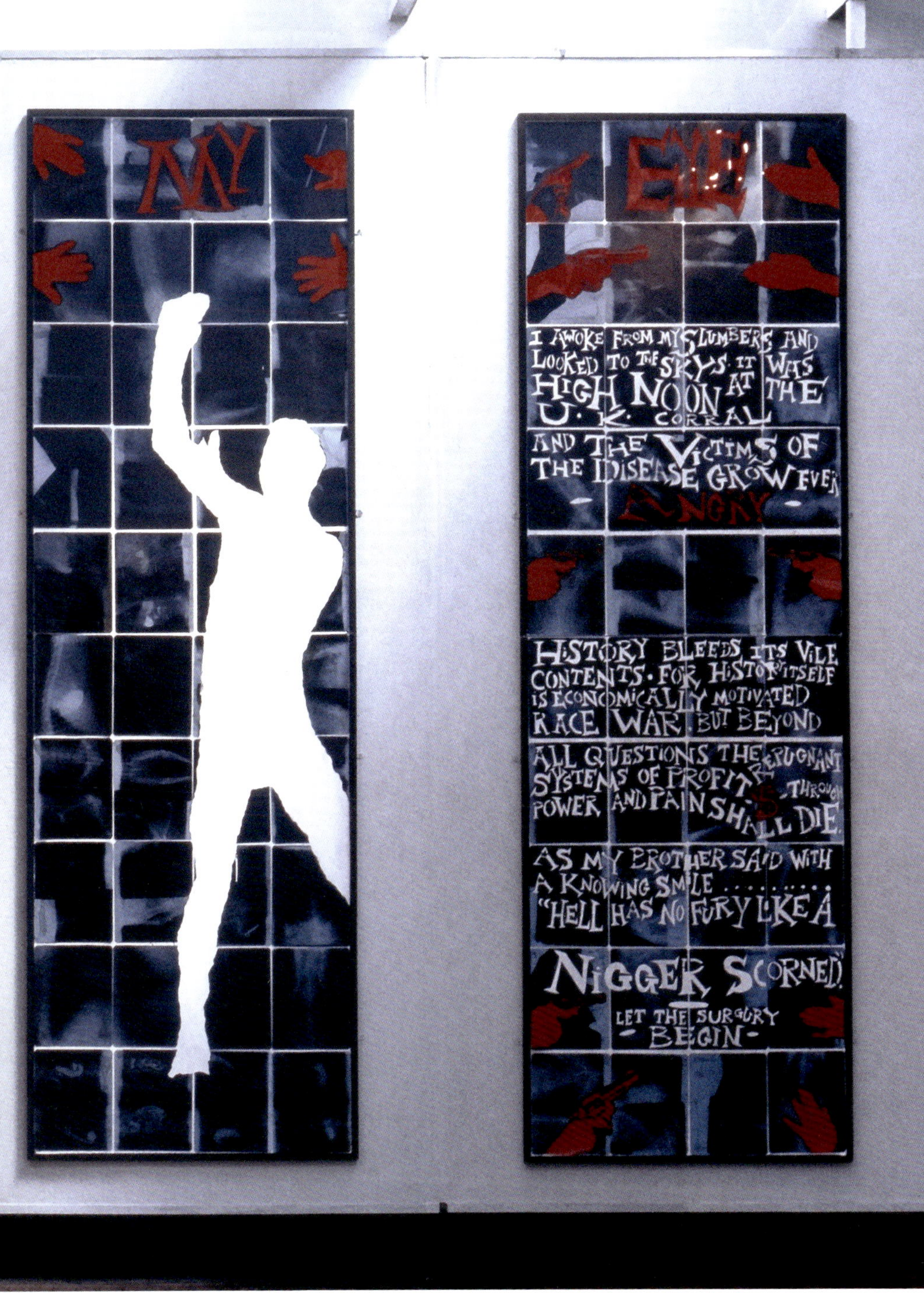

Blood in My Eye, 1986
Mixed media on X-rays mounted on four panels, each: 304 × 122 cm

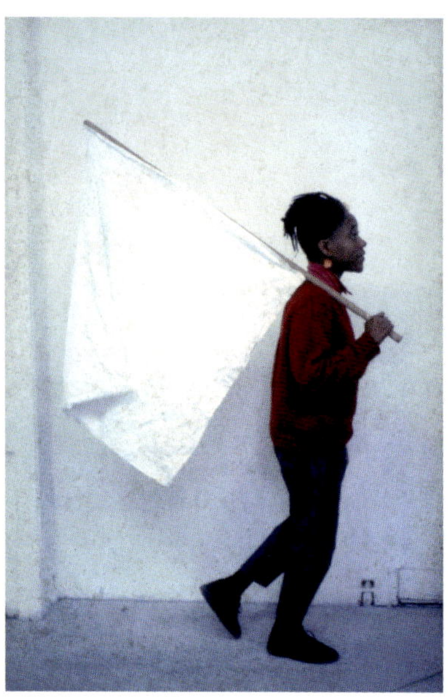

Artist Sonia Boyce carrying a flag in Donald Rodney's studio at Slade School of Art, London, 1987. Rodney used the silhouettes from this series of photographs in a now-lost X-ray work *A Beginner's Guide to Blak History* (1987)

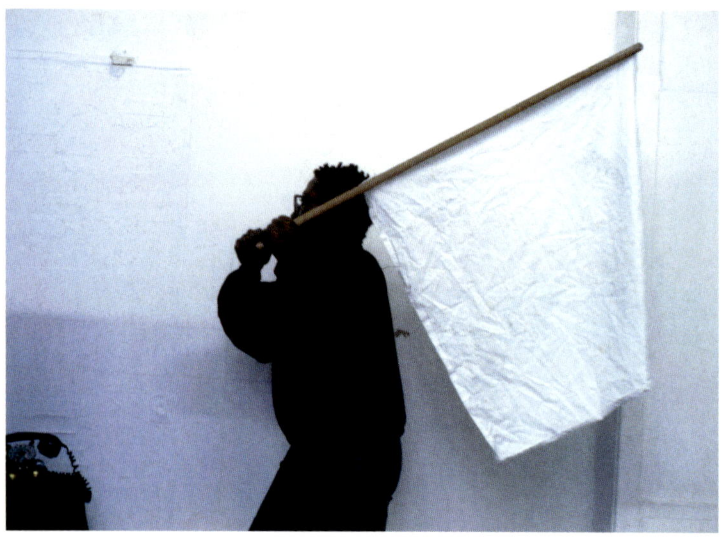

Donald Rodney carrying a flag in his studio at Slade School of Art, London, 1987

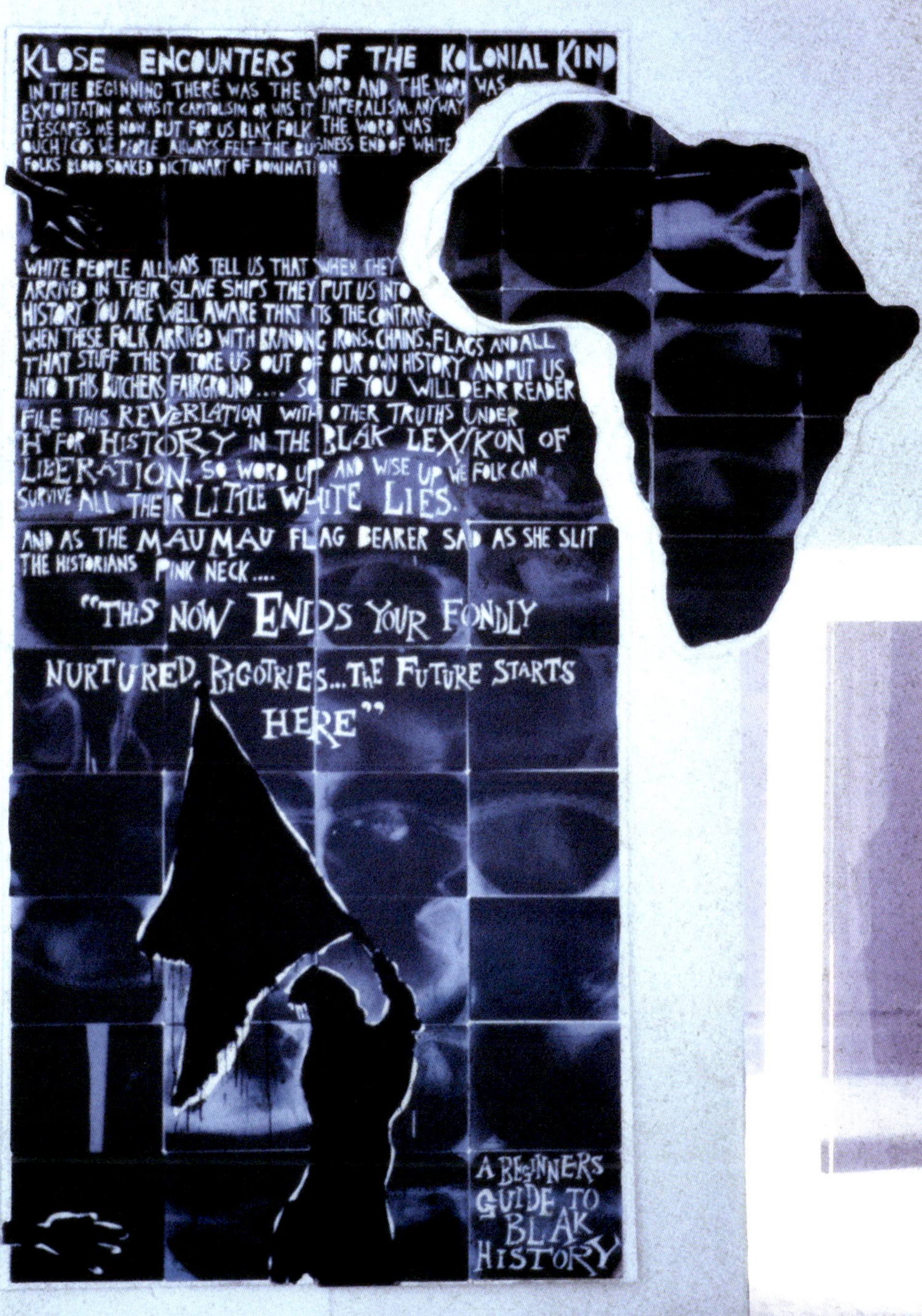

A Beginner's Guide to Blak History (also known as *Klose Encounters of the Kolonial Kind*), 1987
Paint and mixed media on X-rays, dimensions unknown
Installation view at Slade School of Art, London

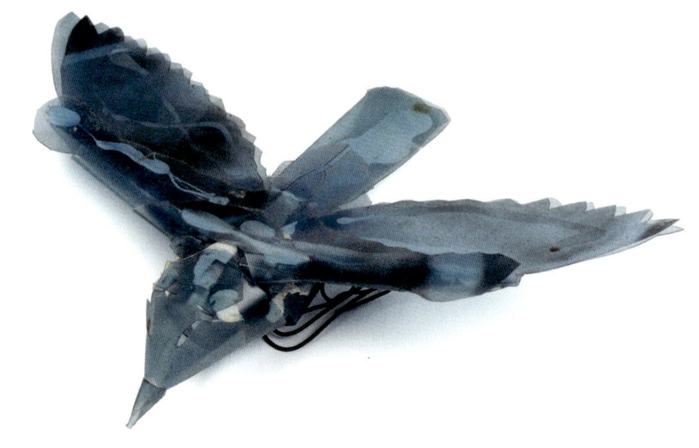

X-ray Bird, 1987
X-rays, glue, wire, 7 × 10 × 3 cm

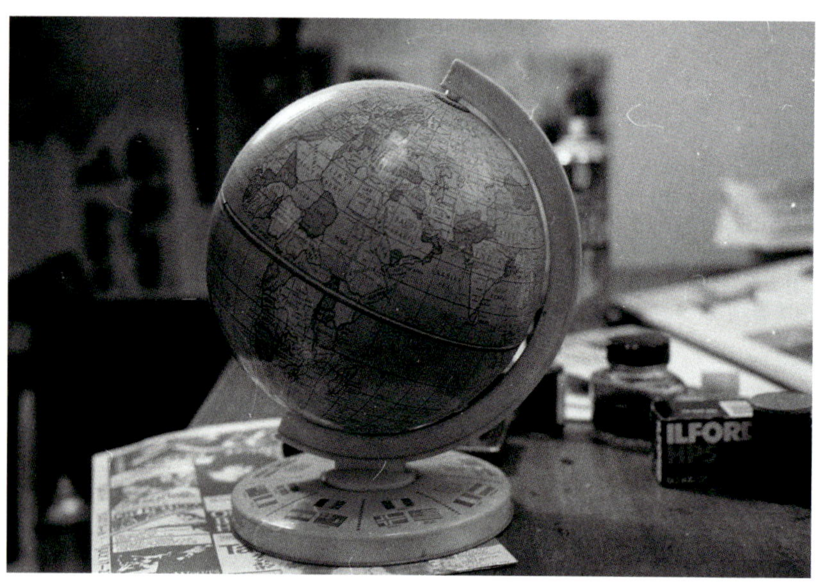

Globe in Rodney's studio at home in London, 1989

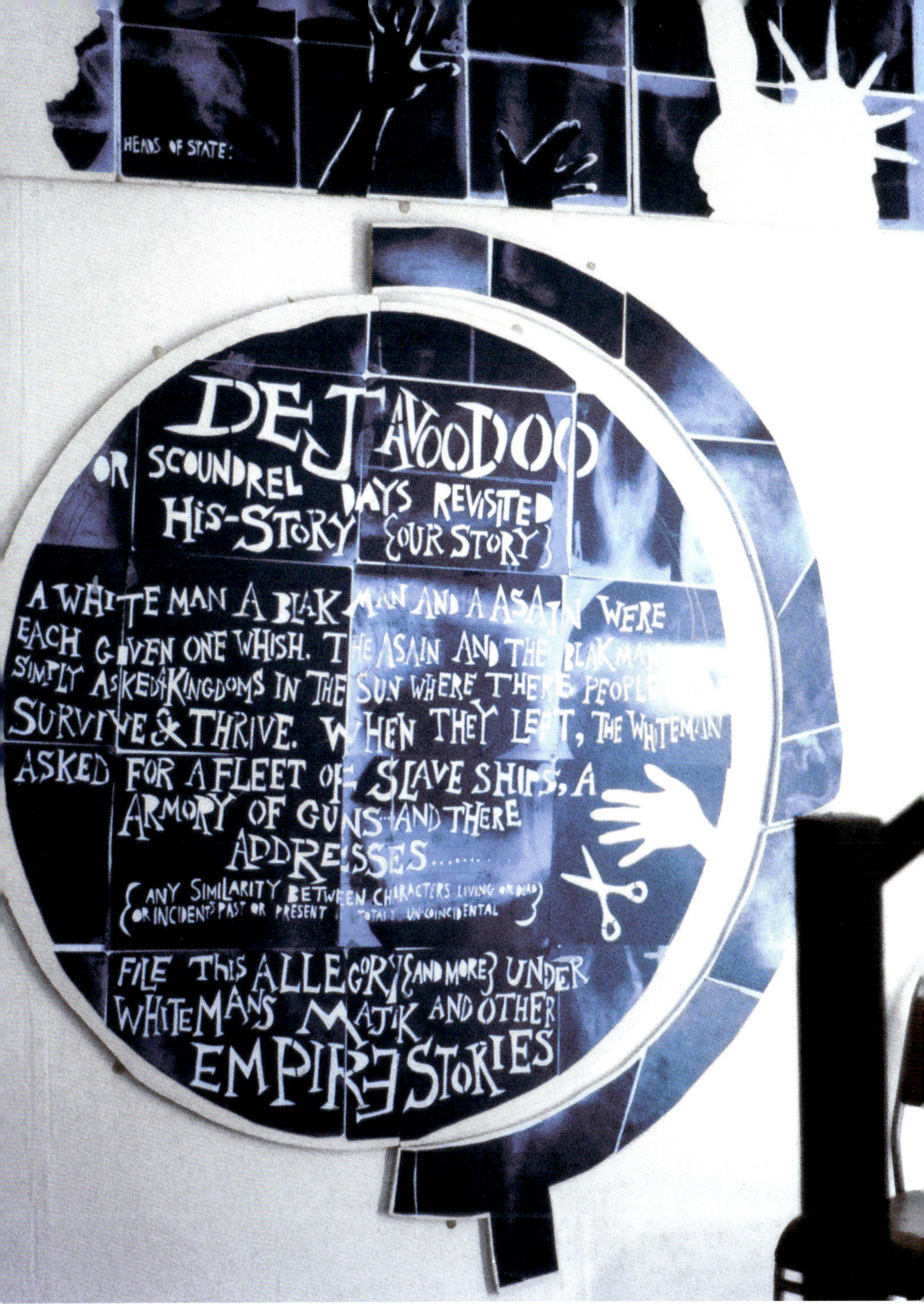

Dejavoodoo , 1987
Paint and mixed media on X–rays on board, dimensions unknown
Installation view at Slade School of Art, London

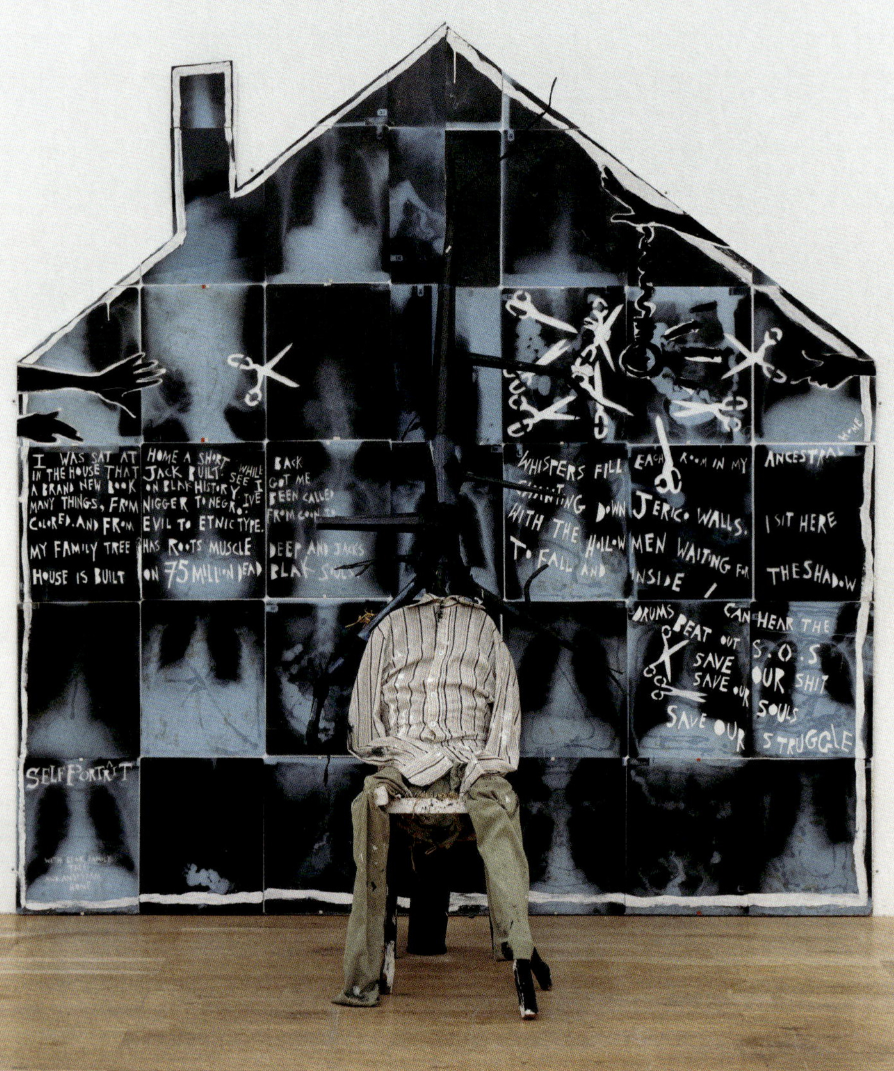

The House that Jack Built, 1987
Mixed media, 183 × 183 cm

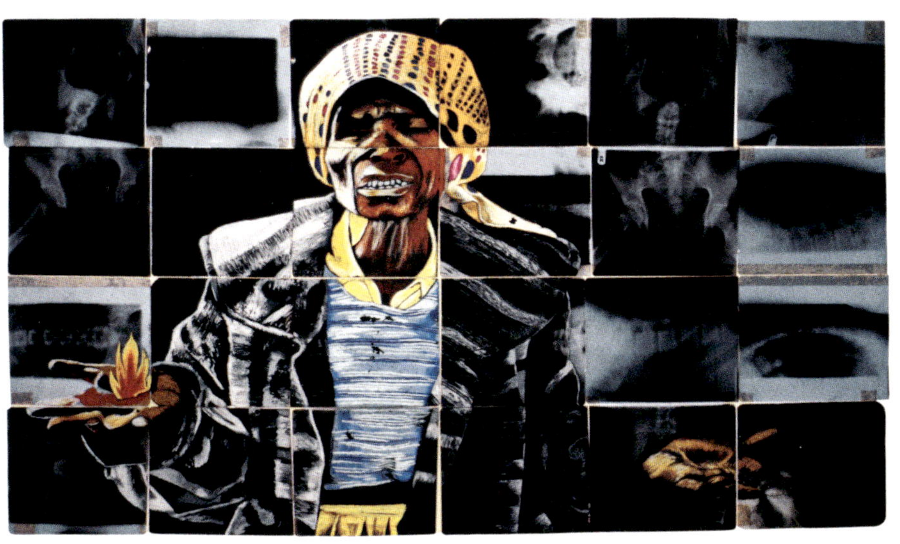

Britannia Hospital 2, 1988
Oil pastel on X-rays, 122 × 244 cm

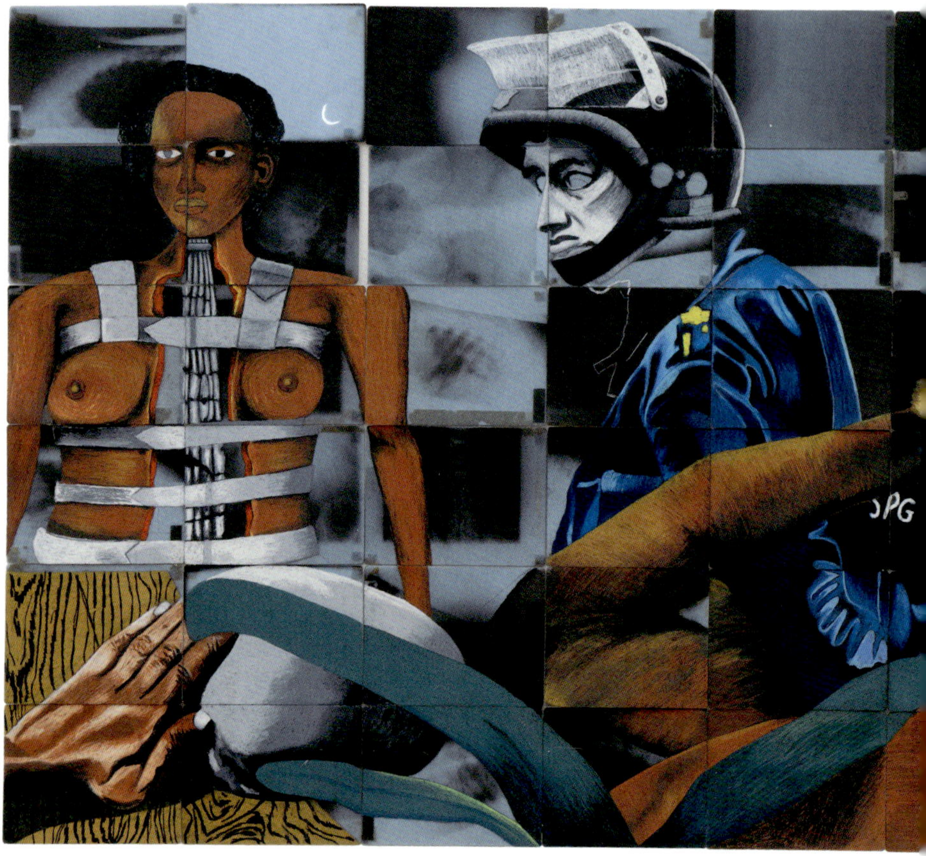

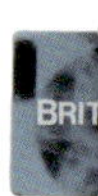
BRIT

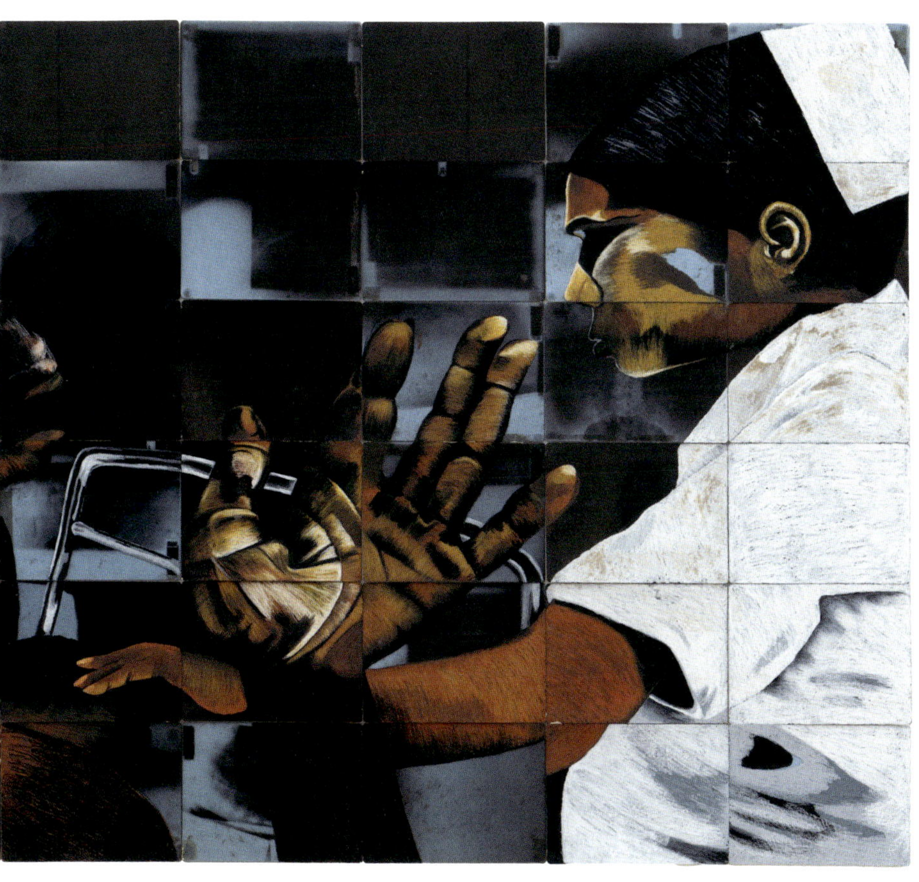

Britannia Hospital 3, 1988
Oil pastel on X-rays, 183 × 447 cm

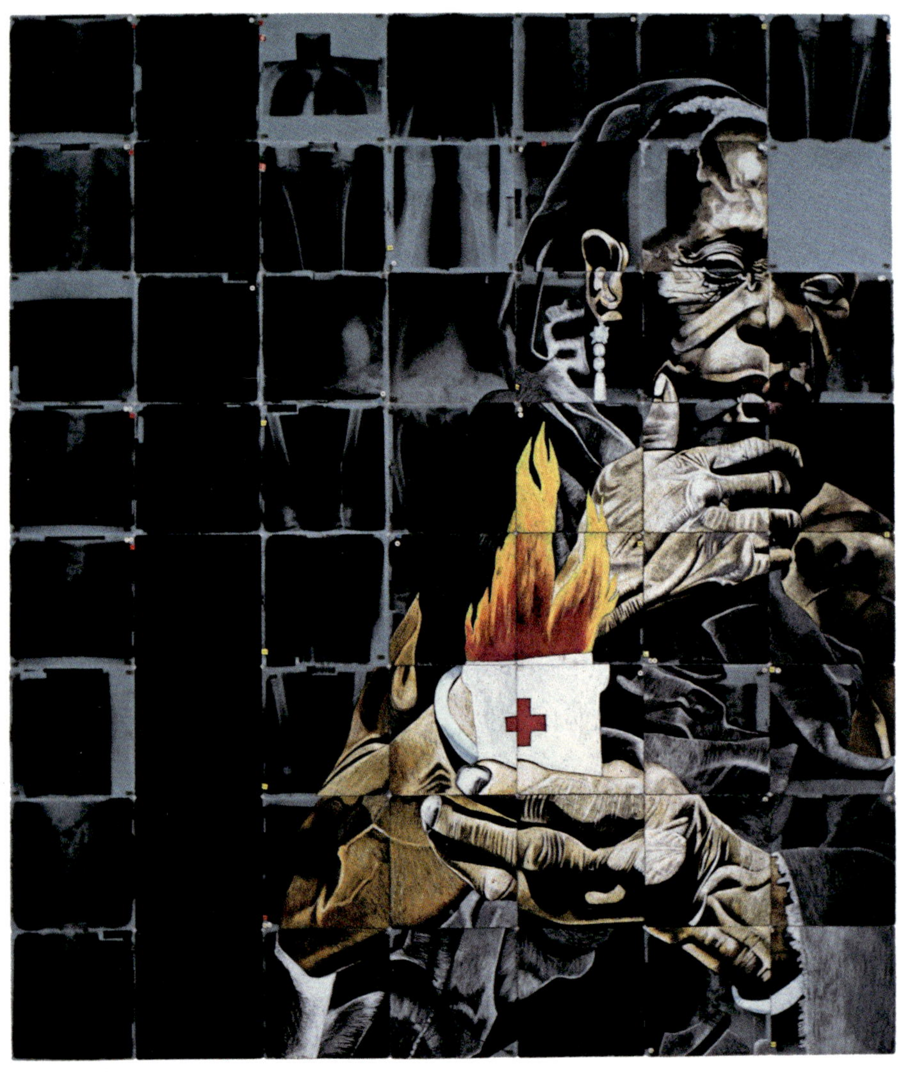

Flame of My Soul, 1988
Oil pastel on X-rays, 183 × 153 cm

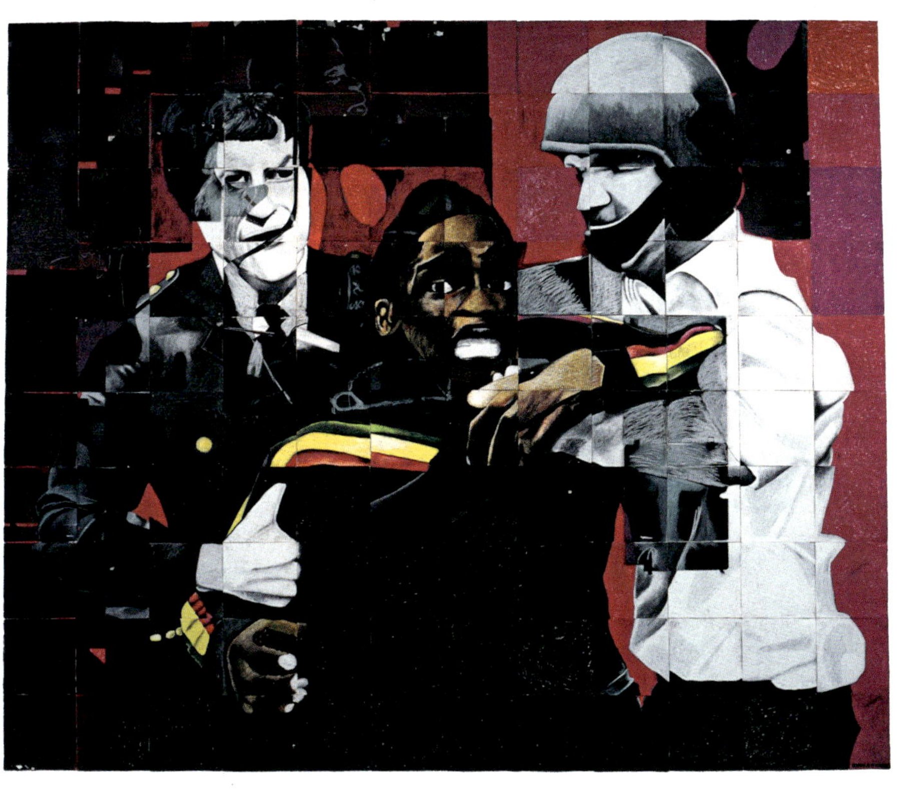

Self-Portrait: Policing the Black Community, Death in the City: Mr. Winston Rose,
Mr Stephen Bogle and Mr. Clinton McCurbin – A Postmodern Postmortem, 1988
Oil pastel on X-rays and paper, 200 × 240 cm

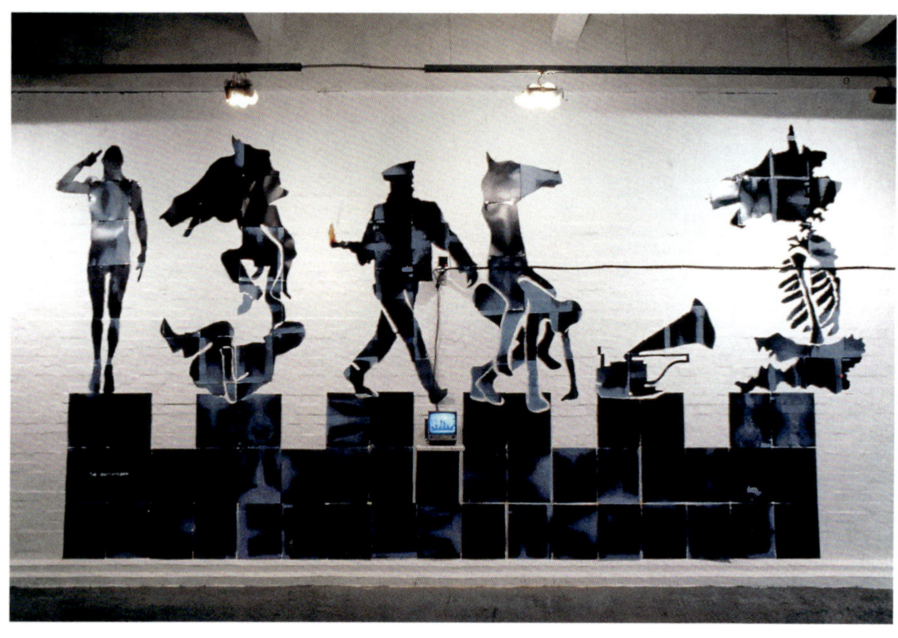

The Watchtower: Citizens stand in British Standard Time: An X-ray History, 1988
Mixed media, X-rays and video installation, dimensions variable
On monitor: *An X-ray Analysis* (detail), 1988

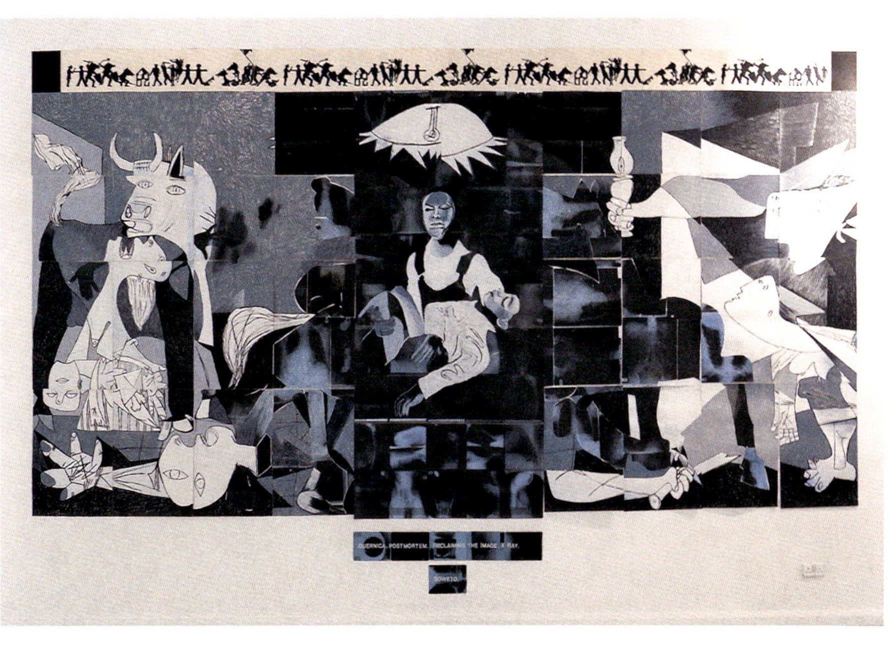

Soweto/Guernica, 1988
Mixed media and X-rays, dimensions variable

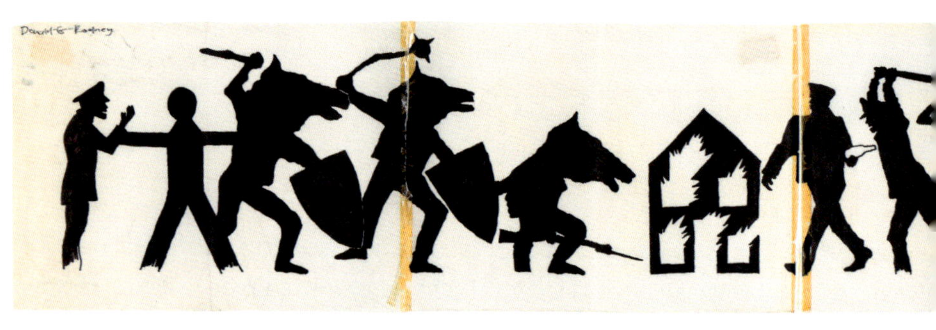

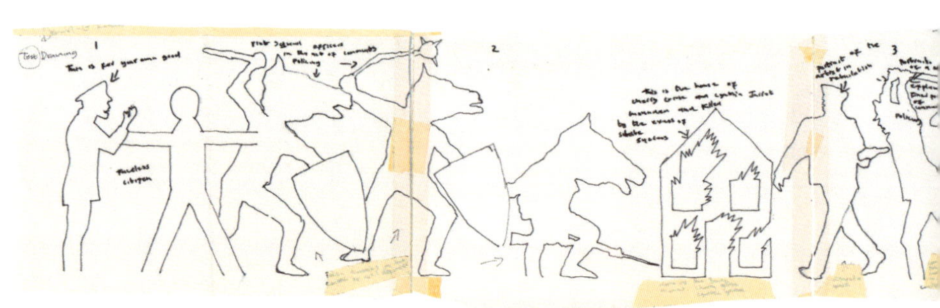

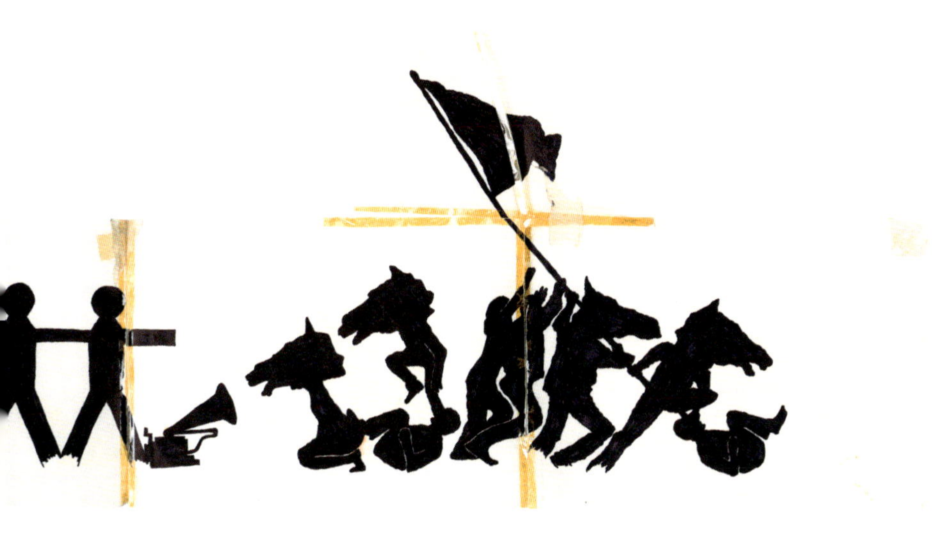

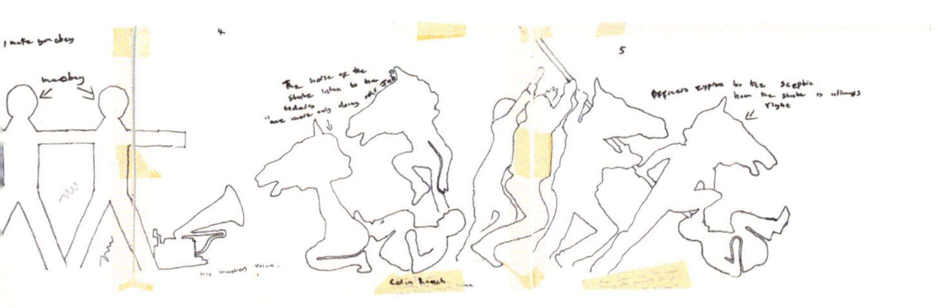

Preparatory drawings for *Soweto/Guernica*, 1988
Ink on paper, above: 34.5 × 146.8 cm; below: 20.5 × 147.5 cm

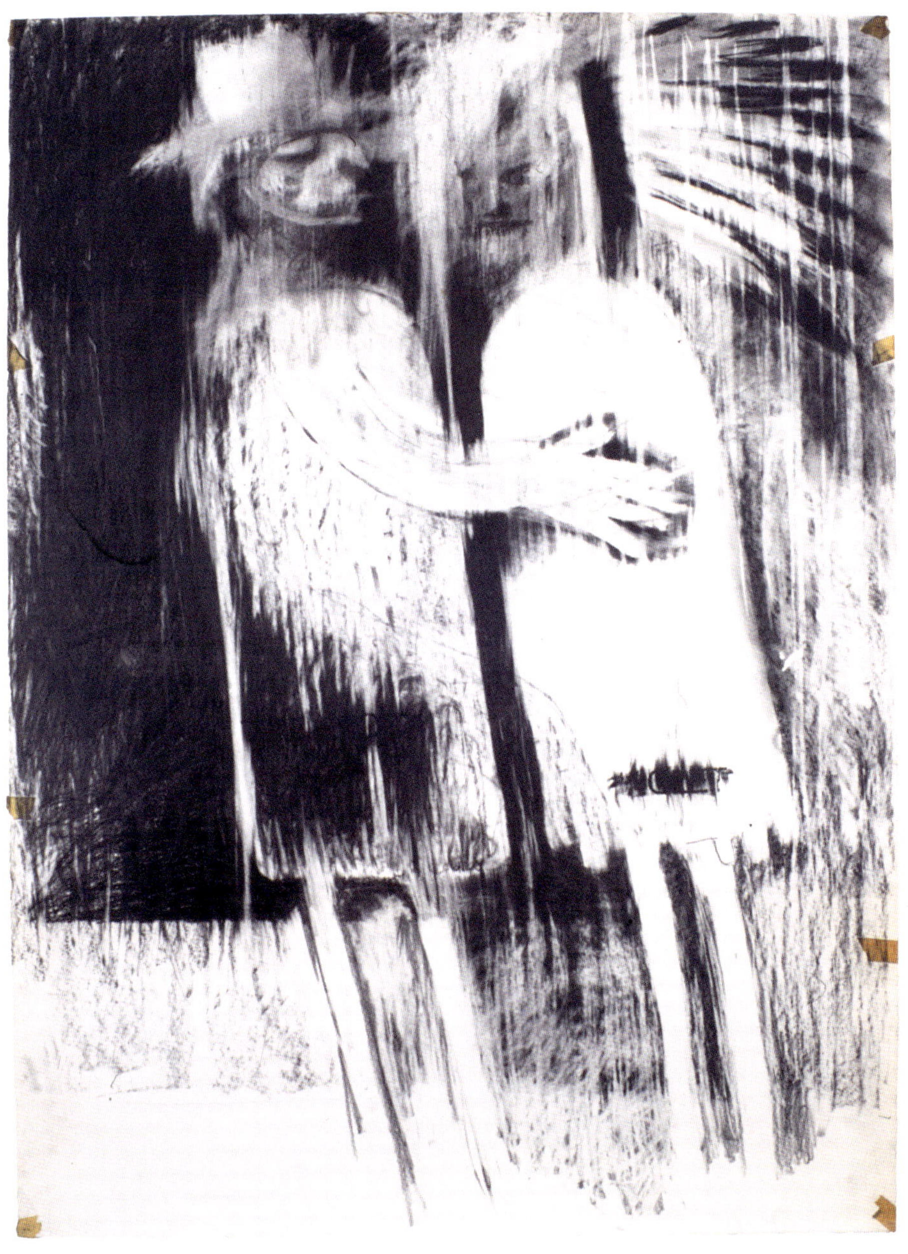

Untitled ('Cowboy and Indian' after David Hockney's
'We Two Boys Together Clinging', 1961), 1989
Charcoal on paper, 156.5 × 120.9 cm

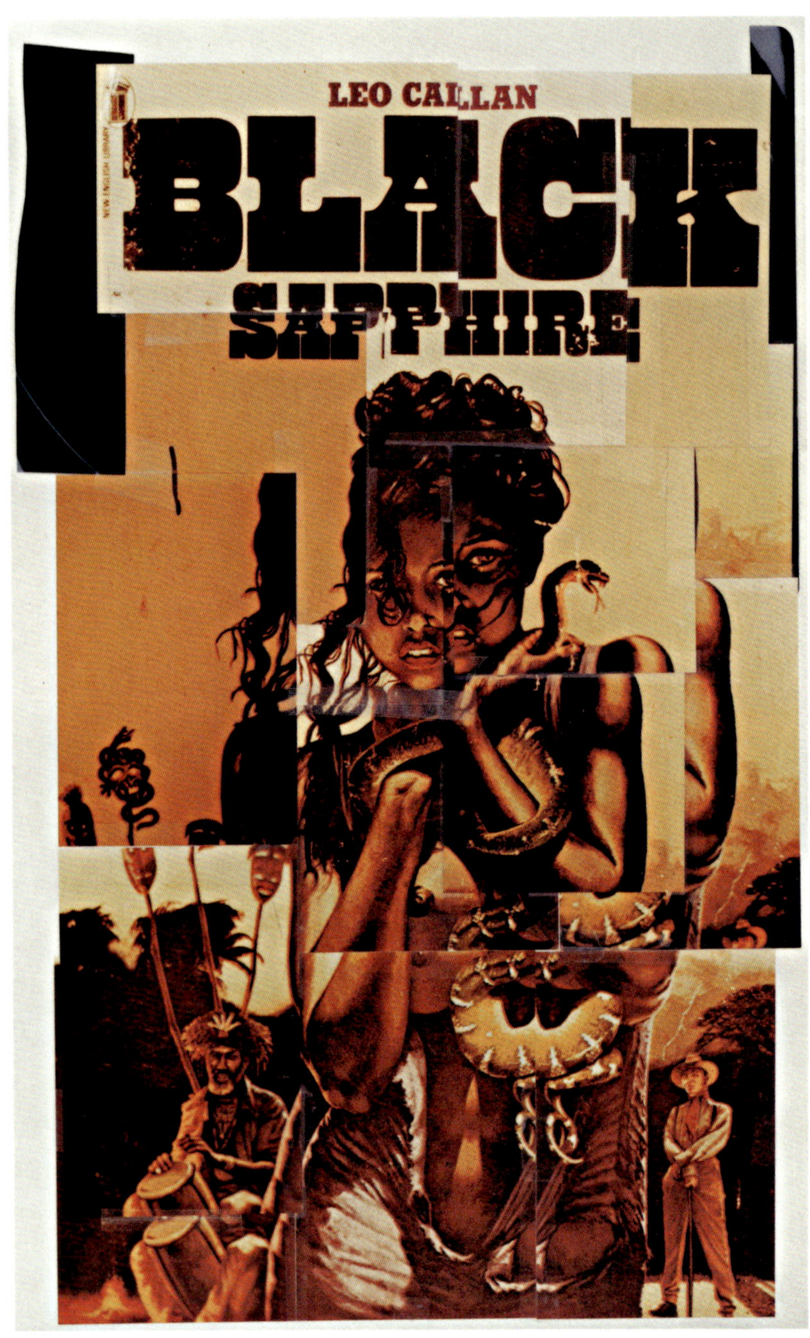

Black Markets Prints (Untitled, Black Sapphire), 1990
Digital giclee print on paper, 59.4 × 84.1 cm

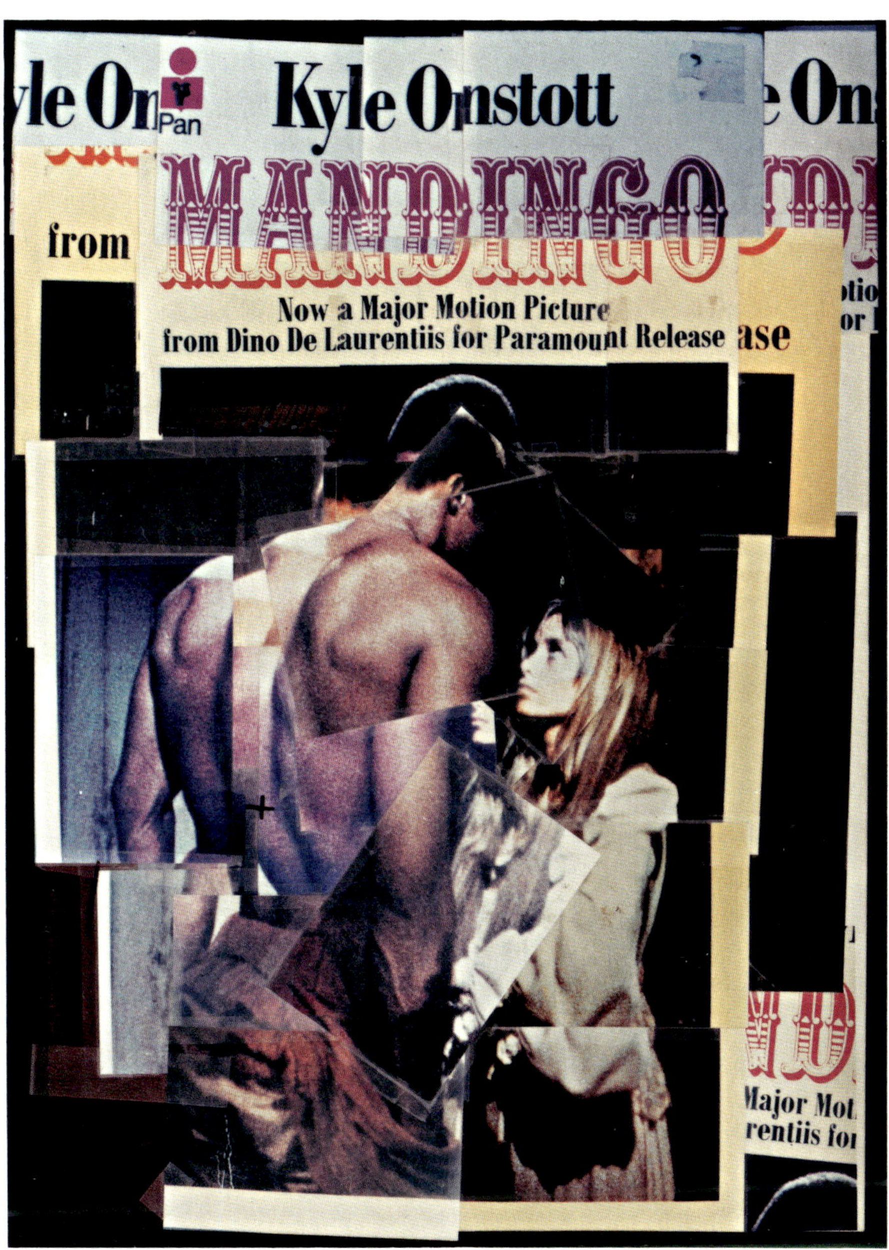

Black Markets Prints (Untitled, Mandingo), 1990
Digital giclee print on paper, 59.4 × 84.1 cm

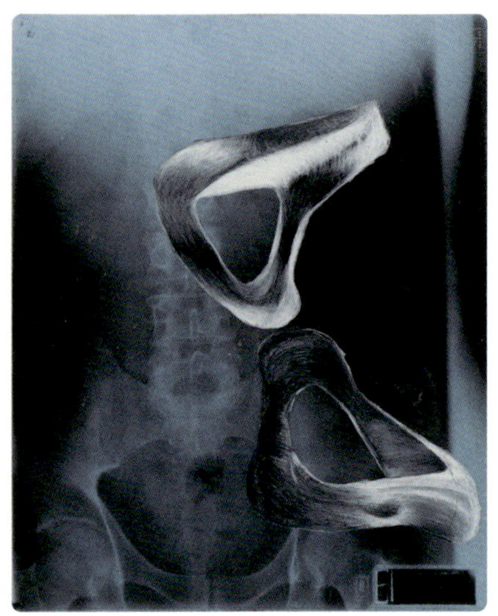
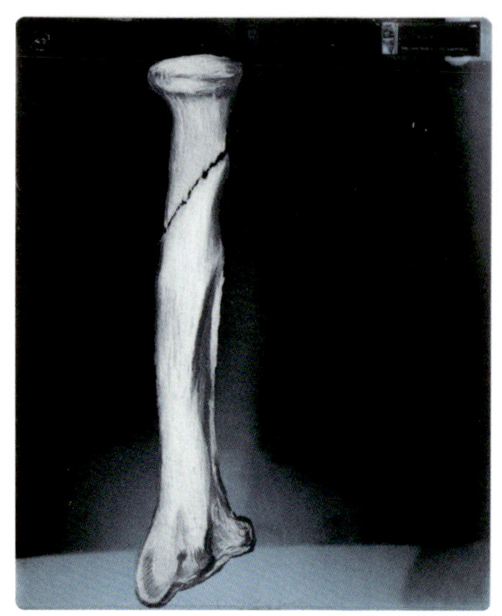
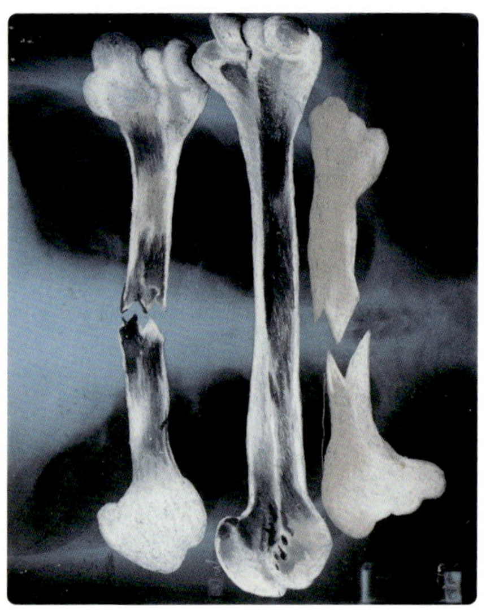
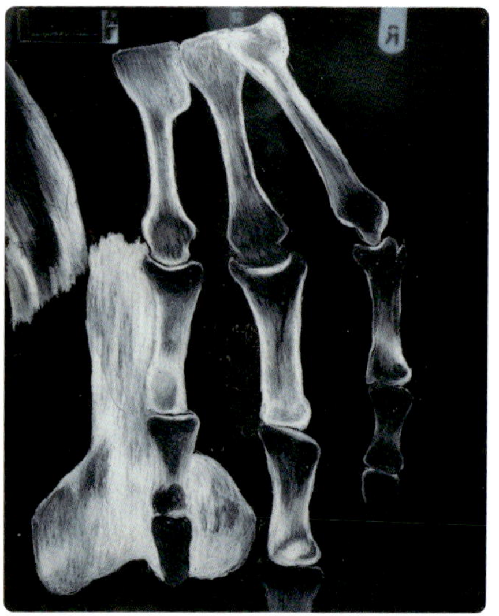

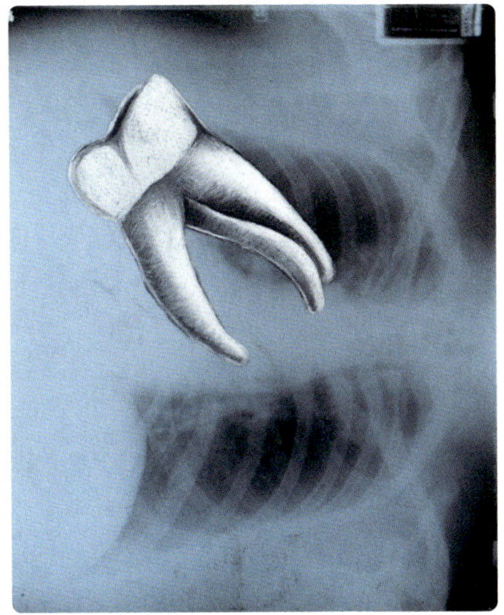
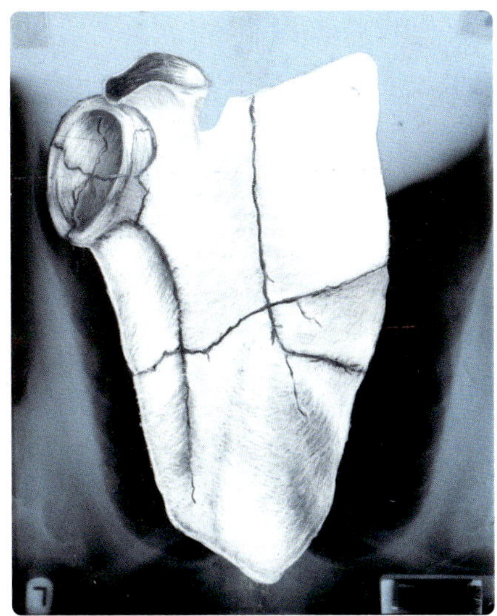
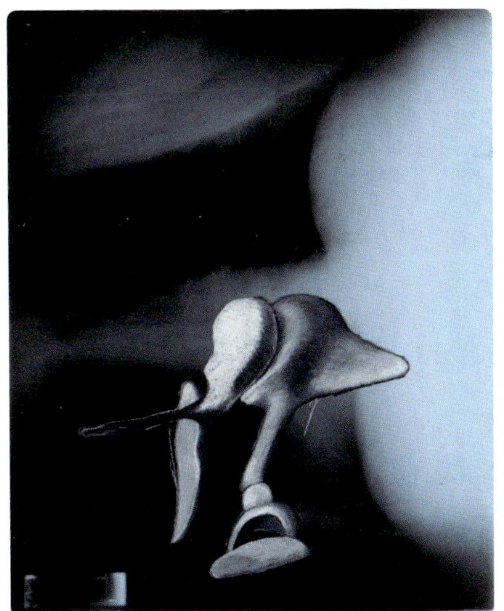
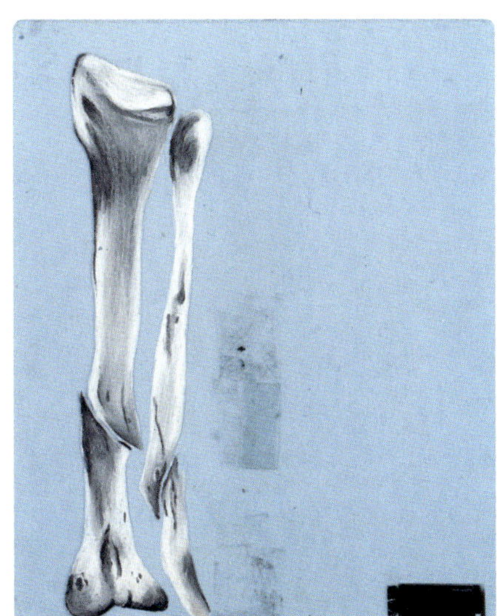

Untitled, c. 1991
8 oil pastel drawings on X-rays, each approx. 30 × 20 cm

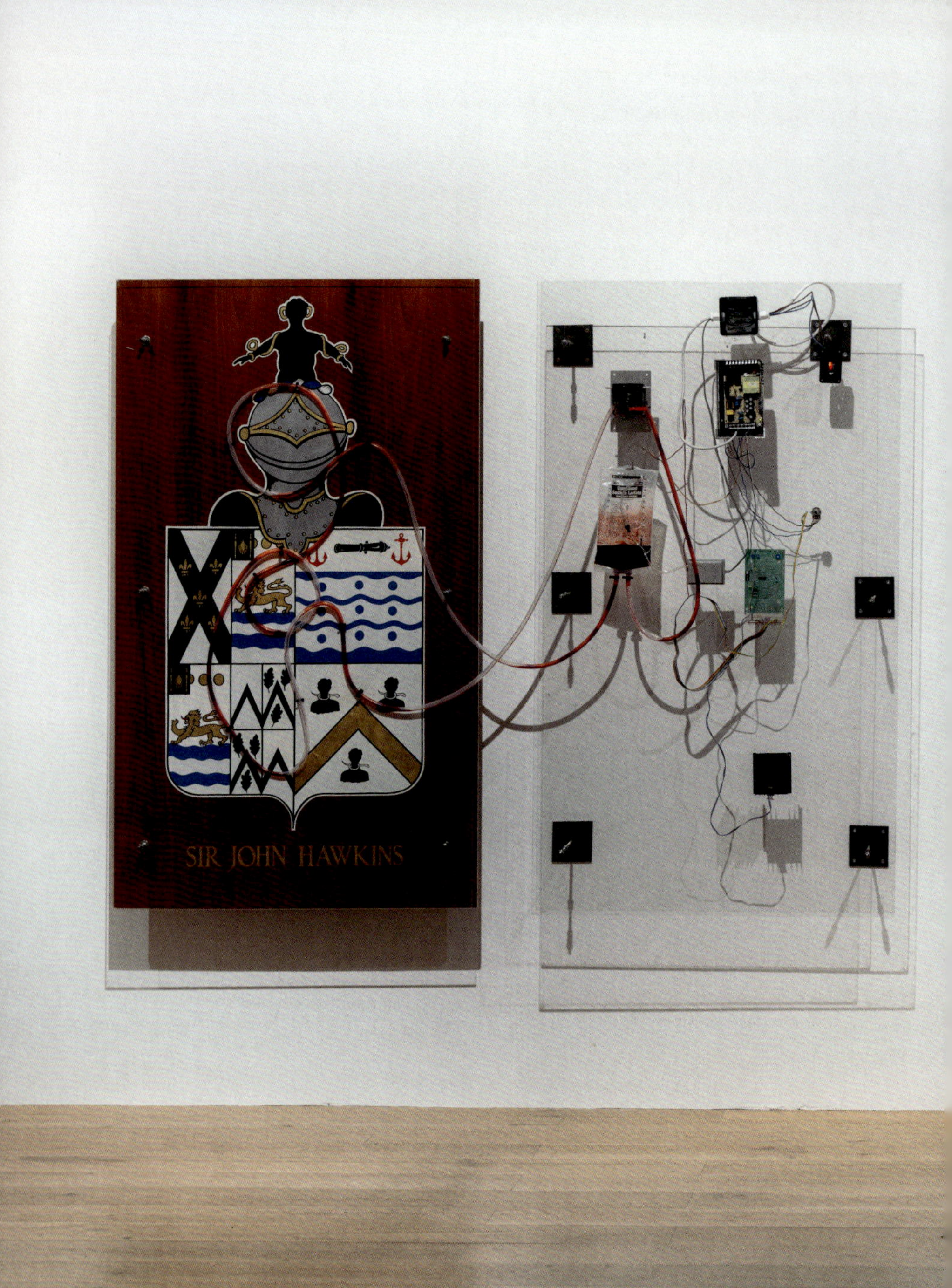
SIR JOHN HAWKINS

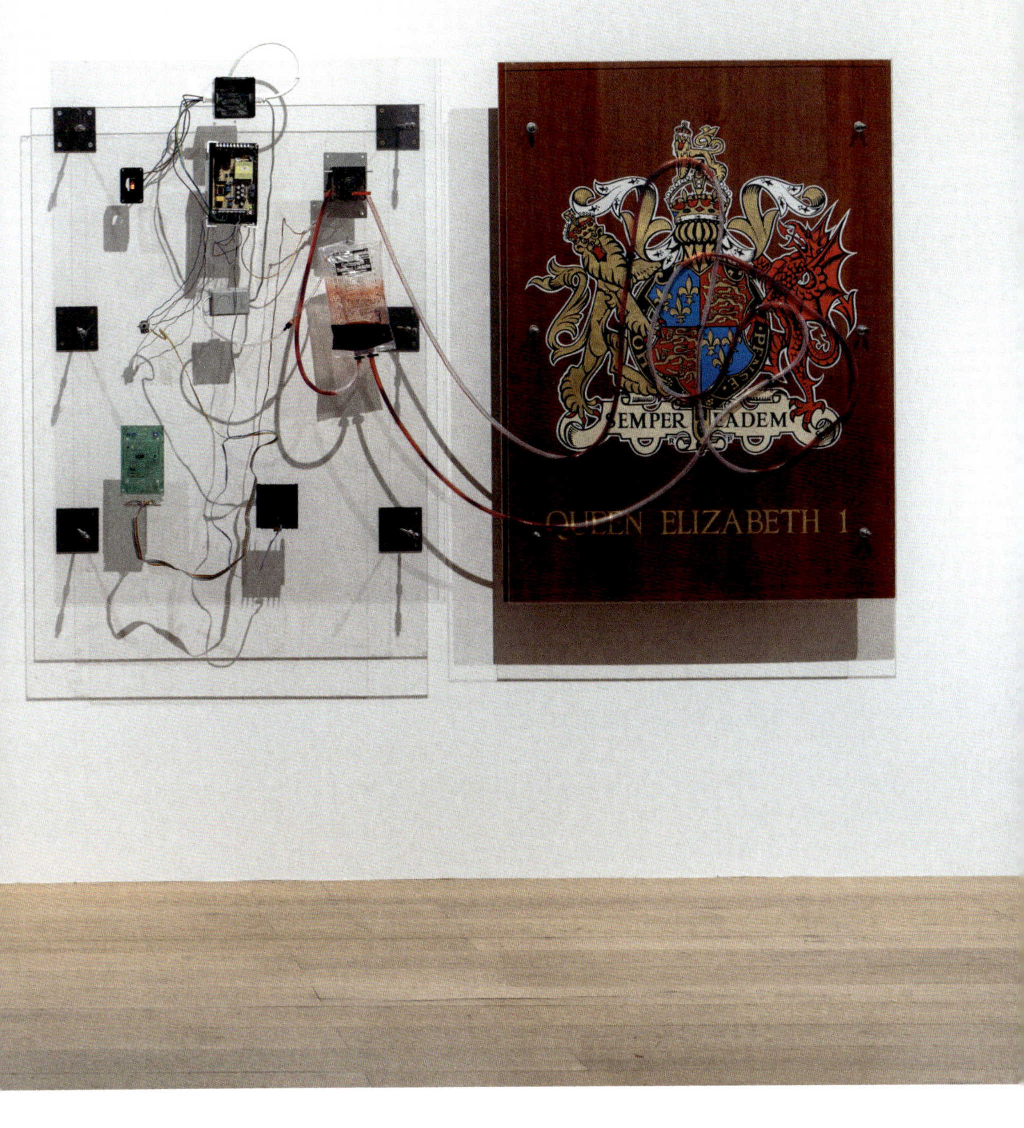

Visceral Canker, 1990
Perspex, wood, silicon tubing, gold leaf, plastic bags and electrical pump
4 panels: 122 × 91 cm; 155 × 91 cm; 122 × 91 cm; 122 × 91 cm

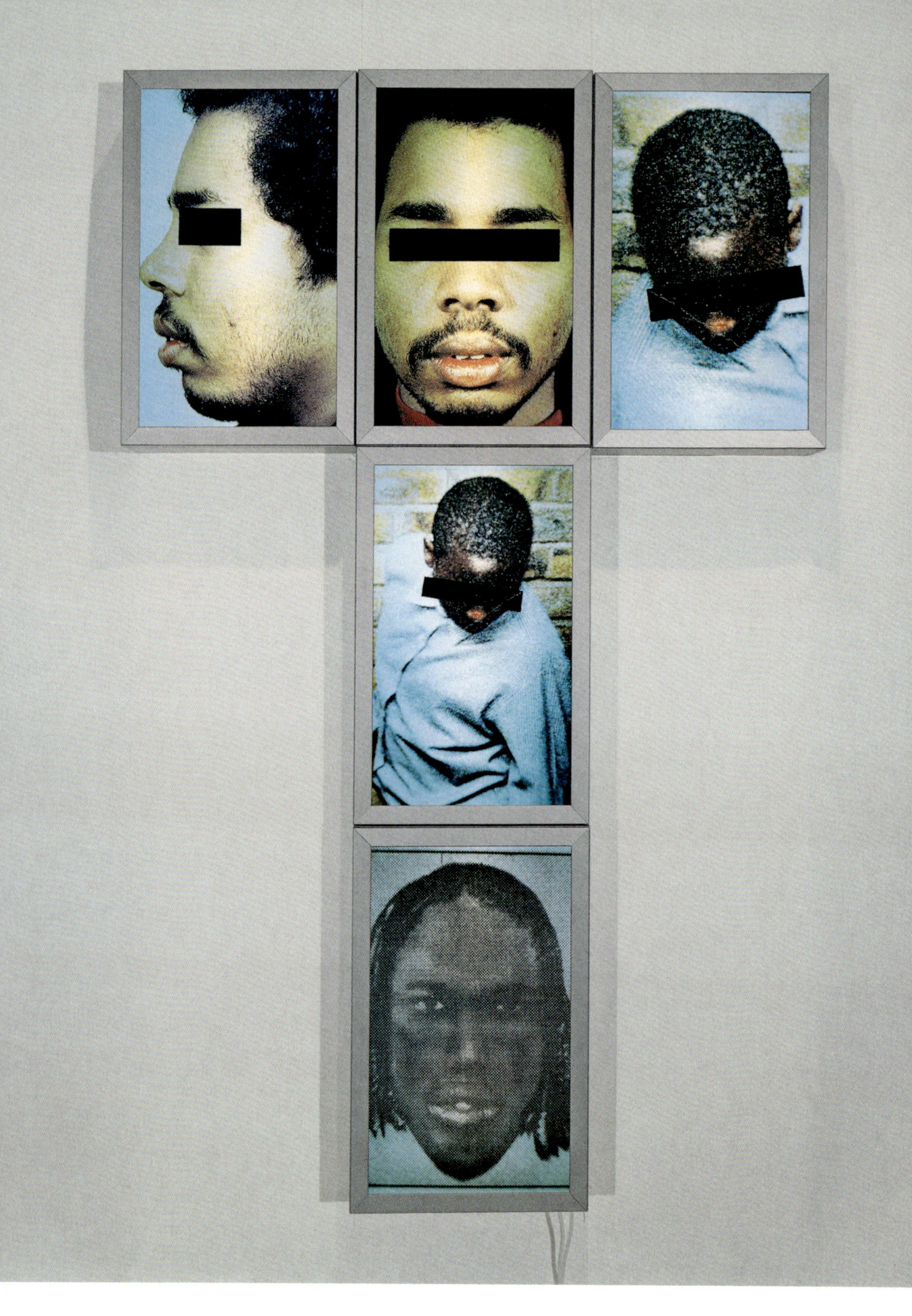

Self Portrait: Black Men Public Enemy, 1990
Lightboxes with Duratran prints, 190.5 × 121.9 cm

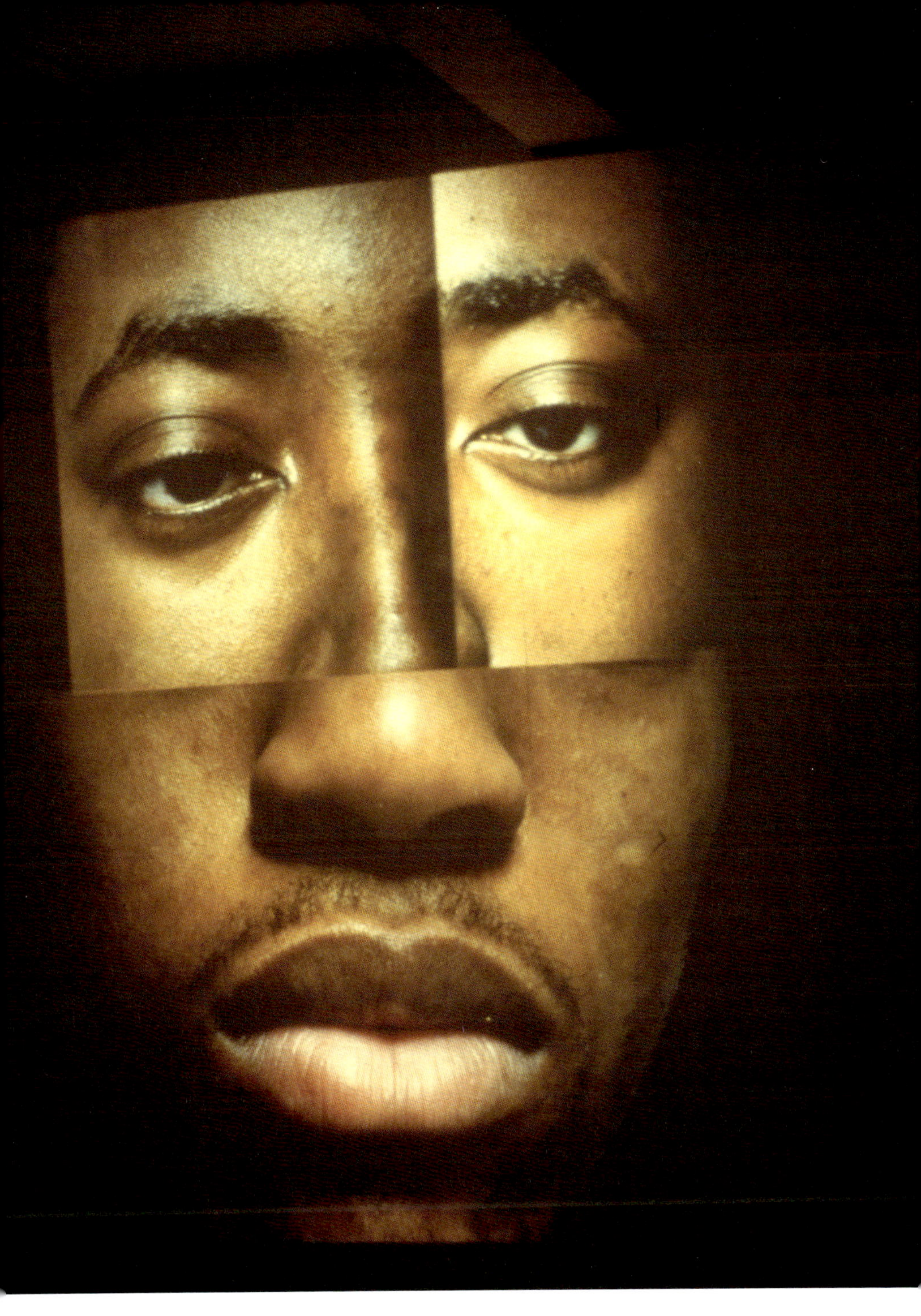

Cataract, 1991
Slidetape work with 240 slides to fit 3 projectors, dimensions variable

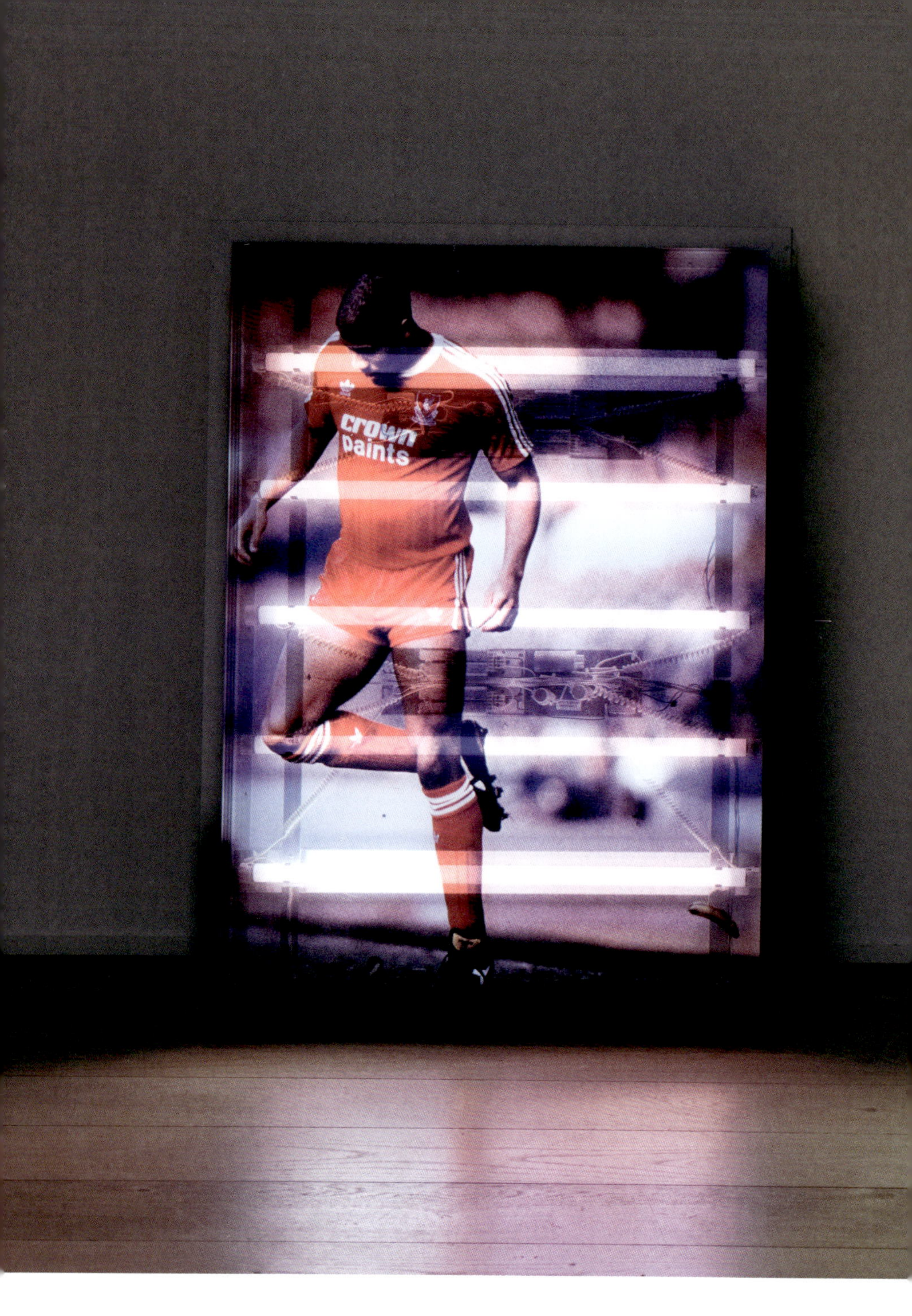

John Barnes, 1991
Duratran print on aluminium framed lightbox with fluorescent tube lights
107 × 80.8 × 16.7 cm

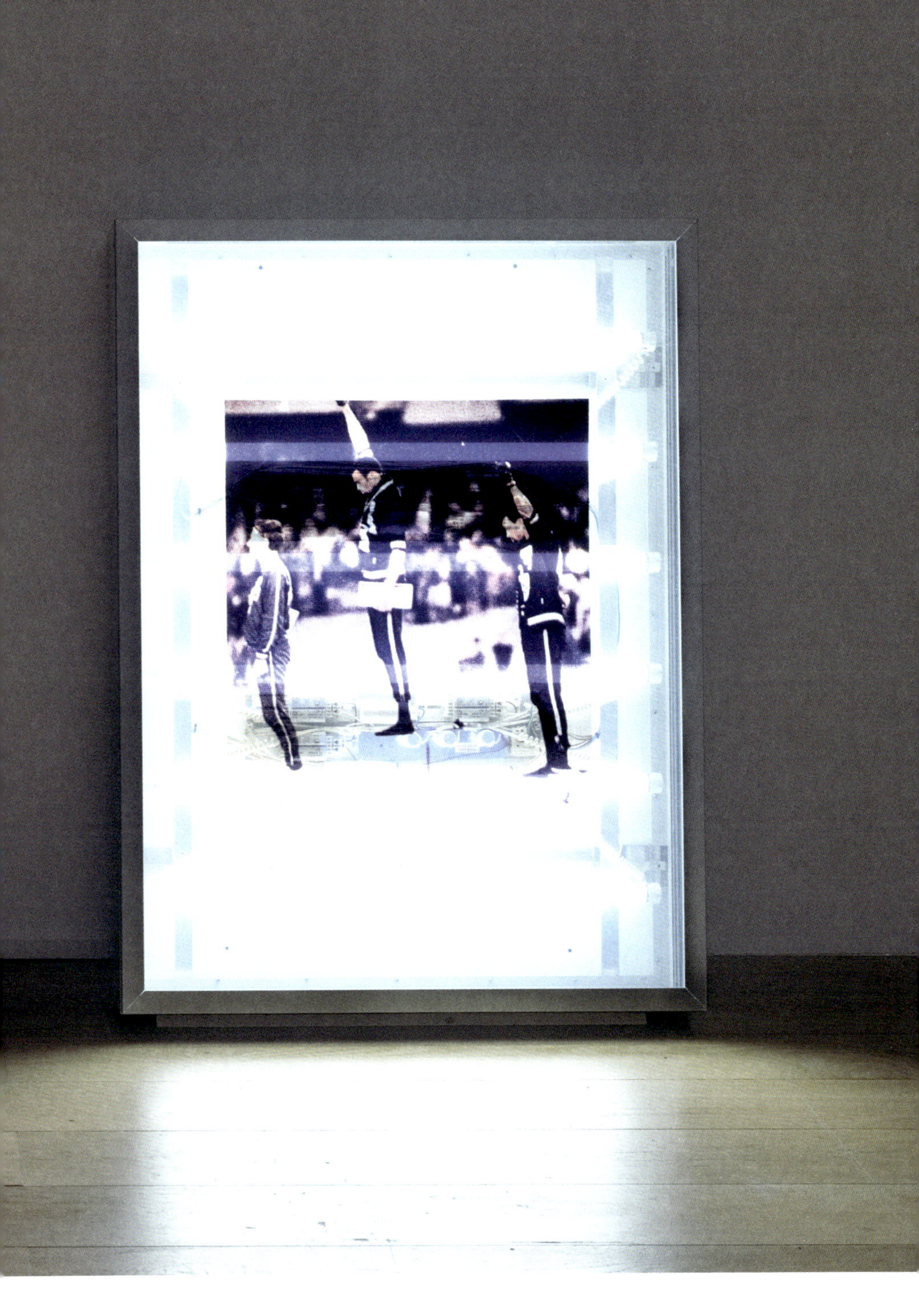

Mexico Olympics, 1991
Duratran print on aluminium framed lightbox with fluorescent tube lights
107 × 80.8 × 16.7 cm

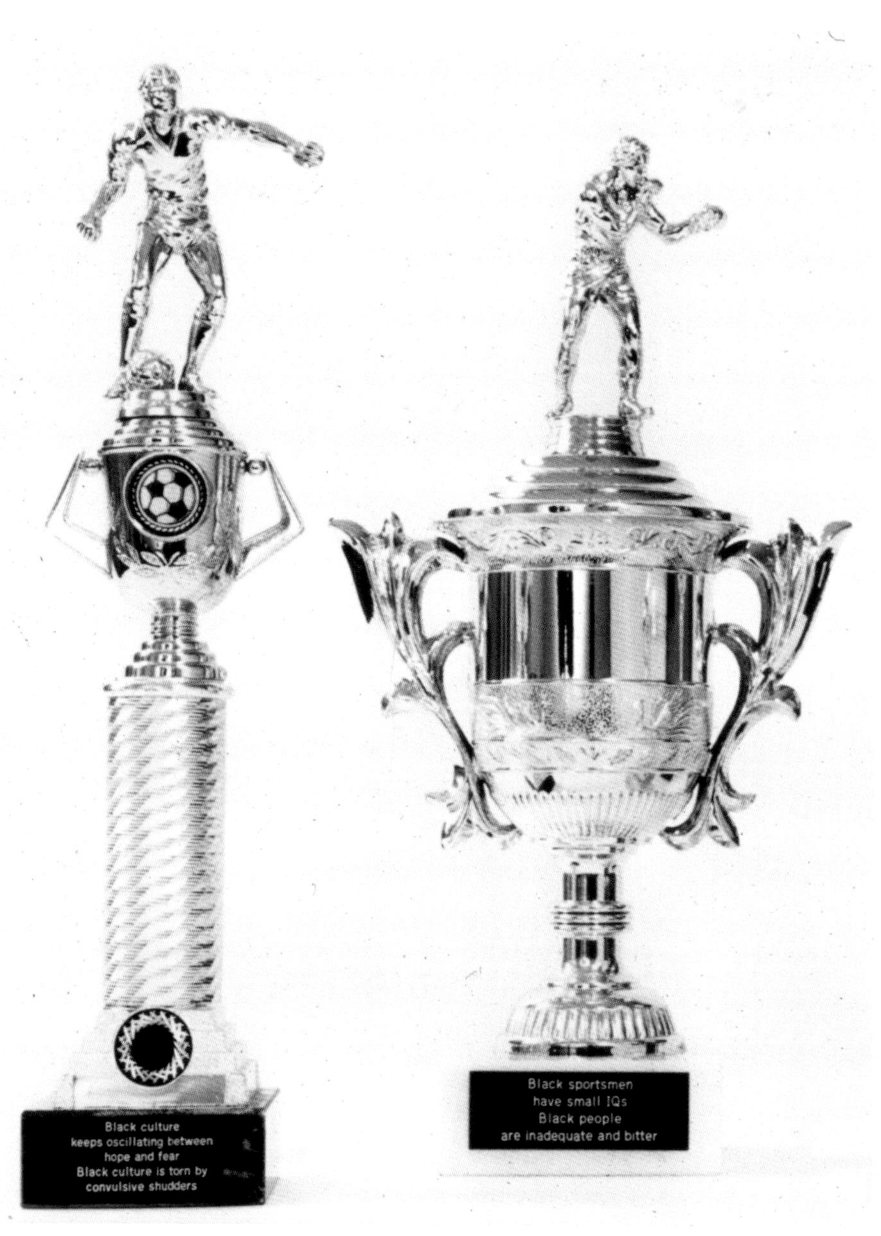

Doublethink, 1992
Trophies with engraved texts, dimensions variable

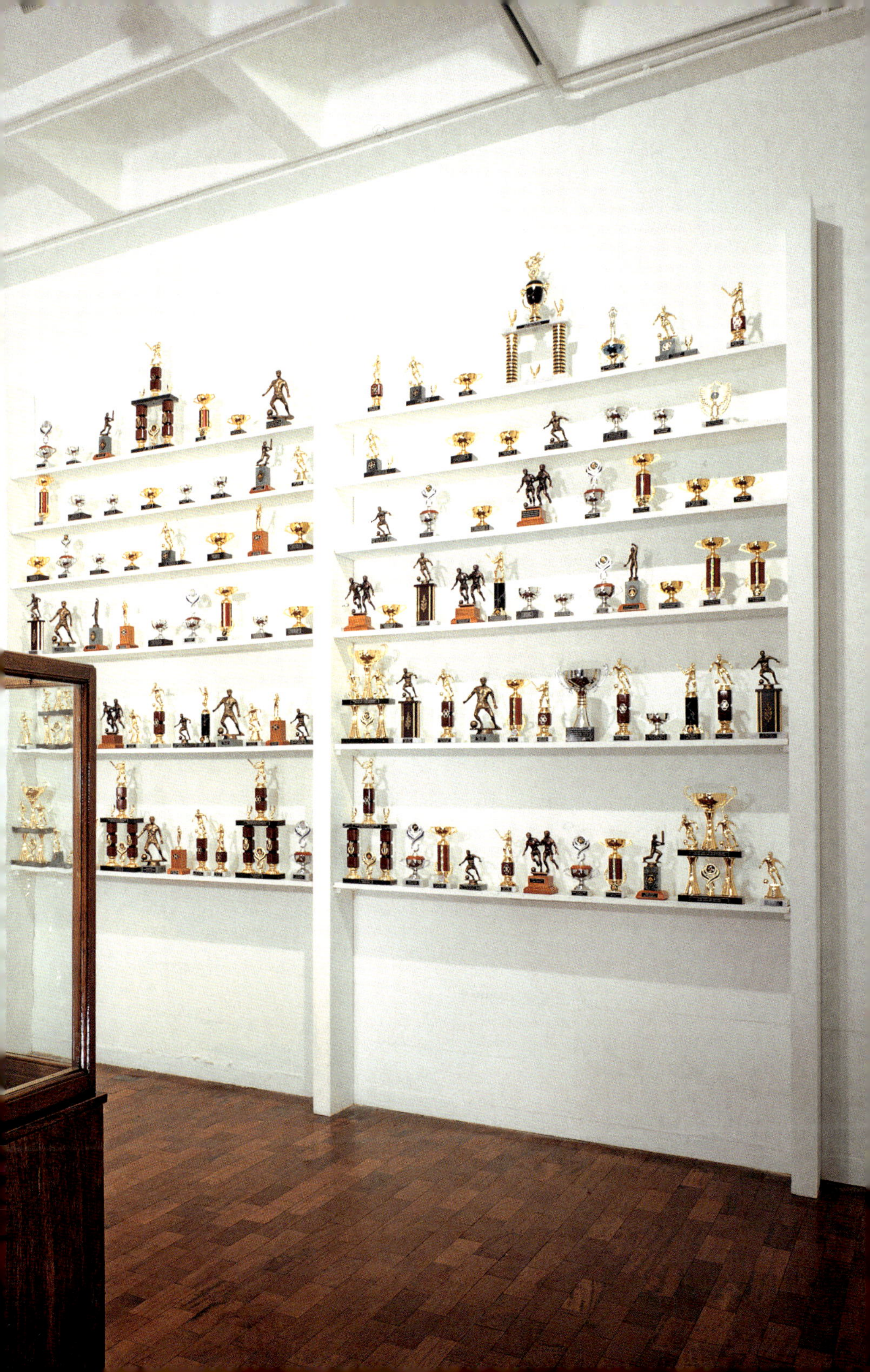

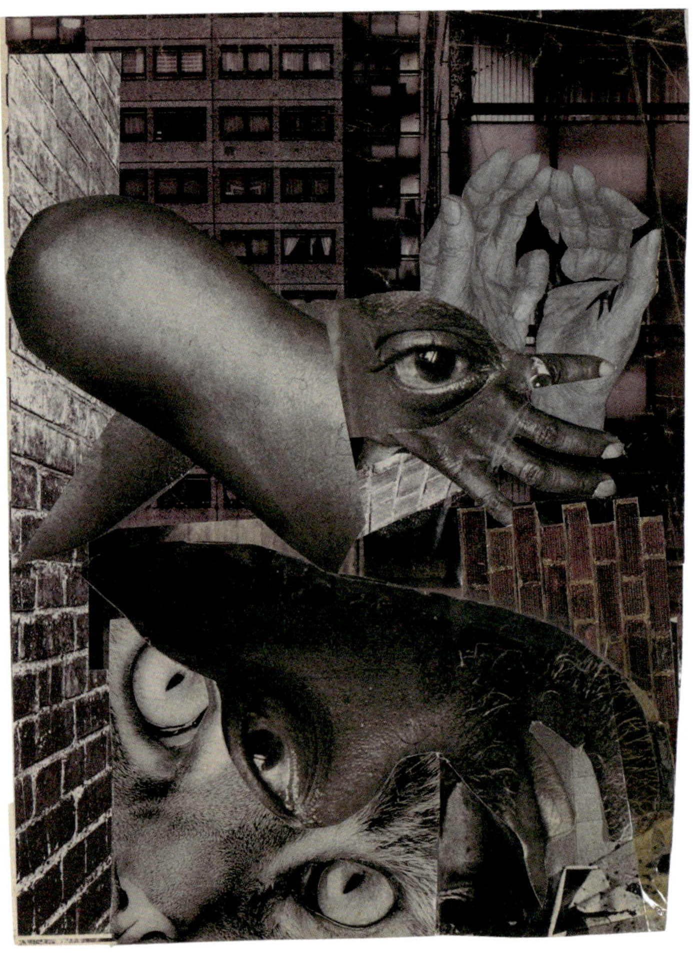

Untitled, 1994
Mixed media and magazine cuttings on paper, 38.5 × 31 cm

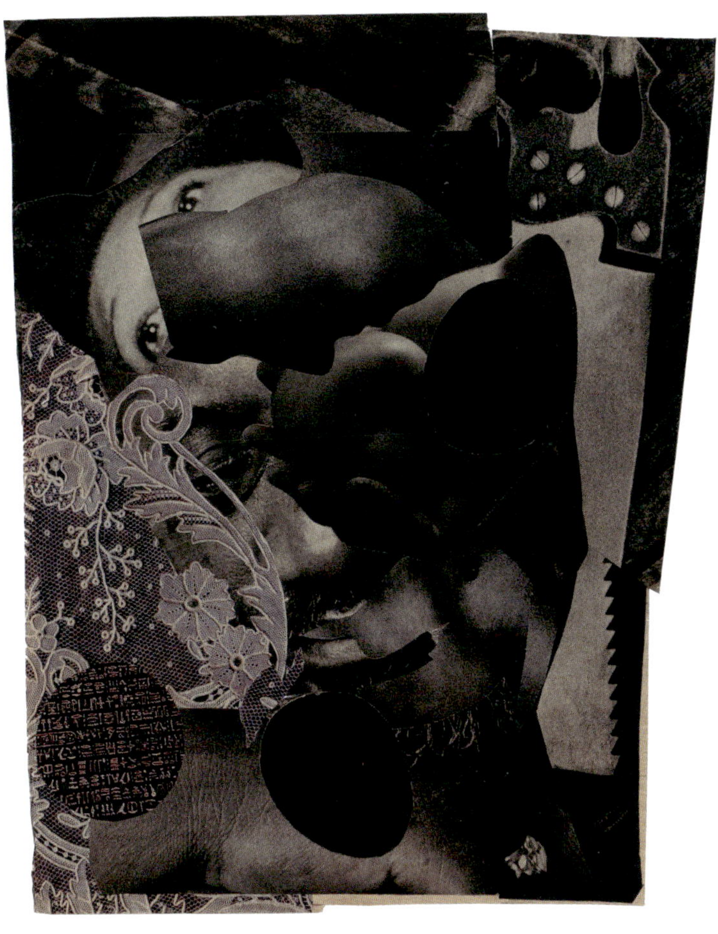

Untitled, 1994
Paper, mixed media, magazines, 44 × 36 cm

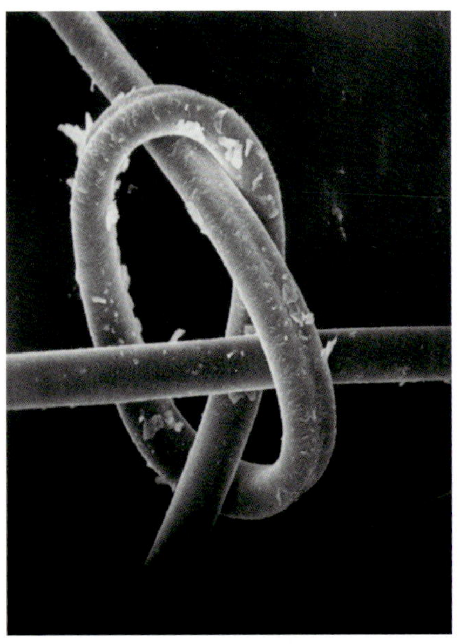
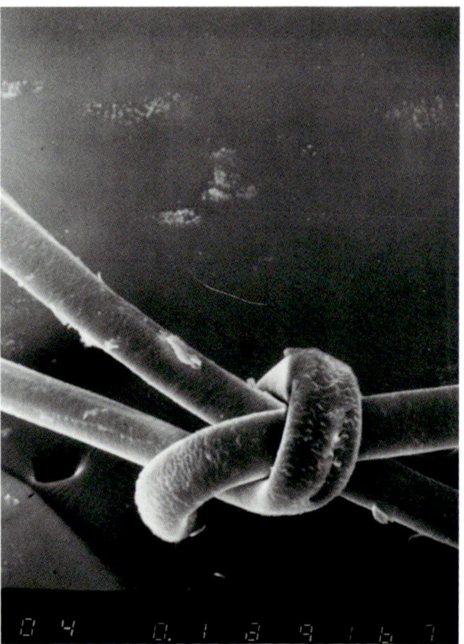
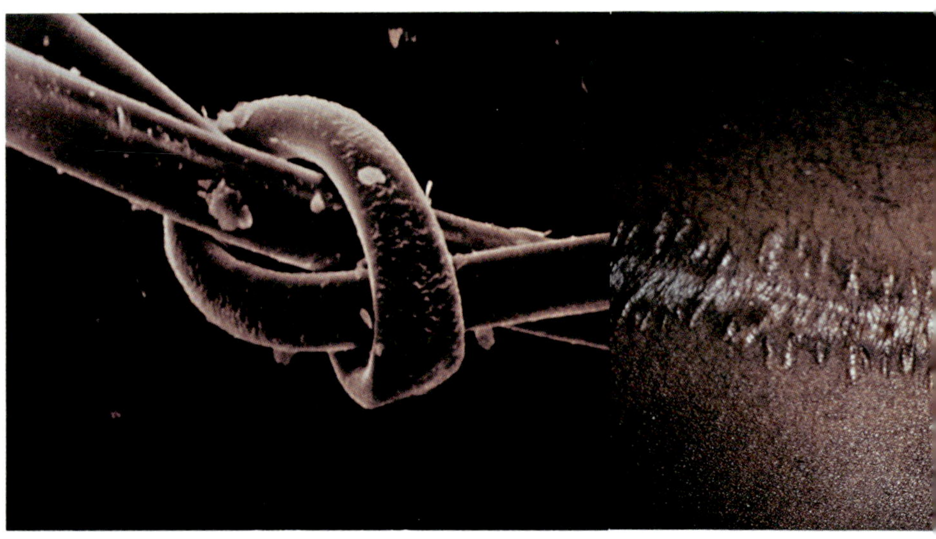

Above: Preparatory photographs for *Flesh of My Flesh*, c. 1996
4 of 12 photographs on paper, each: 42 × 30 cm

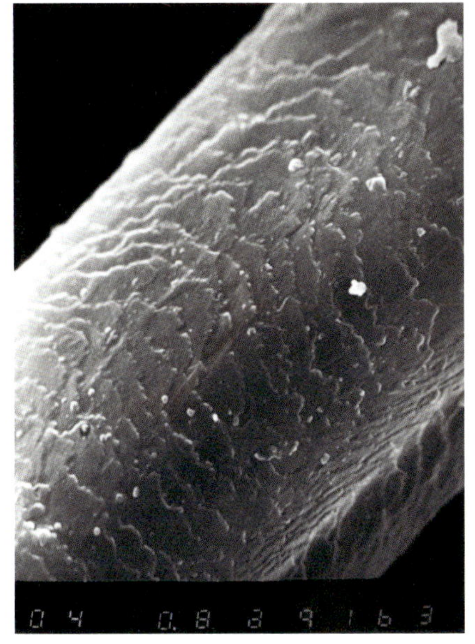
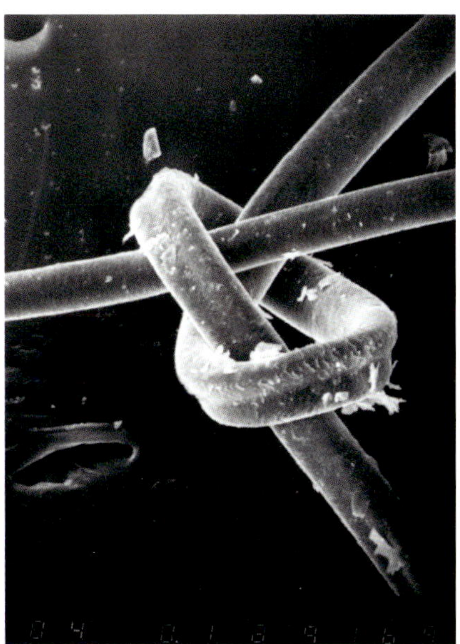
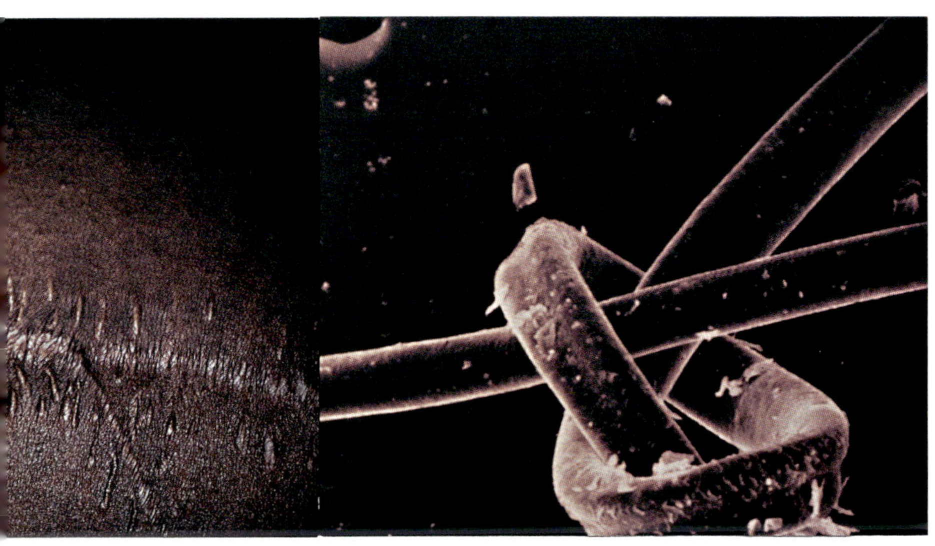

Below: *Flesh of My Flesh*, 1996
Colour photograph on aluminium
Three panels: 139 × 92 cm; 10 × 92 cm; 110 × 92 cm

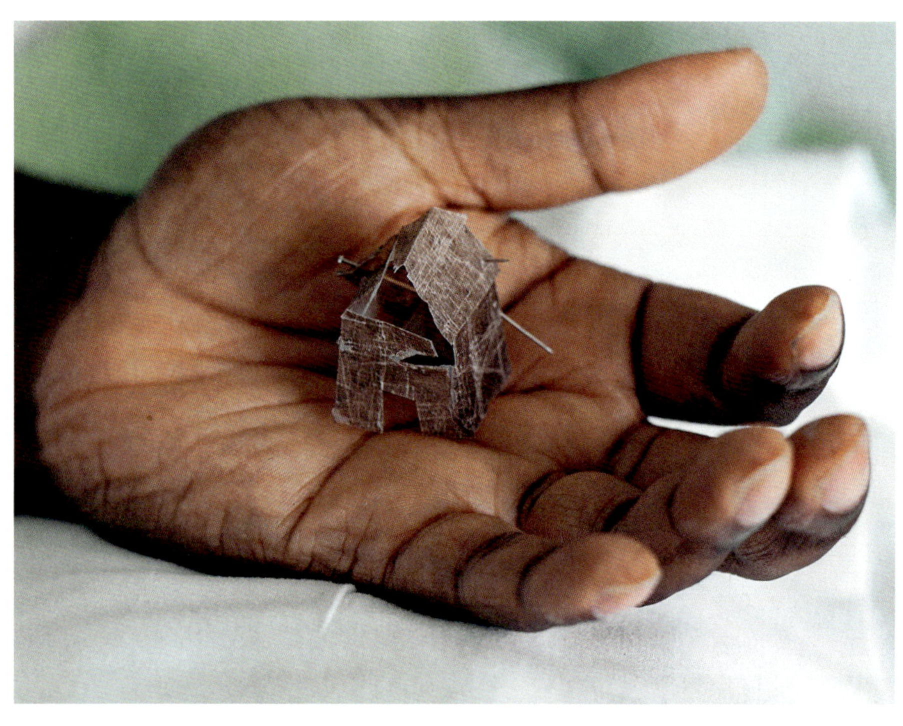

In the House of My Father, 1997
Photograph, 123 × 153 cm

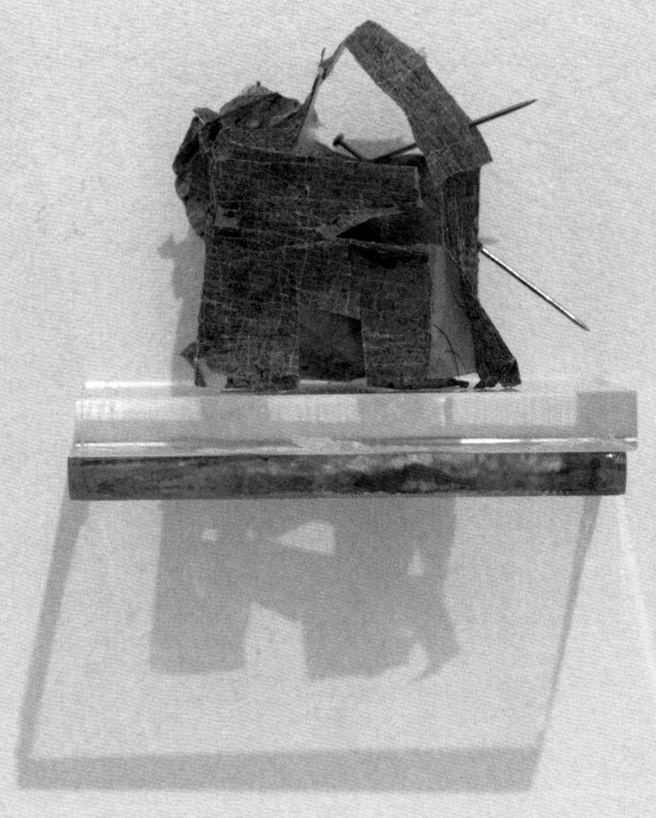

My Mother. My Father. My Sister. My Brother, 1996–97
2 × 3 × 2 cm

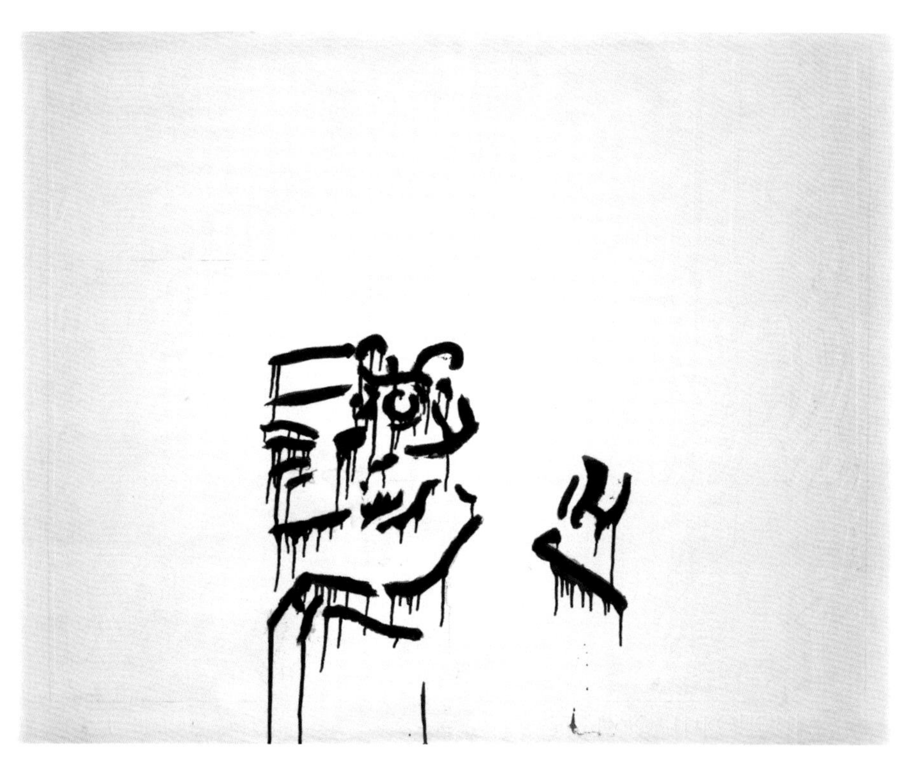

Black Comedy 1, 1997
Vinyl and paint on acrylic sheet, 99.3 × 126.3 cm

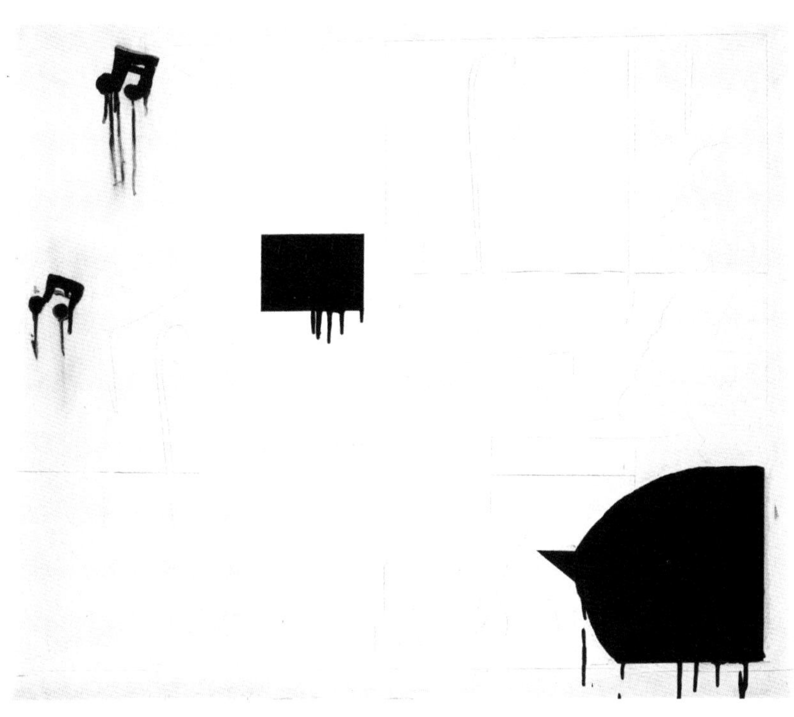

Black Comedy 2, 1997
Vinyl and paint on acrylic sheet, 91.4 × 109.1 cm

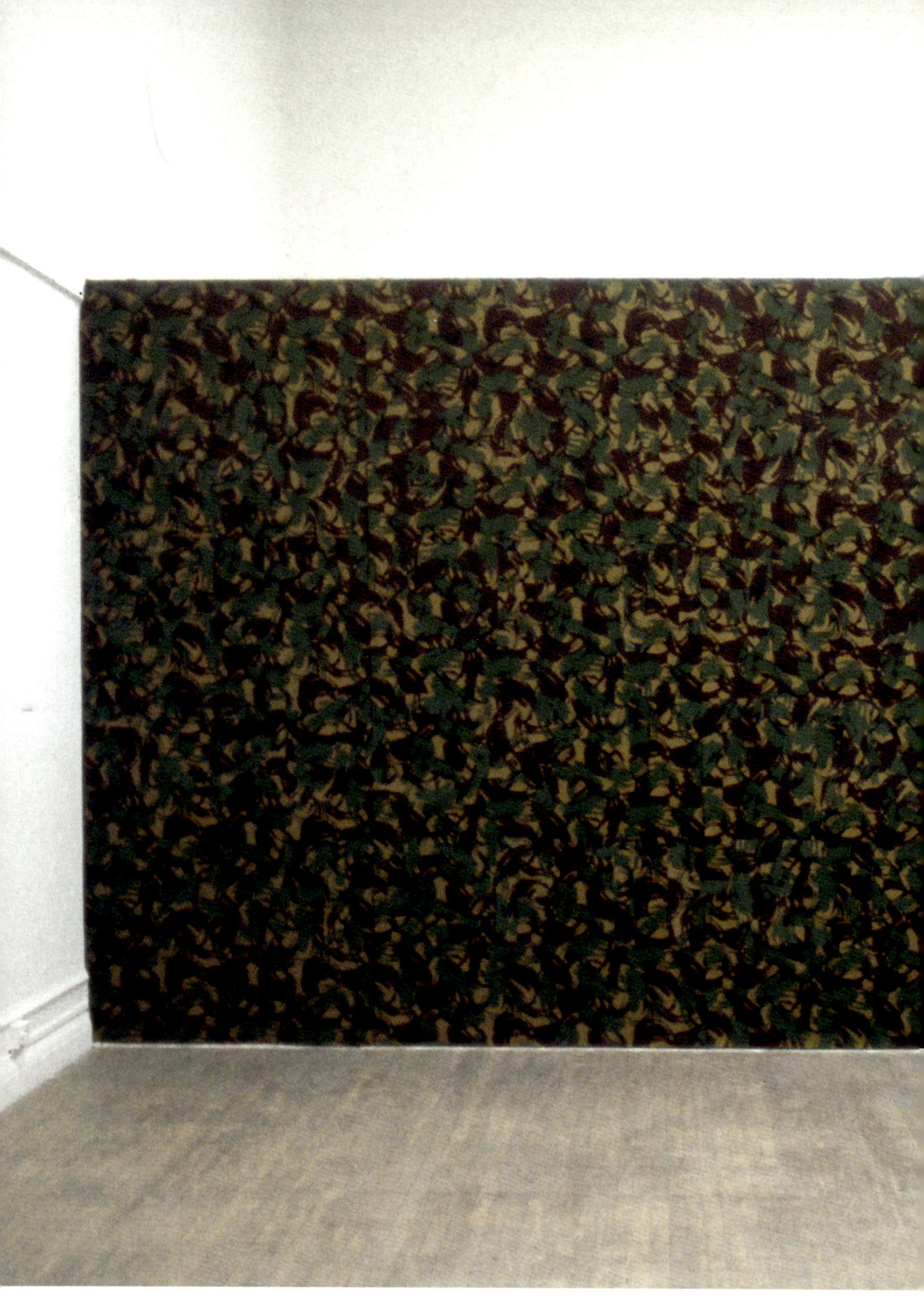

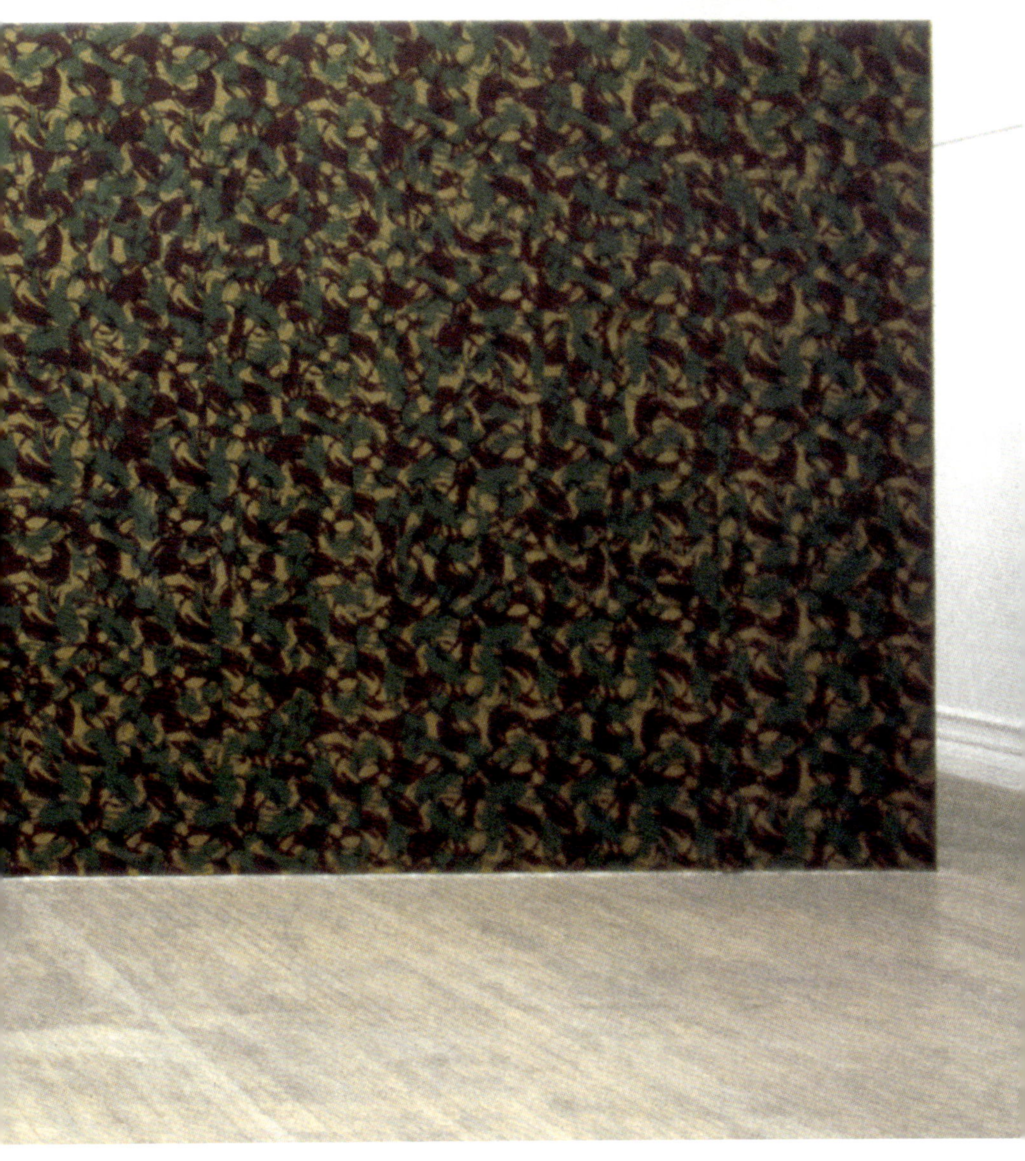

Camouflage, 1997
Textile, 300 × 862 cm

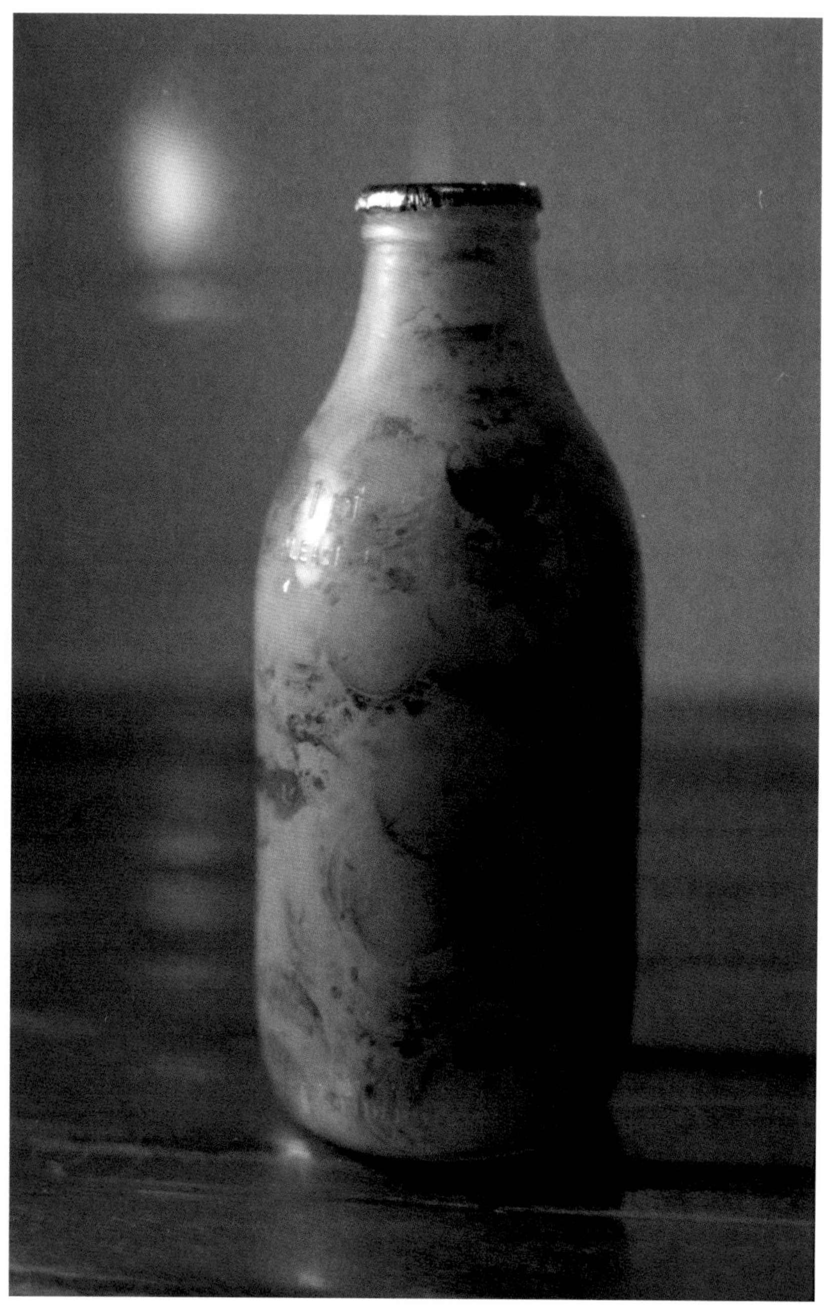

Glass milk bottle filled with milk and coins in Rodney's studio at home in London, c. 1991

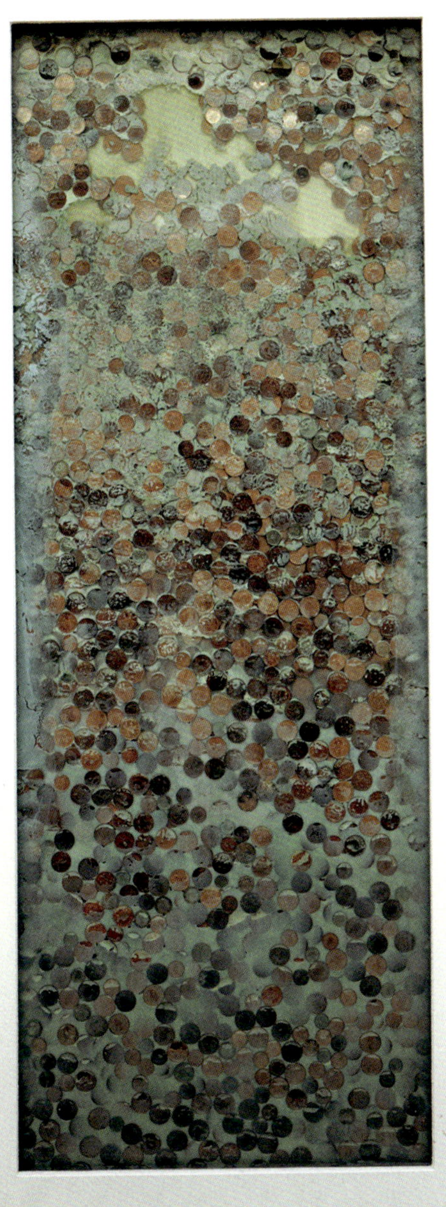

Land of Milk and Honey II, 1997
Milk, copper coins and steel, glass and acrylic vitrine, 168 × 61 × 31 cm

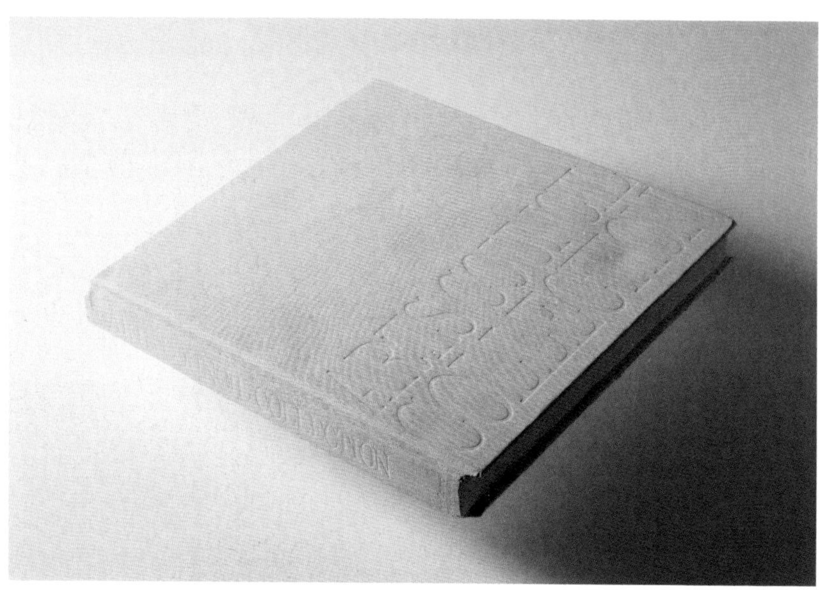

Arts Council (Collection) 1984 – 86, 1997
Plaster cast, 22 × 2 × 1 cm

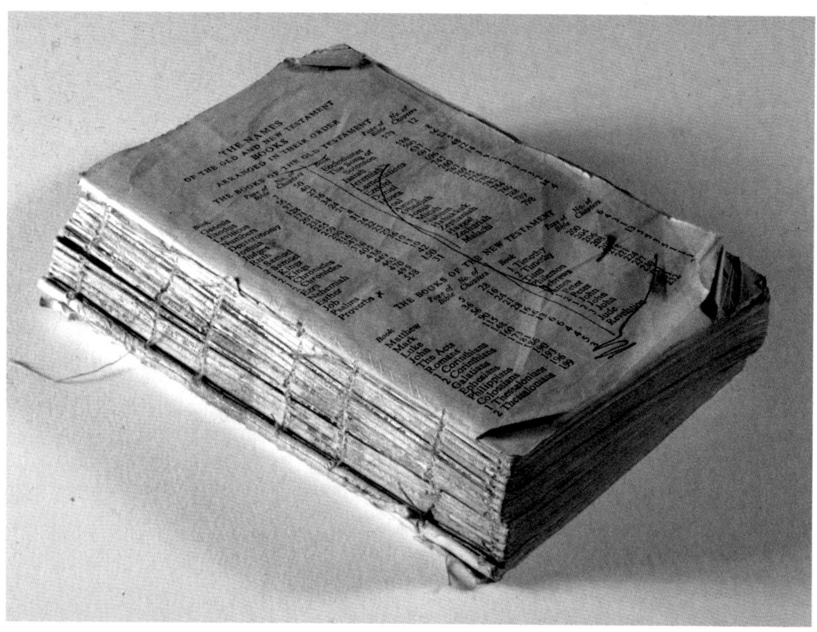

Bible, 1979 – 95
Printed paper, 15 × 10 × 3 cm

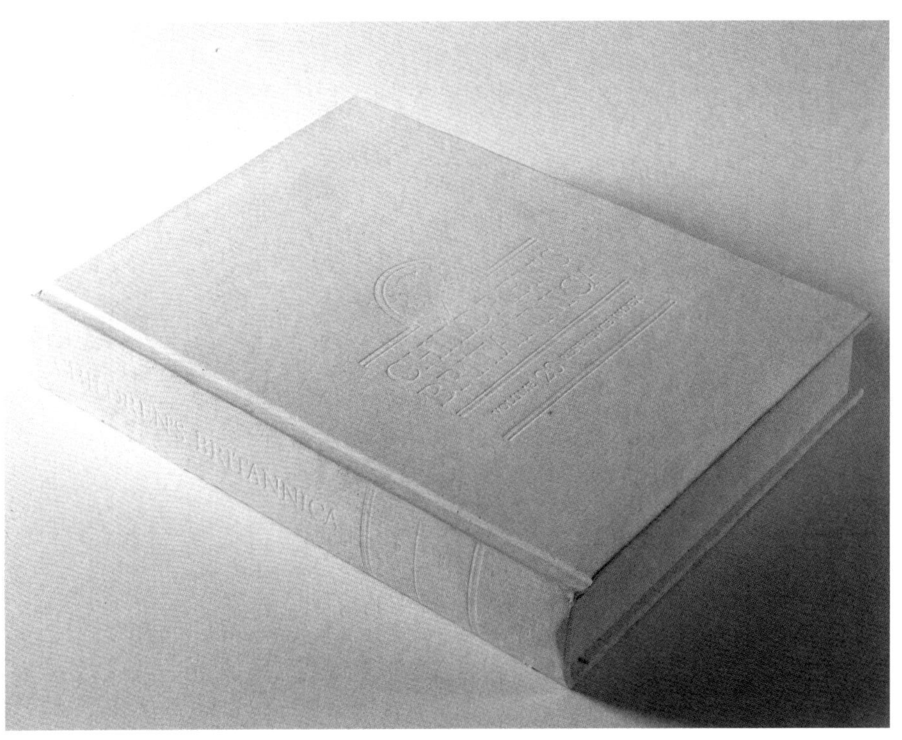

My Catechism (detail), 1997
1 of 20 plaster casts, each: 30 × 22 × 5 cm

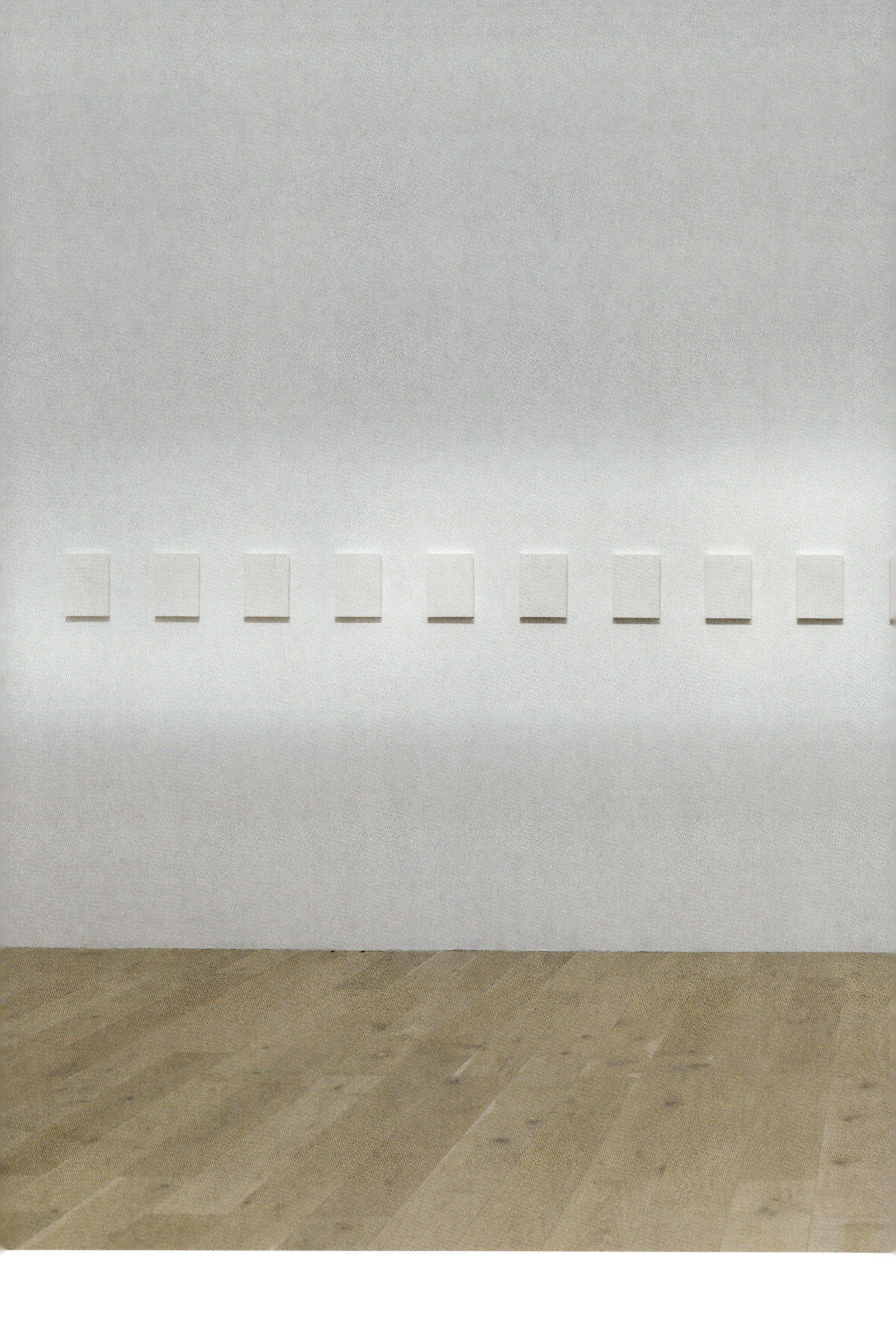

My Catechism, 1997
20 plaster casts, each: 30 × 22 × 5 cm

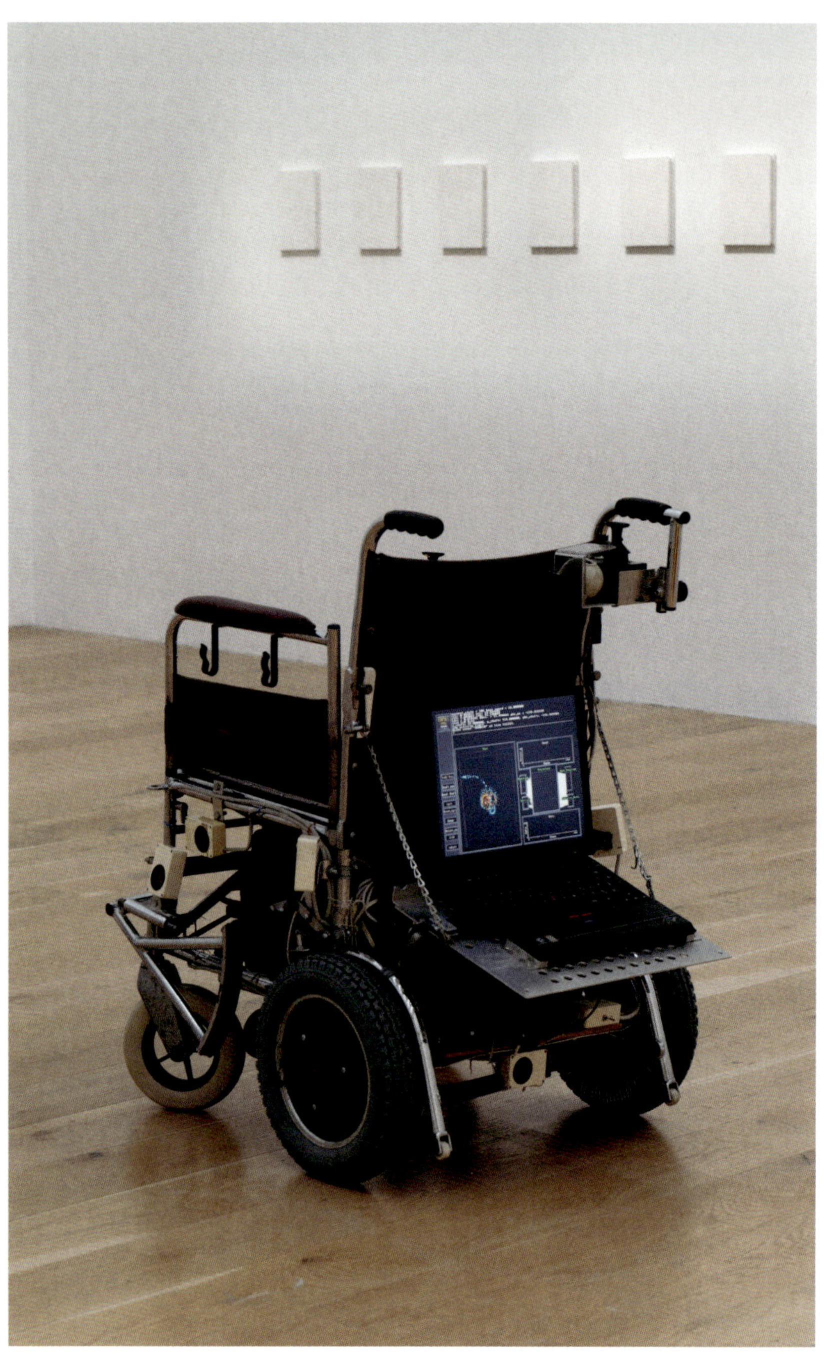

Psalms, 1997
Motorised wheelchair, laptop, 8 sensors and video camera
93 × 65 × 110 cm

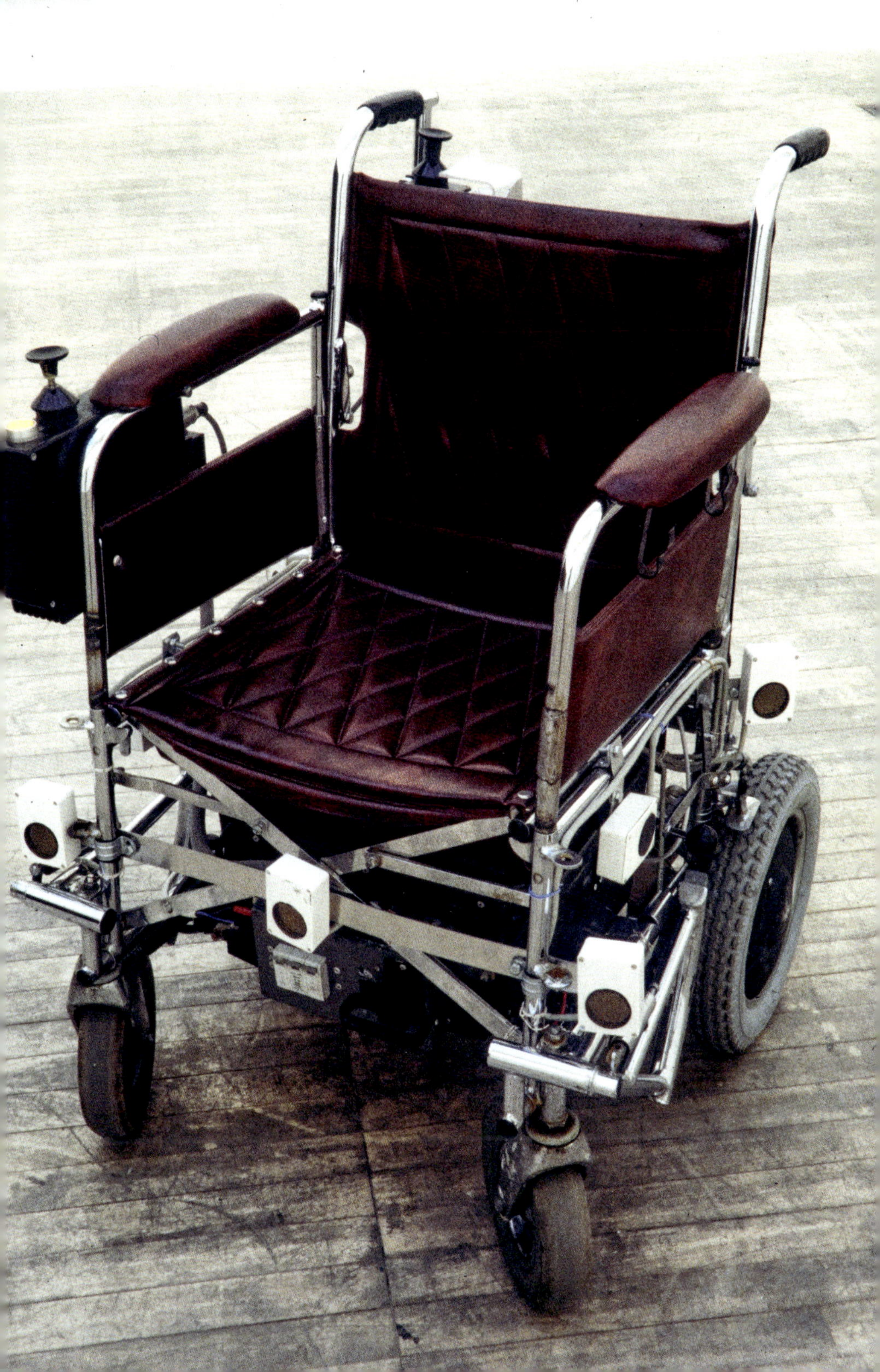

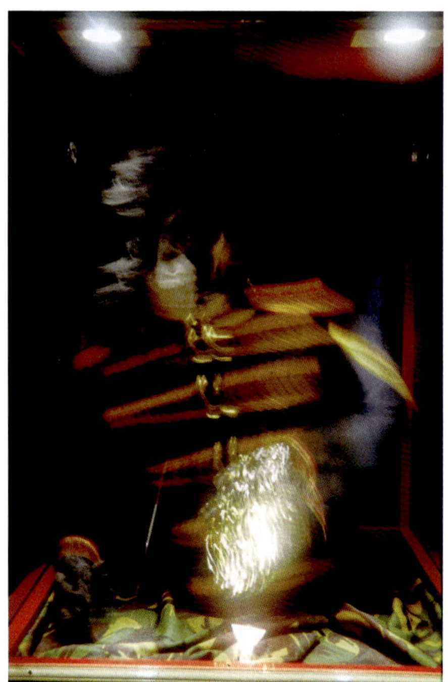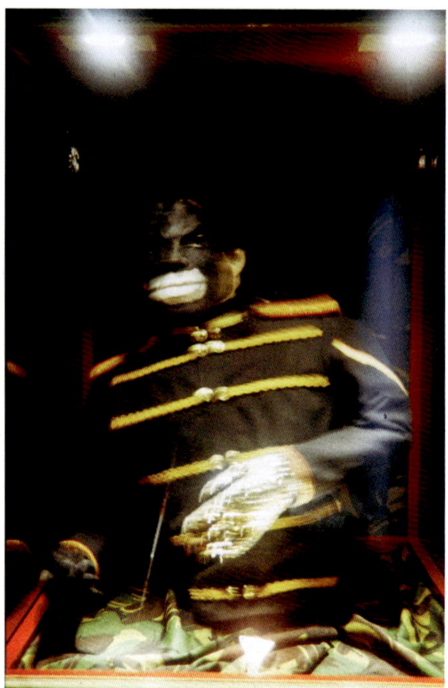

Pygmalion, 1997
Animatronic sculpture, wood and textile
145 × 79.5 × 79.5 cm

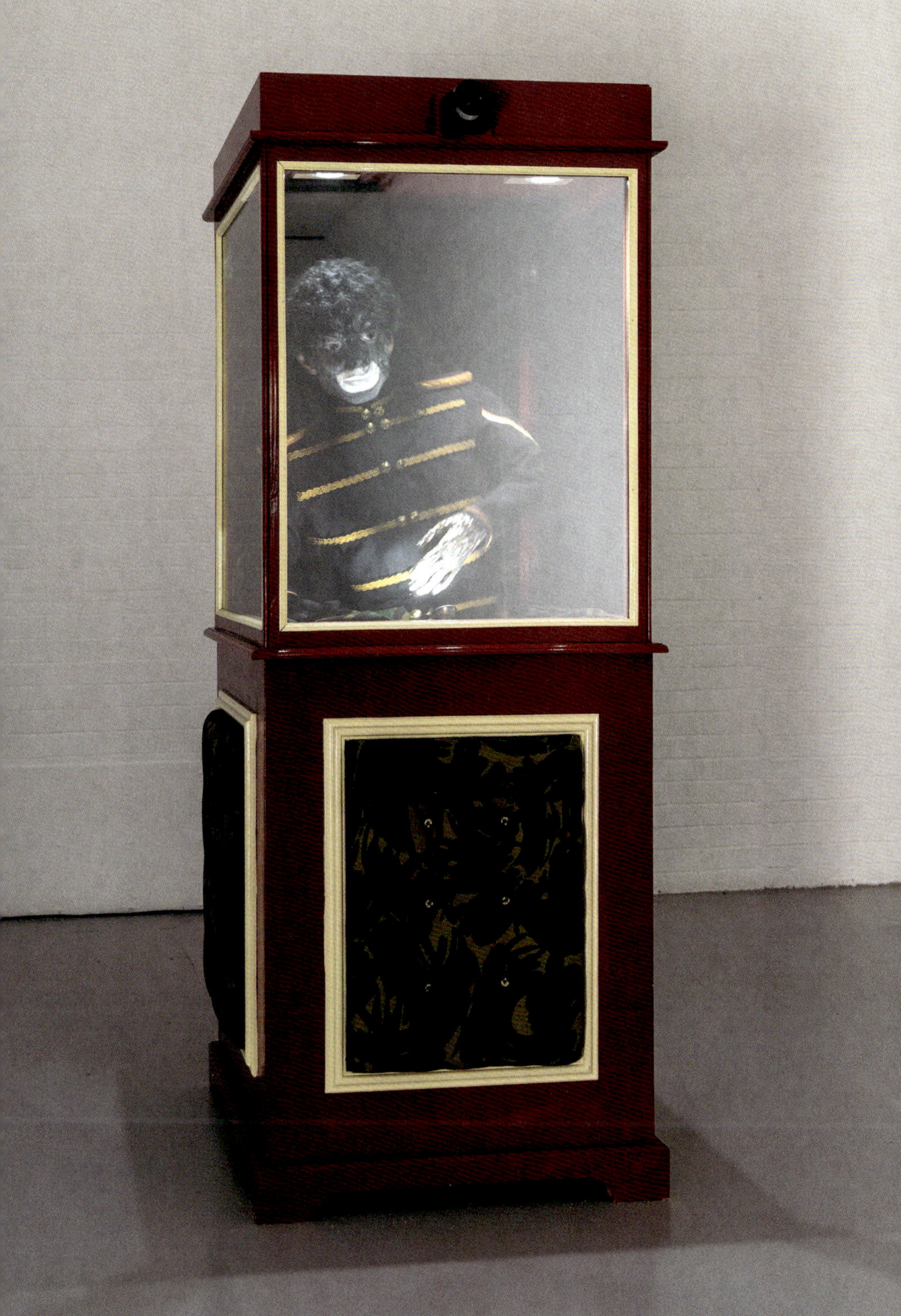

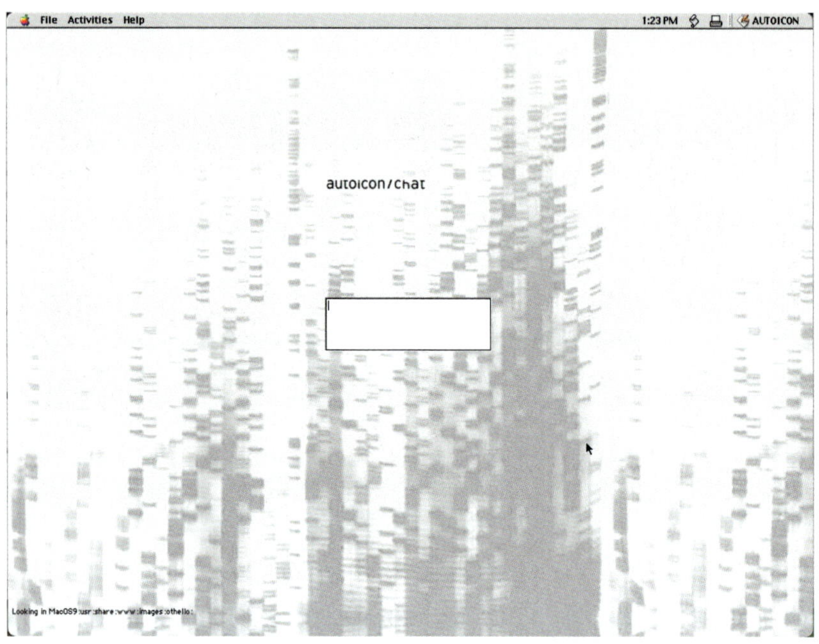

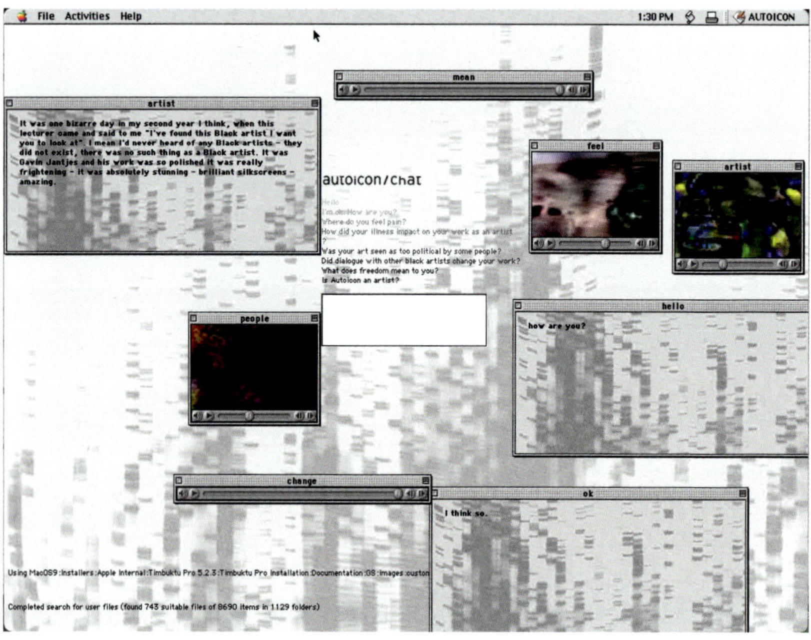

Autoicon, 1997–2000
CD-ROM, digitally transferred, dimensions variable

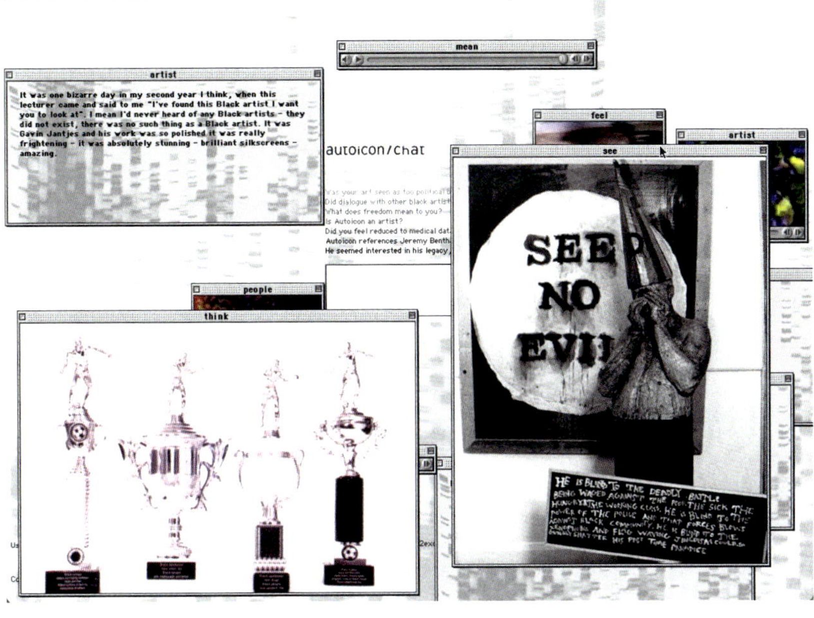

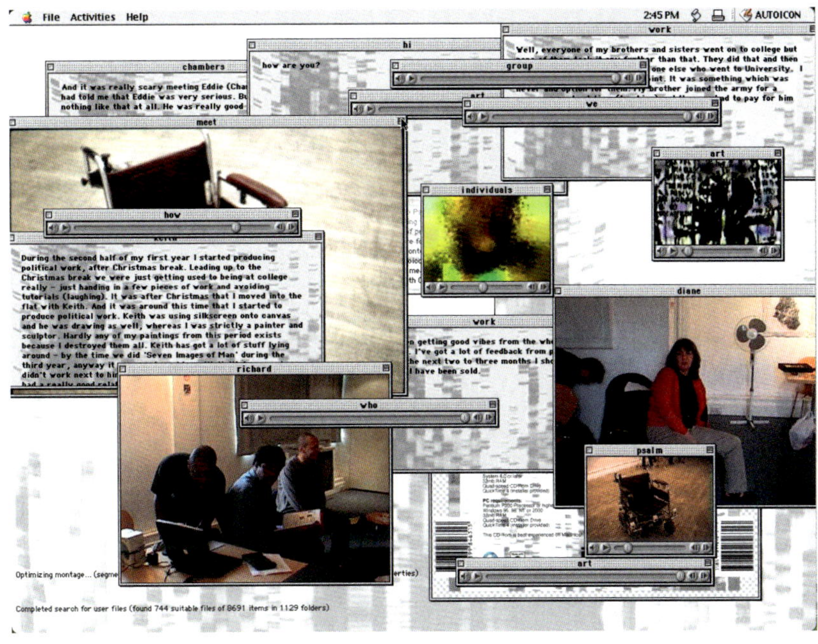

Overleaf: Pages from *Sketchbook Nos.* 1, 2, 5, 18, 24, 26, 28, 30, 31, 33, 1982–90,
Ink and mixed media on paper, each: 20.5 × 15 cm

BLACK

AND

WHITE

memories

browncoloured
black

now hear this Dear Reader
I am the last painter because
with this brush drenched in
the Blood Red of my peoples
pain with this
brush glowing
gold with my
peoples asperations
with this brush
harvest green of
my peoples stolen
land I herald
the spirit of my
generations rebbion.
capitolists
imperialits malls
shall come tumbling
down there is only
one may out for
us now Death or
Victory

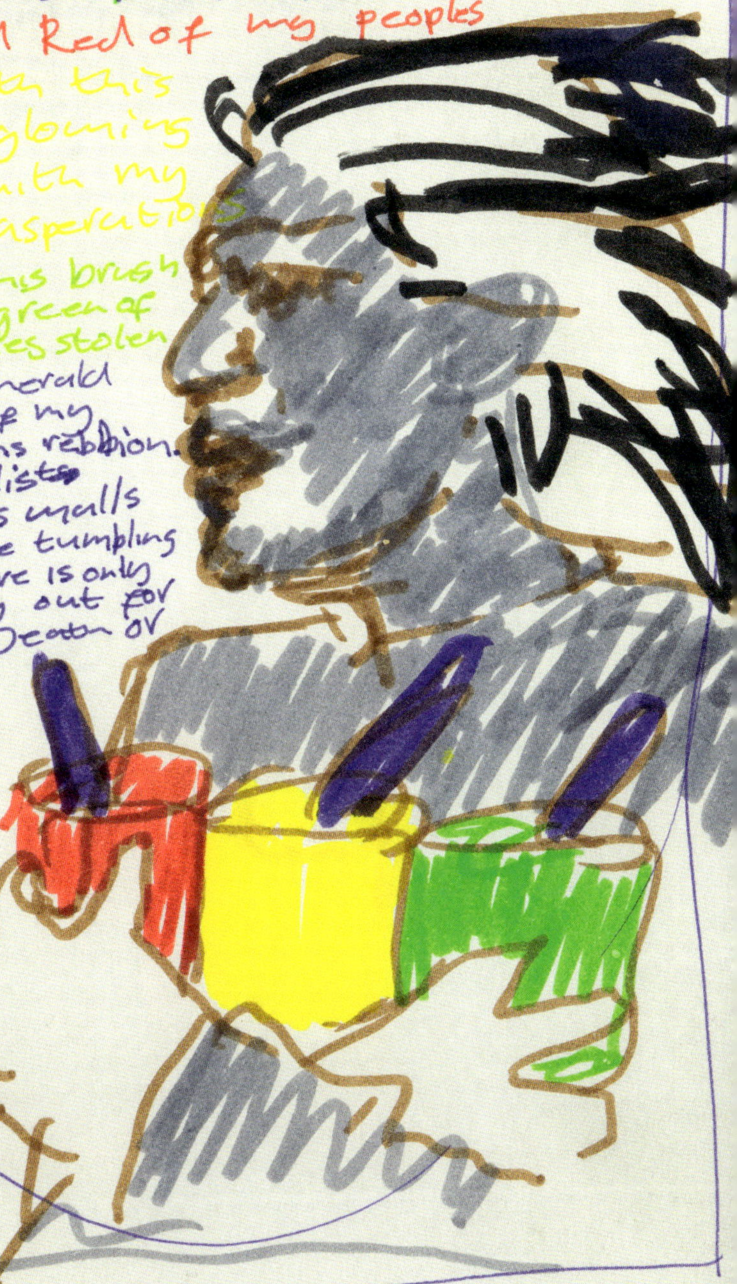

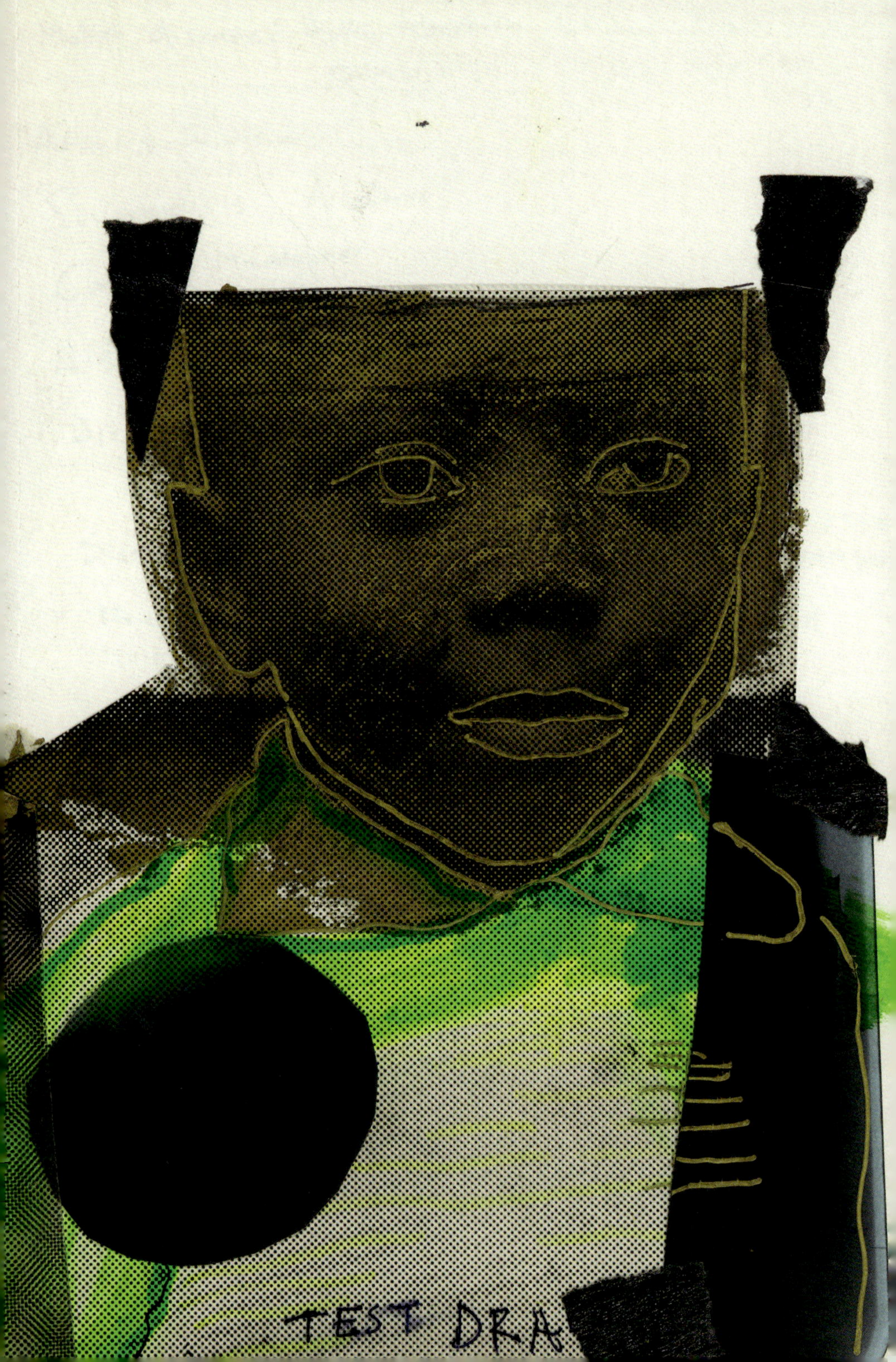
TEST DRA

CRITICAL
INJURY
WOUNDED

BRITANNIA HOSPITAL
Achitecture and Morality.

It was the best of times;
it was the worst of times;
it was the age of wisdom:
it was the age of foolishness
it was the epoch of belief
it was the epoch of incredulity
it was the season of light
it was the season of Darkness
it was the spring of hope
it was the winter of Dispair
we had everything before us
we had nothing before us
we were all going direct to Heaven
we were all going direct the other way

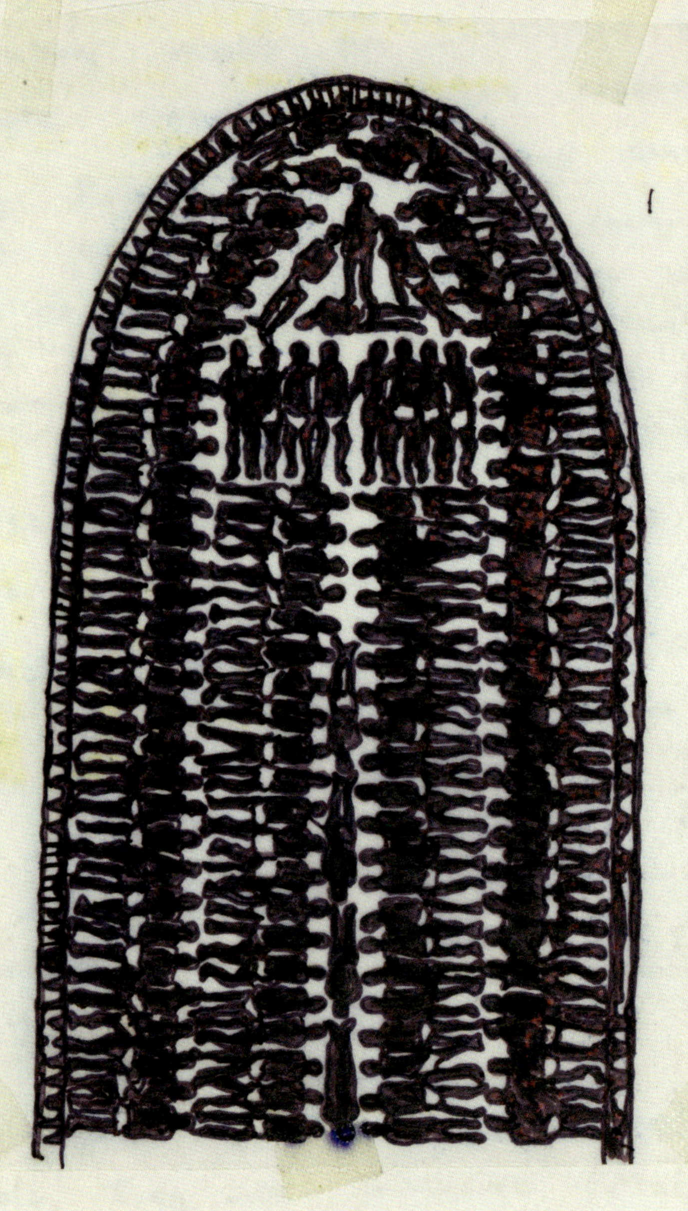

Conceptual patterning

black cells under a microscope

"The Thousand ~~natural~~ shocks that flesh is heir to.
Home as sanctuary as body in a state of Seige
assault in flames baptism by fires black history
as napalmed pages making up with the house
on fire in full smoke.

perhaps on Daler Board
Each square returned
with lead foil.

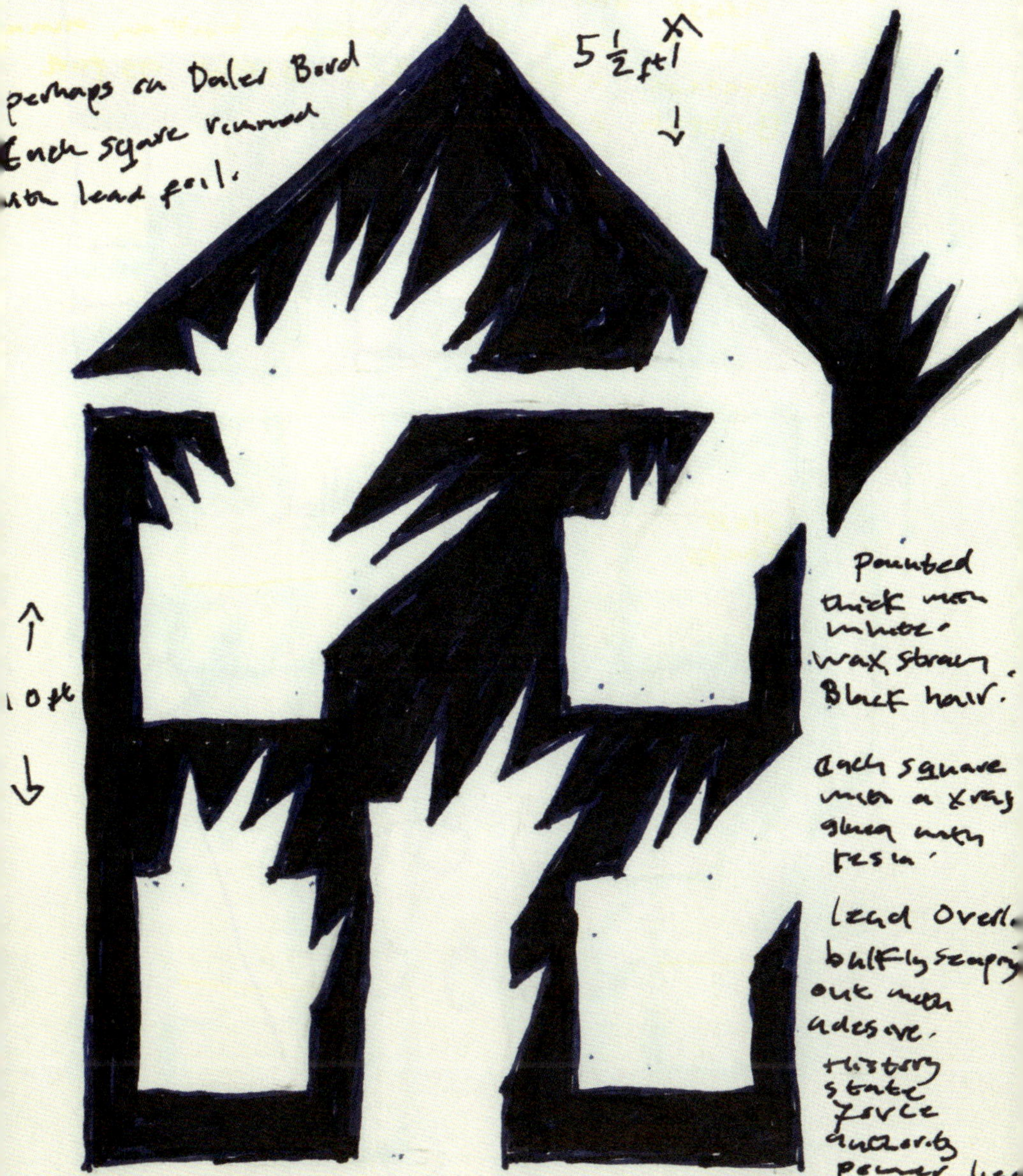

5½ ft

10 ft

Painted
thick non
white.
wax strewn.
Black hair.

each square
with a x ray
glued with
resin.

Lead Over.
butterfly scraping
out with
adesive.
history
state
force
authority
power lies

~~cages soft~~
edges step hair glue page → 7
bar   9½/2
a 5rd

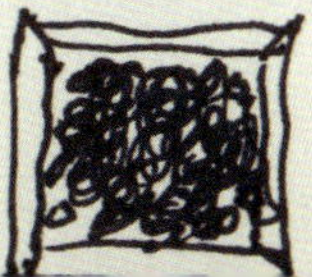

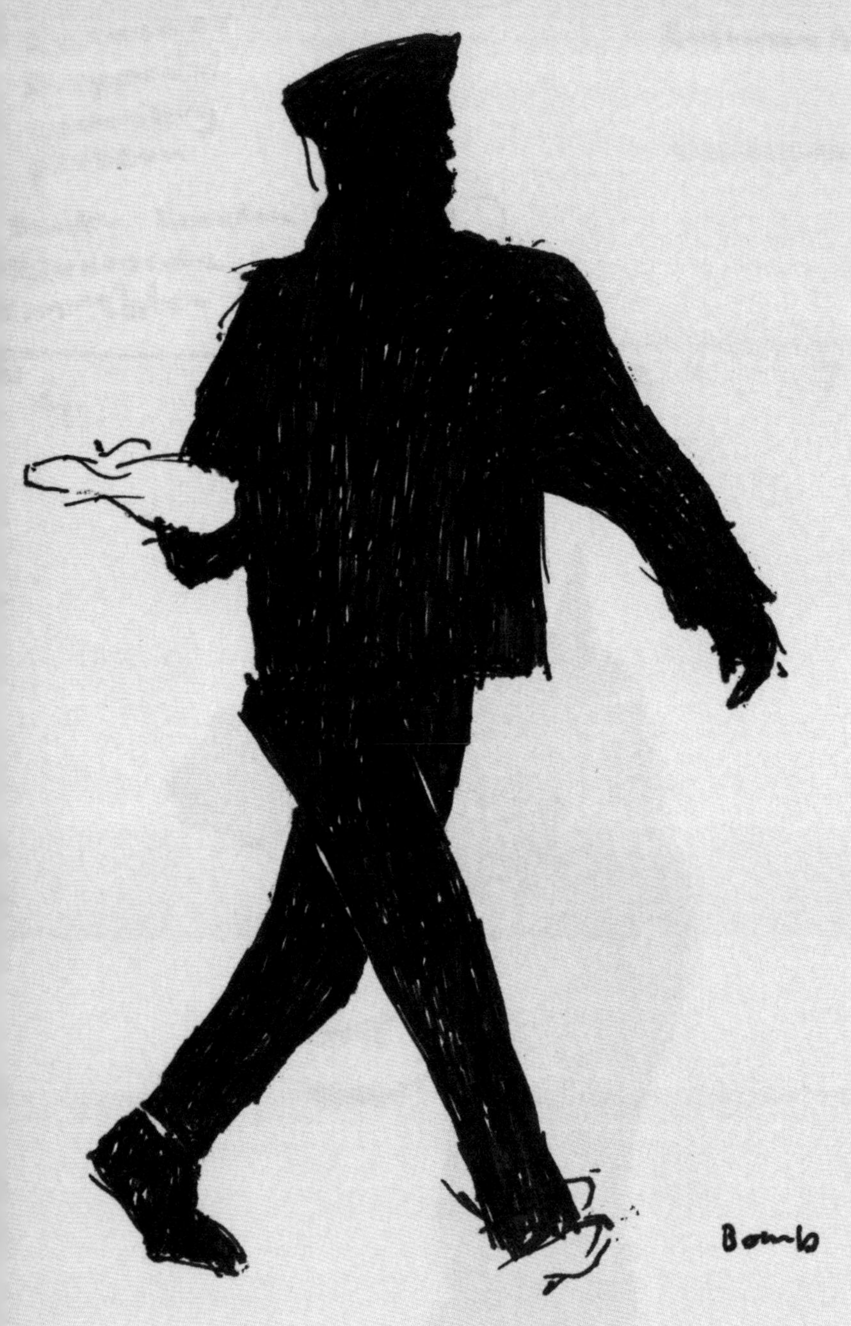

Portrait of the artist taking a political mixture.

SELF PORTRAIT

MY INFUSION
MY ~~APPEARANCE~~ CHARACTERISTICS (FACE)
MY CHARACTERISTICS (EYE)
MY CHEST SYNDROME
MY ~~BONE~~ INFARCTIONS (HIP)
MY INFARCTIONS (SHOULDER)
MY SICKLE CELL
MY SHIP SAILS IN
MY SUGER
MY RACE
MY SEX
MY FEAR
MY SURRVAILANCE
MY TROUBLES
MY CRIME
MY DISEASE
MY MEDICINE
MY CLASSFICATIONS
MY PICTURE
MY PICTURE
MY PICTURE
MY CULTURE
MY INFECTION
MY HISTORY

MY LOVES
MY INJECTIONS
MY BLOOD
MY HEROS
MY FAMILY
MY FRIENDS
MY MYTHOLOGY
MY GAZE
MY INVISIBILITY
MY SOUTH
MY ANTHROPOLIGY
MY POLITICS
MY SOCIAL PLACE
MY URBAN GHETTO
MY CONTRADICTIONS
MY ISOLATION
MY FASCINATION
MY THEORIZING

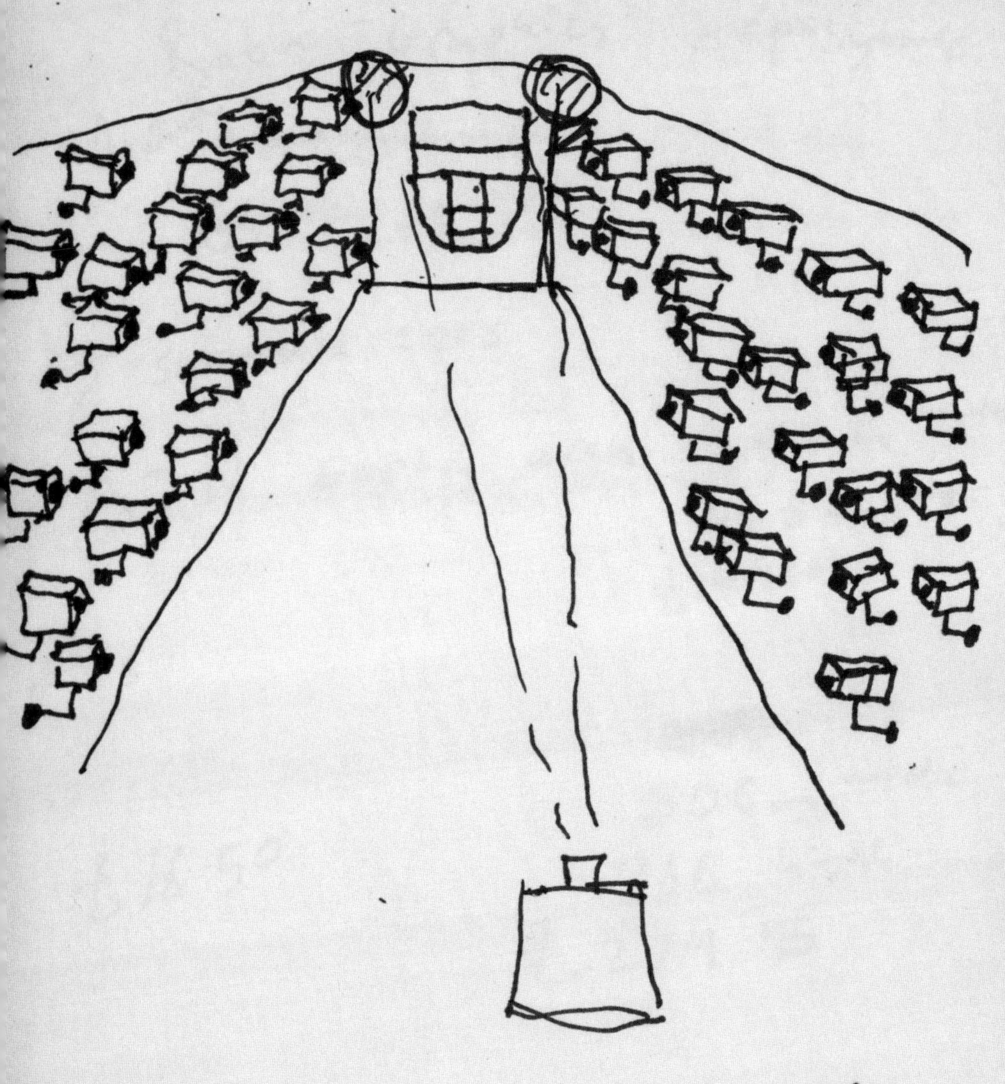

40 dummy video cameras
with red indicator lights
montaged projected of black
male face in Identikit format
2 convex mirrors.

Looking for Eldorado: Donald Rodney's Early Sketchbooks

Janice Cheddie

'Donald critiqued history, art history, but he also demanded his place in it
… So having these sketchbooks in the Tate, having them online, is more
demanding of his place in art history.' Diane Symons[1]

Donald Rodney's forty-eight sketchbooks, made from age 22 (in 1982)
until his death (in 1998), are the most comprehensive known resource
regarding the development of a Black British artist's working practices. Tate
acquired them after Rodney died, and they were eventually digitised and
made publicly available on the museum's website; until recently they were also
available for viewing on a large digital screen in the public gallery dedicated to
the Tate Archive.

The early sketchbooks trace how Rodney began his journey of
appropriating, critiquing and transforming British art through complex
collages of art history, historical sources, music and 1980s popular culture. Yet
despite recent widespread interest in Rodney's art and the work of the widely
influential Blk Art Group (of which he was a core member; the sketchbooks
amply document his membership), the sketchbooks have largely been left
out of critical analysis and are seldom referred to, specifically in relation to
the production of the works regarded as finished.[2] This oversight reflects
wider theoretical concerns. How are artists' sketchbooks positioned within
examinations of their oeuvres? How much can we read into them regarding
an artist's creative development and the process by which they carry out
their work?[3] And what is the sketchbook's relation to the archive? Is it to be
considered as a Derridean 'supplement' that adds to the work but also signals
an absence?[4] Or would we more fruitfully consider the sketchbook as part of
the artist's biography or autobiography?[5]

Throughout his life, Donald Rodney suffered from sickle cell anaemia,
resulting in frequent hospitalisations. Despite this, he was able to establish a
creative practice that, when it could not take place in his private workspace,

moved to the public hospital ward. In 1997, Rodney's friend and creative collaborator Virginia Nimarkoh documented the artistic, cultural, social and technical materials that surrounded his hospital bed, which reflected his socially engaged practice. Nimarkoh's inventory, which appeared in the publication accompanying Rodney's final exhibition during his lifetime, '9 Night in Eldorado', illustrates how the artist's surroundings, wherever they happened to be, became his studio.[6] Nimarkoh and Diane Symons, Rodney's often-uncredited collaborator, both state that Rodney's sketchbooks were key to conversations around the realisation of his work. Rodney's nontraditional practice explored many visual, textual and political themes, making the sketchbooks a rich resource for discussions on the development of inclusive and participatory art-making practices among the Blk Art Group and beyond.

The early sketchbooks are text-heavy, the topics ranging from discussions of slum housing, racism and education to personal notes. They manifest a deep concern with language and the spatial placement of text on the page, and contain abundant experiments with different pens, inks and stencils.[7] This emphasis on the written word directly mirrors Rodney's early finished works. Rodney's interest in developing a new theory of knowledge through text and image is evident for instance in *Lexicon of Liberation* (1984), which features coloured photocopied tiles on a red background that imitate the tiles often used for teaching children the letters of the alphabet. The repetition of the tiles, in varying angles, creates a defined and familiar structure to highlight the systematically Eurocentric nature of British education and language systems.

Rodney was born in Birmingham in 1961, at a time when Black people in the UK were described as Negro or Coloured; by the end of the 1960s, informed by US civil rights struggles and the Black Power movement, the term 'Black' had come into widespread use. Rodney's childhood home was on Marshall Street in Smethwick, an emerging multiracial neighbourhood. In 1964, Peter Griffiths was elected a Conservative Member of Parliament (MP) for Smethwick, having campaigned on the slogan 'If you want a nigger for a neighbour, vote Labour.' Shortly before his death in 1965, Malcolm X visited Marshall Street as part of his evolving solidarity with people of colour across the globe to support antiracist organising.[8] Rodney's lived experiences were thus markedly different from the previous generations of Black and brown artists – artists such as Aubrey Williams, Frank Bowling, F. N. Souza, and Rasheed Araeen – who arrived in Britain in and around 1948, a moment of mass Commonwealth immigration into the UK.

The sketchbooks provide valuable insights into this context and its impact on Rodney's visual practice. The artist's exploration of shifting linguistic definitions of race can be seen in *Brown Coloured Black* (1983, p. 67), which started as a series of text-based experiments in black ink and stencils in

                    Looking for Eldorado

Sketchbook No. 5 (p. 120): 'I was brown, I was coloured, I am black.'[9] Each of the three panels in the completed work features the same childhood photograph of Rodney. The piece is a meditation on how any particular racial term classifies and surveils the Black body. The shifting terminology and the artist's visual layering point clearly to how labelling can make us lose sight of the individual humanity of the Black child.

The year Rodney made *Brown Coloured Black*, he was living with fellow Blk Art Group member and Trent Polytechnic student, Keith Piper, at 3 Lindsay Walk, Hyson Green, Nottingham, which doubled as the headquarters of Blk Art Group.[10] It was a multiracial working-class public housing estate that in 1981 had been the epicentre of riots against police harassment and brutality. This address features on the inside cover of Rodney's early sketchbooks and also appeared on the poster for 1982's First National Black Art Convention, a historically significant gathering of politically Black (African, Caribbean, Asian) visual art students from across the UK, often cited as the birth of the British Black Arts movement. Rodney's sketchbooks provide documentary evidence of the profound impact of his friendship and collaboration with Piper (as in *The Next Turn of the Screw* [1987]) and how this relationship impacted the development of his radical artistic voice.

How We Gonna Make the Black Nation Rise?

'Suddenly I became aware of what I wanted to say and who I wanted to say it to. I no longer had to use the language given to me by Western art traditions.' [11]
— Donald Rodney

The Blk Art Group, which also included Marlene Smith, Claudette Johnson and Eddie Chambers, was founded in 1979 and initiated conceptual, artistic, cultural and political interventions that critiqued Britain's colonial legacies. Seeking to widen curatorial and artistic practices and modes of creative working, it advocated for socially engaged practices and protested the exclusion of non-white artists from Western art historical narratives – important developments that laid the groundwork for the establishment of our current global art scene. All members of the Blk Art Group became influential figures in contemporary British art. Rodney's self-proclaimed radicalisation has often been read in relation to the racialisation of the Black body, and British society and art history's historical amnesia around legacies of slavery, empire and colonialism. While these social and historical areas no doubt informed his work, my reading of Rodney's assertion of radicalisation is that it was also about reimagining what a socially engaged Black art practice could be.[12]

Rodney's first explorations in this vein began with the iconography
of Rastafarianism, 'a compelling countercultural expression'[13] for young
Black British people in the 1970s and 1980s. In *Sketchbook No. 2* (p. 121),
an image of a dreadlocked Rastafarian man accompanies a text by Rodney
reiterating the Rastafarian belief that an artist is not only an image maker,
but a cultural leader spreading knowledge about Black history and culture
for Black people.[14] Rodney's experimentation with the colours of Pan-
Africanism and Rastafarianism quickly moved into wider studies of visual
language and typography. For instance his reference in *Sketchbook No. 3* to
'How We Gonna Make the Black Nation Rise?', the popular 1982 hip-hop
song by Brother D and Collective Effort, signals the displacement of reggae
by hip-hop as the dominant countercultural narrative for young Black people
in the early 1980s.[15] This shift in the early sketchbooks from the Rastafarian
pastoral tones of an imagined precolonial Africa to more industrial, urban
visual aesthetics – the cut-and-mix styles of early hip-hop music, street art
and graffiti art – presaged the predominance of black ink in Rodney's later
sketchbooks and increasingly monotonal final works.

Within Rastafarian philosophy, the Black experience is a fluid space of
becoming. It traces a narrative that begins with precolonial Africa, to the
current situation of formerly enslaved Black people trapped in the West/
Babylon, removed from their history and culture, to Black people being
physically and spiritually reconnected with a mythical Africa. Black identities
operating in these imagined spaces are spoken of as simultaneously individual
and collective. The British Jamaican sociologist Stuart Hall later theorised
a concept of Blackness and race as historical states of emergence rather than
fixed biological categories. These ideas likely played a role in opening up
a conceptual space for Rodney to develop a critical distance between his
individual identity and such social and historical constructions of the Black
male figure.

A critical dialogue between individual and collective experience is
explored in Rodney's reimagining of Ford Madox Brown's *The Last of England*
(1855) in *Sketchbook No. 1*.

This book dates from 1983, when Rodney was twenty-two, making
this among his earliest disruptions to privileged British historical and art-
historical narratives. The work in question by Brown is Pre-Raphaelite in style
and is a sympathetic portrayal of a white middle-class couple leaving England
in a time of economic crisis; the title refers to their final mournful look back at
the iconic White Cliffs of Dover. It is often read as autobiographical, reflecting
Brown's own circumstances.[16] The title Rodney gave his sketch changes the
'last' in the title to 'first', and the drawing, as we glean from the caption ('My
mother and father standing together on the wet and lonely deck of the sailing

                    Looking for Eldorado

...asts of England
...d Madox Brown Prevaphelities,

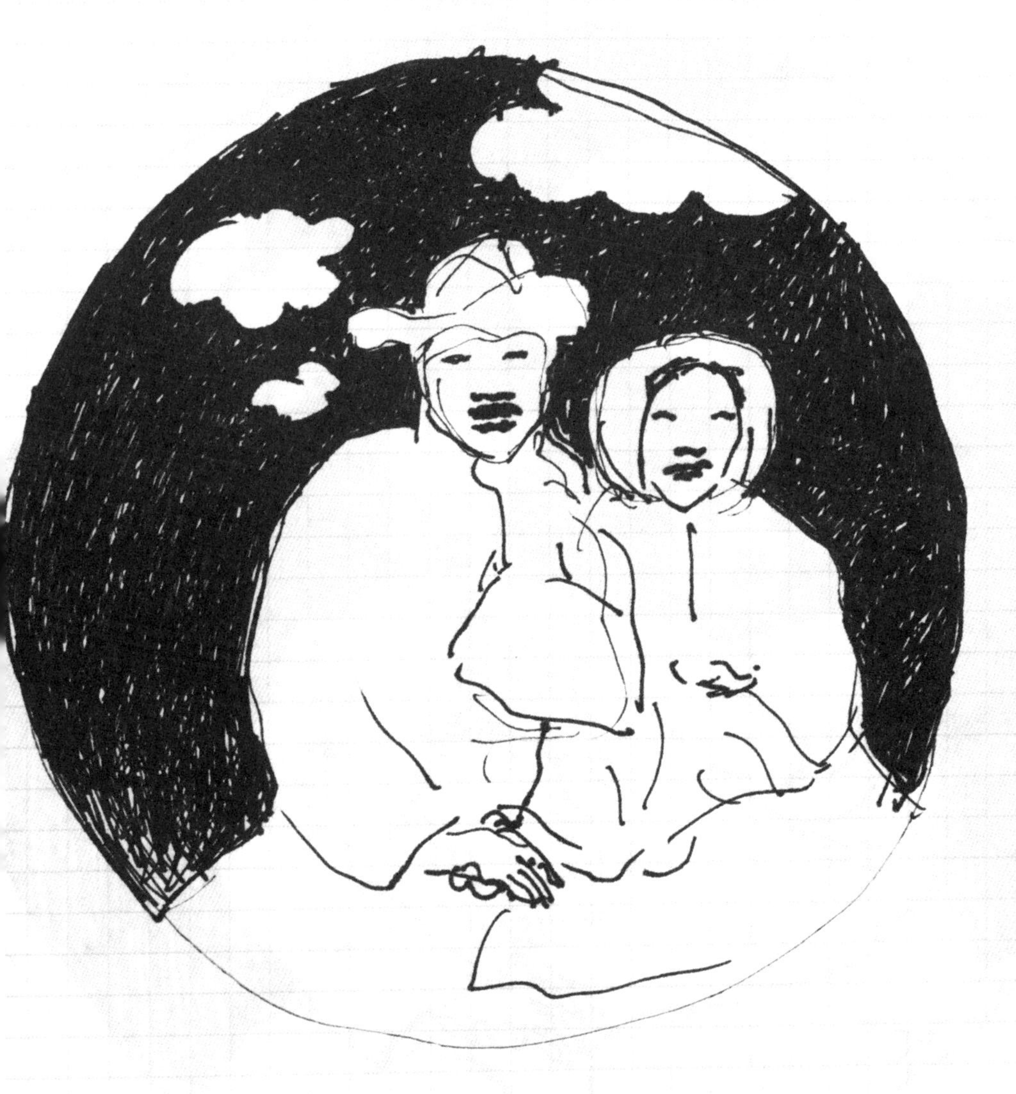

First of England
my mother and father standing
on the wet and lonley deck
of the Sailing ship the Empire
windrush

ship the *Empire Windrush*'), shows his parents' arrival in England via the HMT *Empire Windrush*.[17] Although *First of England* was never translated directly into a completed artwork, it manifests key visual and narrative concerns that Rodney did develop in later finished works – namely questions of migration, (auto)biography, history and visual language.

Rodney's title signifies not simply a shift of perspective or of geographical direction; it is a bold insertion of his parents into England's history by positioning them as British citizens arriving on England's shores. His adoption of Brown's circular framing, usually interpreted as sentimental, stresses the couple's unity and invites the viewer's empathy for these people who have sacrificed so much to make their journey, only (as we now know) to face a cold and unwelcoming Britain. Through the replacement of a white couple with a Black one, Rodney counters Brown's classist and gendered assumptions about the human capacity for loss and longing. And, significantly, he changes the name of the ship from *Eldorado*[18] to *Empire Windrush*, one of the first vessels to bring Caribbean migrants to postwar Britain. But his romantic autobiography is completely fabricated. His parents did not sail on the *Empire Windrush*, nor did they even travel together. Like many Black working-class Caribbean migrants, they came to the UK separately. Travel of this kind was prohibitively expensive in the 1950s, and it was typical for families to send one person ahead, who, once established with a job, would send money overseas via remittances to pay the travel costs for the rest, one by one. Knowing that *First of England* is more metaphor than autobiography, then, we can infer that Rodney was seeking less to document his family's story than to insert into the tradition of British narrative painting the collective histories of the first generation of postwar Caribbean migrants.

A central framing of the Black subject combines with subjective text in *The Lords of Humankind (Part One)* (1986, p. 67), *Self Portrait: Black Men Public Enemy* (1990, p. 92), and *Self Portrait as Clinton McCurbin* (1988, p. 79). These three works operate as visual acts of remembrance and recognition, exploring the hypervisibility of the Black male within the public realm. Moving between individual and collective Black identities, Rodney's use of the self-portrait is not a substitution for, but a recognition of, shared experience. It positions the Black artist as a critical, but not objective, observer who reinserts into collective cultural memory the precarity of Black lives in a racist society. Clinton McCurbin was a Black man who died, aged 23, after contact with the police. In *Self Portrait as Clinton McCurbin*, Rodney carefully reproduces a smiling family photograph of McCurbin, subverting the police photographs that circulated. Rodney's centering of McCurbin's face and its evident fragility constitute a public act of mourning and memorialisation.

     Looking for Eldorado

The pages of *Sketchbook No. 1* manifest a rapid working through of ideas and materials. Just a few pages after *First of England* sketch, we see Rodney reiterating Brown's name and artwork title above a reference to Conceptual artist Sue Atkinson,[19] thereby bringing critical material and conceptual investigations by contemporary artists together with British art history. Atkinson's mixed-media work is notable for its use of diverse materials, including crayons, washing powder, icing sugar and glue, challenging the boundaries between the political, domestic and artistic spheres. There is a clear affinity between Atkinson's and Rodney's work given the latter's use of nontraditional and/or domestic materials – glue, hospital bed sheets, bleach, wallpaper, wax crayons, mirror, matches, spray paint, photocopies, X-rays, milk – in later works. Indeed, Rodney's sketchbooks reference a wide range of works by other artists, reflecting his development and mobilisation of visual tools within his critical investigations into constructions of Black histories.

In *Sketchbook No. 3*, Rodney does some more rethinking of art historical references by compiling a list of important paintings in the European avant-garde, then using them to construct his own art canon based on references to Black history.[20] 'A Nigger Splash' is an appropriation of the title of David Hockney's 1967 painting *A Bigger Splash* that seeks to highlight the history of slavery. (Bigger is also the main character in Richard Wright's seminal 1940 novel on Black alienation, *Native Son*). 'Splash' here refers not to a swim in a pleasant suburban backyard pool, but to the transatlantic slave trade practice of drowning enslaved Africans by throwing them overboard during an unprofitable sea voyage. To their enslavers, they were worth more as insurance claims than as human beings to be sold.[21] Later in the sketchbook, the references are further fleshed out.[22]

As Rodney's visual style developed, his focus shifted from his parents' imagined joint journey to his father's actual lone voyage.[23] And in 1997, nearly twenty years after his first encounter with Brown's *The Last of England*, Brown was still being referenced, albeit indirectly, through Rodney's use of 'Eldorado' as a metaphor to explore the losses, betrayals, and rejections faced by his father's generation in the title of his final exhibition, '9 Night in Eldorado'. The exhibition publication does not specifically invoke Brown, but focuses on the 1849 poem 'Eldorado' by Edgar Allen Poe, which is about unfulfilled searches for happiness and success. This extended engagement with Eldorado as a visual and textual trope is just one example of how Rodney's early sketchbooks provide a rich resource for exploring his visual experimentation, engagement with the history of British art, and navigations of migration, loss and longing.

First published in *Mousse Magazine*, issue 85 (Fall 2023) 57–61.

1 Diane Symons, 'Donald Rodney: A Practice Unfolding – Animating the Archives', Tate, March 1, 2017, 9:04 min., available at https://www.tate.org.uk/art/artists/donald-rodney-3076/donald-rodney-practice-unfolding.

2 '[Rodney's] sketchbooks played an integral role in his art and contain a mixture of preliminary studies for new artworks, records of past exhibitions and various writings. His drawings and writings bring together diverse personal, cultural, social and political influences.' Tate Archive, https://www.tate.org.uk/art/archive/tga-200321-3/rodney-sketchbooks-and-artwork.

3 'Oftentimes viewed as part of a single artist's body of work – supplementary scraps of material preceding finished pieces – sketchbooks are rarely accorded critical scholarly attention despite their essential role in one's creative process and stylistic development.' Eleonor (Ellie) Botoman, 'Building Community through Brooklyn Art Library's Sketchbook Archive', *Public Services Quarterly* 18, no. 2 (May 2022) 56.

4 Here I refer to Jacques Derrida, '... That Dangerous Supplement ...', in *Of Grammatology*, trans. Gayatri Chakravorty Spivak (1967; repr., Baltimore: Johns Hopkins University Press, 1997) 141–43.

5 See Martha Barratt, 'Autobiography, Time, and Documentation in the Performances and Auto-Archives of Carolee Schneemann', *Visual Resources* 32, nos. 3/4 (October 1, 2016) 282–305.

6 Virginia Nimarkoh, *9 Night in Eldorado* (exh. cat.) (South London Gallery, 1997) n.p.

7 See for instance Donald Rodney, *Sketchbook No. 5*, 1983–84, p. 81, https://www.tate.org.uk/art/archive/items/tga-200321-3-5/rodney-sketchbook-number-5/81.

8 Stuart Jeffries, 'Britain's Most Racist Election: The Story of Smethwick, 50 Years On,' *The Guardian*, 15 October 2014, https://www.theguardian.com/world/2014/oct/15/britains-most-racist-election-smethwick-50-years-on; Perry Blankson, 'When Malcolm X Came to the West Midlands,' *Tribune*, 10 March 2022, https://tribunemag.co.uk/2022/03/malcolm-x-smethwick-peter-griffiths-racism-1965.

Footage of Malcolm X visiting Marshall Street appears in John Akomfrah's documentary *Handsworth Songs* (1986). In a 1994 interview with Ruth Kelly, conducted as part of the research degree 'The Blk Art Group in Historical and Cultural Context,' Open University, Rodney stated that he had no recollections of his family experiencing racial harassment. But it's very likely that Rodney, the youngest member of the family, was shielded from discussions around racism.

9 Donald Rodney, *Sketchbook No. 5*, 1983–84, p. 83.

10 Now Nottingham Trent University.

11 Donald Rodney, 'Identity, Culture and Power', in *State of the Art: Ideas and Images in the 1980s*, ed. Sandy Nairne (London: Chatto & Windus in collaboration with Channel 4 Television, 1987) 235.

12 See Donald Rodney, *Sketchbook No. 2*, 1982–85, p. 9.

13 Eddie Chambers, *World Is Africa: Writings on Diaspora Art* (London: Bloomsbury Visual Arts, 2020), xxvi.

14 Donald Rodney, *Sketchbook No. 2*, 1982–85, p. 9.

15 Donald Rodney, *Sketchbook No. 3*, 1983–84, p. 19. This is considered by some cultural commentators the first openly political hip-hop song. It is interesting to note that one line in the lyrics uses the Rastafarian 'I&I.'

16 Lionel Lambourne, *Victorian Painting* (London: Phaidon, 1999) 356. Rodney was born and raised in Birmingham, and it is highly likely that he saw the painting at the Birmingham Art Gallery.

17 See Donald Rodney, *Sketchbook No. 1*, 1983.

18 In *The Last of England*, the ship's name *Eldorado*, is clearly visible.

19 Donald Rodney, *Sketchbook No. 1*, 1983, p. 23.

20 Donald Rodney, *Sketchbook No. 3*, 1983–84.

21 This practice is depicted in J. M. W. Turner's *The Slave Ship* (1840).

22 Donald Rodney, *Sketchbook No. 3*, 1983–84.

23 Donald Rodney, *Sketchbook No. 2*, 1982–85.

     Looking for Eldorado

Intertwining Histories in Donald Rodney's Untitled ('Cowboy and Indian' After David Hockney's 'We Two Boys Together Clinging', 1961], 1989

Gregory Salter

In a drawing from 1989, Donald Rodney appropriated and adapted David Hockney's painting *We Two Boys Together Clinging* from 1961. It is both an enigmatic response to the racial politics of 1980s Britain and an unexpected and provocative intertwining of histories of race, colonialism and sexuality.

In Donald Rodney's 1989 drawing *Untitled ('Cowboy and Indian' After David Hockney's 'We Two Boys Together Clinging', 1961)* (p. 85), a cowboy places one arm on a Native American with an ambiguous touch. He stands slightly taller than the other figure and looks down, his lips pursed, perhaps in speech or perhaps, even, to offer a kiss. The Native American's body faces the cowboy, though his head is turned; he seems to look back out to us while offering an ear, or a cheek, to the other figure. The two figures are simply drawn. Their bodies are curved oblongs supported by thin, footless legs, and their identities are indicated by stereotypical headgear – a Stetson hat for the cowboy and feathered headdress for the Native American. Rodney has formed the bulk of these figures out of an absence or subtraction of pencil marks. The Native American's body is largely unmarked paper, though areas of dark shading emphasise the touch of the cowboy's hand. The cowboy's hat, body, and sections of the Native American's headdress are modelled out of erased areas of pencil. Behind the cowboy, there is a dark rectangle of thick, scrawled pencil marks, towards which he almost appears to pull or guide the Native American. Their two heads, meanwhile, are formed from subtler, softer shading into uncanny masks. Between their heads, and partly obscuring the Native American's face, is another area of frantically erased pencil – a kind of anxious absence that separates the two men.

This essay seeks to address the histories and resonances of this enigmatic drawing. It begins with Rodney's focus on the figures of a cowboy and a Native American, which reflects his general interest in this theme – it appeared in several of his paintings in the early 1980s, though this later work returns rather unexpectedly to the subject in ambiguous ways. It then addresses the drawing's curious appropriation of the queer British Pop artist David Hockney's painting *We Two Boys Together Clinging* from 1961. Rodney has mutated Hockney's representation of homosexual love into a personal drama between the cowboy and the Native American, that bears queer traces. Finally, it explores how the drawing is also a continuation of Rodney's preoccupation with masculinity, placing it in comparison with another representation of Black masculinity in Wolverhampton Art Gallery's collection Keith Piper's *Go West Young Man* (1996).

Cowboys and Indians

The figures of the cowboy and Native American first appeared in Donald Rodney's work in 1982. In the painting, *Sadly The Redskin Has His Reservations* from September of that year, a Native American and a cowboy meet in a desert landscape. The Native American is depicted with paint on his brown body and face. A band stretches across his forehead, though it is painted with the same blue of the sky, giving the strange effect of separating the top of his head from the rest of his body. He holds out an open hand with six digits to the cowboy on the other side. The cowboy, painted with bright pink skin, is depicted in a checked shirt, neck scarf and black Stetson, and he holds his own hand out to shake that of the Native American. His eyes are wide and his face is dominated by a curving, sharp grin created out of thick lines of black paint. Running along the side of his face and hat, Rodney has twice written the phrase 'The white man smiles'. Across from him, the Native American smiles too, though his horizontal band of teeth read more like an anxious, forced grimace. Alongside the Native American's body are the words of the title: 'Sadly the Redskin has his reservations'.

This is an image of power, wielded with a degree of superficial cooperation but also duress. The cowboy's manic, unsettling grin and the Native American's resigned offering of his hand betray this. The 'reservations' of the title, of course, do not just refer to feelings of doubt and reluctance. 'Reservation' was the term given to small parcels of land that were granted

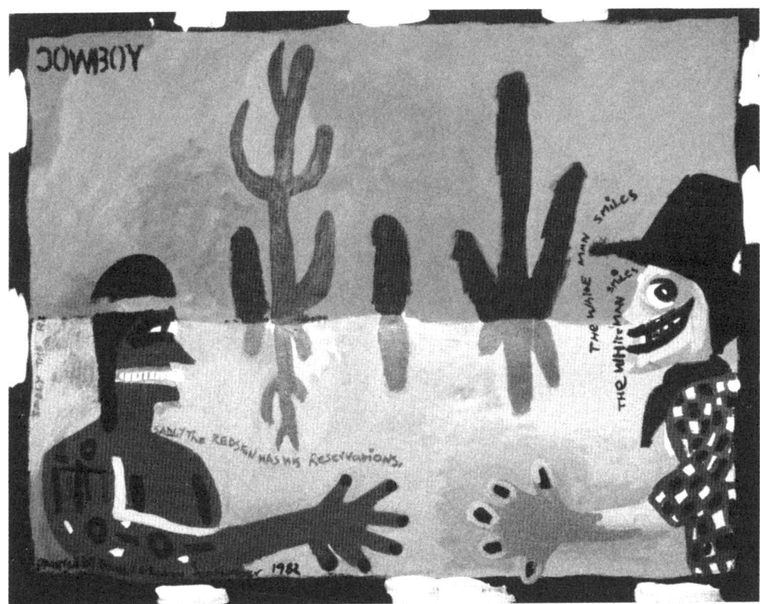

Sadly the Redskin Has His Reservations, 1982
Oil on canvas, dimensions unknown

to Native American tribes by the US government following the American Revolutionary War of 1775–83. This process was undertaken initially through peace treaties that were frequently signed under duress by Native Americans. The term continued to be used for land occupied by Native American tribes, even after the US government began forcibly relocating them to land to which they had no historical connection.[1] Rodney's painting and its title appear to dramatise this process of negotiation and forced migration.

The tentative, yet unsettling, agreement that is being reached in *Sadly The Redskin Has His Reservations* reaches a violent climax in another of Rodney's paintings of September 1982, *How the West was Won* (p. 65). We are back in the simple desert space of the former painting – a bright sky, beaming sun and luminous yellow sand. A white cowboy – depicted with pink skin, blonde hair and a familiar hat, though now wearing all black – grins almost demonically, with his smile reaching up and across one side of his face and curving off the other side. His arm is raised; originally this held a red plastic toy gun, which Rodney had glued to the surface of the canvas, though this has since been lost. It was aimed at the head of the Native American on the right of the painting. He is depicted frontally, with feathers emerging from a band around his head and his mouth turned down into a frown. Travelling along the contours of the cowboy's body and hat are the words 'The only good Injun

Gregory Salter139

is a dead Injun'. While *How The West Was Won* and *Sadly The Redskin Has His Reservations* were produced at the same time, it is unclear as to whether they are meant to be read 'in sequence' – as a moment of (forced) negotiation giving way to violence and murder. However, the paintings simply and powerfully evoke the power and histories of the 'cowboy and Indian' theme.

Part of this power comes from the paintings' distinct combination of a childlike style, popular culture and mass media, and direct politics. These are intentionally childlike works, intended in part, we can assume, to evoke the artwork produced by children at school. This is borne out in the simplistic, flat rendering of the landscape, the simplified faces, expressions and bodies of the figures, and the inclusion of explanatory text, down to Rodney also including his full name and the specific date of production (all that is missing, perhaps, is his age). The choice of subject matter also evokes childhood, as the cowboy and Native American are subjects we might expect children to focus on in their artworks. This subject has filtered into the worlds of children since the beginning of the twentieth century through the Western film genre. Rodney's work alludes to this: he paints a black border with white marks around each work, giving them the appearance of individual frames from a reel of film (again, this suggests that we might want to read the works as part of a filmic narrative). *How the West was Won* was also the title of a highly successful, Western epic of 1962, which starred John Wayne, Gregory Peck and Debbie Reynolds, amongst others. Additionally, the inclusion, at one time, of the red toy gun in *How the West was Won* also underlines the link between the subject and childhood, evoking pretend games of 'cowboys and Indians' between children. We might also draw some links between Rodney's work and Roy Lichtenstein's paintings that focused on scenes of war and violence from comic books – such as his large yet detached and cool *Whaam!* (1963) – though Rodney's painting makes more explicit use of dark, biting humour and has a more complex interplay of references and emotions. In these paintings, Rodney allows the resonances of his subject matter – its links to childhood, film, play, and pop culture – to rub uncomfortably alongside the connotations of power, coercion and eventual violence that are inscribed within them.

I have looked back to Rodney's 1982 paintings as it is important to acknowledge their significance at the early point in his career; it is striking and surprising to find the same subject re-emerge, suddenly, in his art seven years later. I want to suggest here that while the 'cowboy and Indian' subject was something to interrogate for its own historical and early 1980s resonances, it became increasingly useful as a broad metaphor or dynamic that had resonances beyond simply itself. For example, the meeting of two opposing figures also occurs in Rodney's *Master and Servant* (1986), a work created in ink, bleach and wax crayon on hospital sheets. In this work, a white worker in overalls on the left shakes hands with a man in a suit on the right, who looks like a business owner; underneath, the text 'MASTER & SERVANT' seems to imply a disruption of class power, with 'MASTER' aligned with the worker and 'SERVANT' aligned with the man in the suit. However, between the two figures are some words that are attributable only to the suited man:

'DEAR CHEQUE BOOK. I HAVE HIM NOW, MY UNWITING [SIC] PAWN AGAINST THE ENGLISH WORKING CLASS. YOU SEE OUR CONGLOMERATE PLANS HAVE WORKED. THE POWER OF COLLATERAL MIXED UP WITH THERE [SIC] OWN IRRATIONAL XENOPHOBIA WILL SEE THE FOOLS VENTING THERE [SIC] ANGER ON THE JEWS, SPICKS, WOPS, COONS, AND PAKIES. & ME THE UNACCEPTABLE FACE SHALL PULL THE STRINGS. SHAKE THE HAND. I'M THE MASTER.'[2]

Rodney's text underlines that it is the suited man who is in control. His words imply that he makes a scapegoat of migrants and people of colour so that white workers might vent their anger at them, rather than figures of capitalist power such as himself. The handshake, then, between the white worker and the suited boss has echoes of the tentative negotiation in *Sadly The Redskin Has His Reservations*. Both relationships are built around coercion and compromise that merely reproduce existing systems of power, of race or class.

Beyond *Master and Servant*, Rodney's work of the mid-to-late 1980s consistently engaged with incidences where coercion and control of people of colour sprung, suddenly, into violence. His *Soweto/Guernica* (1988, p. 81), adapted Picasso's famous 1937 representation of the Spanish Civil War to speak of the 1976 Soweto Uprising, where Black South African schoolchildren demonstrated against the introduction of lessons taught in Afrikaans and were met with violent force from police. Hundreds of the student protestors were killed. For his work, Rodney placed the figure of Mbuyisa Makhubo carrying her son Hector Pieterson after he was shot by police at the centre of the violent chaos that Picasso depicted in Guernica. At the same time, the effects of contemporary police brutality in Britain also became a prominent aspect of Rodney's practice. For instance, Wolverhampton Art Gallery holds the preparatory drawings for the frieze of *Soweto/Guernica* (pp. 82–83), which contains representations of acts of police brutality in combination with rampaging half-horse, half-human figures (in a nod, perhaps, to the Parthenon Marbles at the British Museum). With these other works in mind, the ambiguous embrace of the Native American by the cowboy in Rodney's *Untitled* drawing begins to take on broader possibilities. The cowboy's touch might be an echo of the grinning cowboy's offered hand in *Sadly The Redskin*

Has His Reservations or the duplicitous handshake offered by the suited man in *Master and Servant*. The Native American is welcomed into an embrace that contains, controls and perhaps dooms him, a fate that Rodney may well have seen playing out within class and racial struggles in both Britain and the wider world during the 1980s. The figures of the cowboy and the Native American in his drawing, then, are rooted in the ongoing cultural resonance of Westerns and the histories and power relations they evoked. But they are also, perhaps, increasingly mobile symbols of the dynamics of race and class in society more widely.

Black/queer/pop

I have so far paid little attention to the connections between Rodney's *Untitled* drawing and the artwork that provided some inspiration for it: David Hockney's *We Two Boys Together Clinging* (1961). However, his appropriation of Hockney introduces questions about Rodney's connections to Pop Art and British art history more widely. It brings connotations of sex and desire into an image of racial power. I would like to argue that the traces of queerness that inevitably remain here might shape our understanding of this drawing in new or unexpected ways.

Rodney's quotation of Hockney's work puts him in dialogue with Pop Art and, more generally, British art of the recent past. This is a consistent though

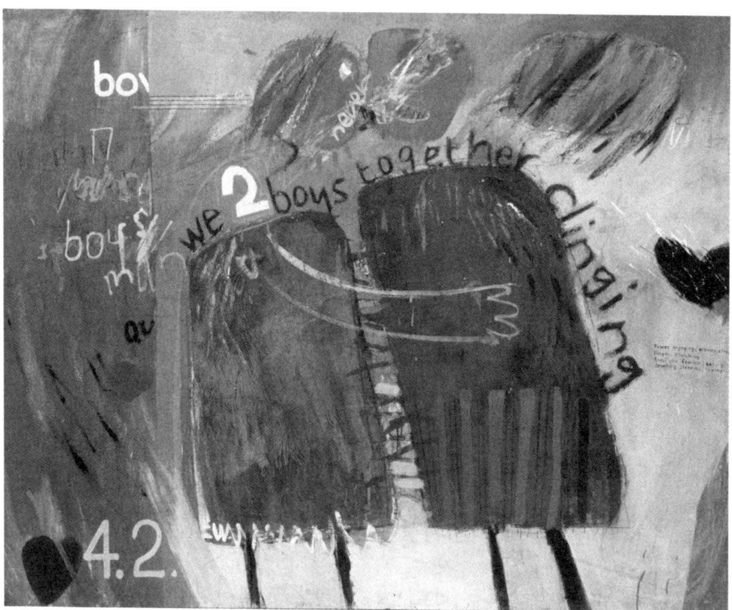

David Hockney, *We Two Boys Together Clinging*, 1961
Oil on board, 121.9 × 152.4cm

                    Intertwining Histories

so far under-acknowledged aspect of his art. In his sketchbooks during 1988 and 1989 – around the point at which he produced his *Untitled* drawing – there is evidence that Rodney was also reflecting on the work of another British Pop artist, Richard Hamilton. He consistently riffs on the title of Hamilton's famous collage *Just What Is It Makes Today's Homes So Different So Appealing?*, produced for the 'This Is Tomorrow' exhibition at the Whitechapel Gallery in London in 1956. Rodney's version of the title becomes 'What Is It That Makes Today's Black Homes So Fragile So Vulnerable So Open To Attack' and appears to have formed the basis of ideas for an installation.[3] One of the adaptations of Hamilton's title is followed by a sketch of a policeman entering the home of Dorothy 'Cherry' Groce. She has been knocked to the floor and the policeman, in riot gear, stands over her.[4] On 28 September 1985, Groce was shot by a policeman and paralysed below the waist as they sought her son during an early morning raid; the incident sparked the Brixton riots later that day. A week later, Cynthia Jarrett died from heart failure after the police entered her home to search it on 5 October 1985; this triggered the Broadwater Farm riot the following day. It is possible, then, that Rodney's adjustments to Hamilton's title were conceived with these events in mind. These events had certainly filtered into other works by Rodney, such as the poster for his 1986 show 'The Atrocity Exhibition and Other Empire Stories' at The Black-Art Gallery in North London, which depicted both Jarrett and Groce. Two years later, Hamilton's title and its connections to a collaged image that combined aspirational objects and figures of an emerging post-war home and British society more widely became a pointed comment on the fragility of Black lives and homes in 1980s Britain. Rodney transforms the post-war consumer boom and the white figures of Hamilton's ideal domestic interior into police racism and a visceral sense of vulnerability in your own home.

Beyond Hamilton, Rodney also engaged with other canonical figures of post-war British art. His use of collaged X-rays arranged in strict, framed grids, such as in *Blood In My Eye* (1986, pp. 68–69), appears to be a nod to Gilbert & George's pictures. In *Apart Hate* (1987), meanwhile, a pacing dog appears to have been lifted from Francis Bacon's *Dog* (1952) in the Tate (additionally, the X-rayed rib cages recall the hanging slabs of meat from Bacon's 1946 *Painting*). These borrowings from figures including Hamilton, Gilbert & George and Bacon – as well as Picasso in *Soweto/Guernica* – were conscious, political acts. Eddie Chambers puts it like this:

> 'Rodney sought not so much to make work that stood outside of this history; instead, he made work that critiqued that history (in terms of its partiality and bias), whilst simultaneously demanding for himself a credible place within a more equitable and textured history of art.'[5]

In this way, Rodney sought to work critically and actively, both with and against representations that surrounded him, whether that was 'cowboy and Indian' imagery or the work of other artists. It was a way of folding himself, as a Black artist, into this history but also – crucially – troubling it at the same time.

Rodney brings this active, critical approach to appropriation in his references to the David Hockney painting in his *Untitled* drawing. In *We Two Boys Together Clinging*, Hockney created an unapologetic image of homosexual desire (particularly notable given that he was working six years prior to the partial decriminalisation of homosexuality in England and Wales in 1967). The title comes from a poem by the American writer Walt Whitman, who was known for addressing homosexual desire in his poetry of the late nineteenth century. The two figures are locked in an embrace: they lean in to kiss each other (a heart marks the meeting of their lips), the left figure's hand reaches out to touch his partner (just as in Rodney's version), and the closeness of their bodies is emphasised by short brush marks that seem to pull and fasten them together. Rodney's adaptation of Hockney's painting bears its traces of desire. I have previously suggested that we might read the *Untitled* drawing as an image that allows the imbalance of power at the heart of the cowboy and Native American relationship to speak to wider questions of racial and class struggles. It is, still, an image of coercion. At the same time, the drawing's intimacy, the closeness of these figures, is difficult to deny. It is true that Rodney has transformed two queer lovers into two historical foes, but there is an aura of desire – in the cowboy's gentle hand the way the figures' faces are caught in movement towards each other – that intermingles with more readily available meanings. Why has Rodney allowed coercion and intimacy, tension and desire, to become part of the relationship between his cowboy and Native American?

It is worth noting that Rodney explored the intersections between race and sex – and particularly the sexualisation of Black bodies and Black histories – elsewhere in his work. For his contribution to the exhibition 'Black Markets: Images of Black People in Advertising & Packaging in Britain (1880–1990)' held in Manchester in 1990, Rodney produced artworks based on the front covers of pulp novels written by white authors that combined sex and slavery. For example, one untitled work is a colour photocopy of a collage of various photographs of the cover of Kyle Onstott's 1957 novel *Mandingo* (p. 87). The latter had been a wildly successful novel upon its publication, becoming a national and international bestseller and, in 1975, a successful film, directed by Dino De Laurentiis and starring Ken Norton, then at the height of his boxing career. The novel and film take place on a fictional plantation called Falconhurst, which is a slave-breeding plantation (where slaves were encouraged to produce children). *Mandingo* is dominated by the sexual exploitation of slaves by both white men and women, and inter-racial sex forms its anxious heart. The book cover depicts Blanche (played by Susan George in the film), the wife of slave-owner Hammond, gazing up at one of the male slaves Ganymede (played by Norton). In this scene, Blanche blackmails Ganymede into having sex with her. She falls pregnant and gives birth to a mixed-race child, who is immediately killed to avoid scandal. Hammond retaliates by poisoning Blanche and shooting and drowning Ganymede at the climax of the film.

Rodney considered novels and films like *Mandingo* as means for a white audience to restage the past:

> 'They are a type of fact/fiction utilising genuine historical fact combined with eroticised romanticism of that time. The books revolve around plantation life but usually have key characteristics that link them all, black stereotypes of sexual omnipotence; graphic depictions of a sado-masochistic nature and the fear/thrill of miscegenation.'

His response was repeatedly to photograph the cover of *Mandingo*, both in and out of focus, as a means of 'distorting and dulling the images'; he saw this as a way of seeking 'the truth below the surface', of resisting the rewriting of Black history.[6] Through his use of individual, collaged photographs of sections of the Mandingo cover, its image becomes distorted and fragmented, but also the object of intense study. Rodney emphasises the focus on the Black body's physicality and sexuality (his photos are arranged to broaden Ganymede's shoulders and lengthen his arm), while honing in on Blanche's look of both lust and power. Rodney seeks to underline the complex and troubling intermingling of Black history and sexuality here.

There are certainly elements of Rodney's concern with interracial desire in the *Untitled* drawing, though his focus has shifted from pulp re-imaginings of slavery to locating the possibility of interracial, same-sex desire in the figures of the cowboy and Native American. While the *Untitled* drawing lacks the obvious references to white fantasies that inhabit the *Mandingo* collage, it is appropriate, I think, to hold on to Rodney's sense that sexuality and desire's meeting with histories of race, might distort or complicate those histories. In the *Mandingo* collage, that distortion was fundamentally harmful; in the *Untitled* drawing, it is Rodney himself who creates this distortion through his use of the Hockney painting and so we might want to consider this as more tentative and even playful. At the same time, the undercurrents of desire between the cowboy and Native American feel neither idealistic (too much remains of coercion, of the power relations between these figures), nor mocking. Instead, we might suggest that the traces of desire that Rodney allows to infiltrate this image allow these figures to inhabit a closeness and separateness at the same time. The Native American, coerced and destroyed elsewhere in Rodney's work, is, instead, coerced and desired here in the drawing. A Western cliché of good (cowboys) versus evil (Native Americans) becomes a much messier, open-ended narrative of closeness (think of the 'clinging' of Hockney's title, the cowboy's touch) and desire.

Rodney was not homosexual, but his artworks and sketchbooks demonstrate an engagement with the work of queer artists, including Hockney but also others, and some overlaps in terms of subject matter and approach. His sketchbooks include small, quick studies of works such as Francis Bacon's *Two Figures* (1953) (which depicts two men having sex on a bed) and Andy Warhol's *Dick Tracy*, 1960 (Tracy was a personal sex symbol to Warhol; as he put it, as a matter of fact, 'I fantasised about Dick's dick').[7] Again, I am not suggesting that Rodney had a particular interest in the homoerotic connotations of these images, but, at the same time, they held enough interest for him to record them in his sketchbook. Additionally, Rodney makes several copies of David Wojnarowicz's burning house image in his sketchbooks, which he used as a stencil for street art before it appeared in later paintings.[8] Wojnarowicz was inspired to create it after coming across a set of stencils of 'international symbols' for signs like 'train crossing', 'no smoking' and so on; his response was to 'invent some symbols that are international but haven't been invented', like the burning house.[9] Wojnarowicz's burning house could be linked to his rejection, as a queer man and a victim of childhood abuse, of the nuclear family, and it might more broadly be tied to a desire to undermine given structures of society, such as the home. Houses recur in Rodney's art and sketchbooks – they are, at various moments, aflame, broken, forcibly entered, unhomely but also necessary. While the burning home may have been a symbol of queer alienation for Wojnarowicz, it may well have worked as a jumping-off point, for Rodney, for thinking through the fragility of Black homes, racial and social unrest and a feeling of homelessness. Elsewhere, Rodney took a more critical approach to queer imagery, juxtaposing a detail of the anonymous Black male's penis from Robert Mapplethorpe's controversial *Man In A Polyester Suit* (1980) with a tiny toy figure of *The A Team*'s Mr. T cast in bronze as a means of exploring stereotypes about Black masculinity in a 1991 work titled *Bête Noire*.

Rodney's art has also drawn parallels with contemporary queer experiences in the 1980s and 1990s. He had sickle cell anaemia, a disease that only affects Black people, and this became an aspect of his artworks, particularly as his health worsened during the 1990s (though Eddie Chambers has rightly highlighted that this has generally overshadowed the other elements of Rodney's practice).[10] Some critics drew links between Rodney's illness and the AIDS crisis, such as Amanda Sebestyen, who commented, 'Donald Rodney also suffers from sickle cell anaemia, which, like AIDS, is little understood because it only affects people who are themselves seen as disease within our body politic'.[11] Sickle cell and AIDS appear to have merged in public consciousness as diseases of the blood. Rodney's installation *Visceral Canker* (1990, pp. 62, 90–91) for example, was to include tubes that circulated blood around the coats of arms of Queen Elizabeth I and John Hawkins, the first English slave trader. He was refused permission to use his own blood, as it was considered a hazard to the public. Chambers refuses a simplistic alignment of Rodney's sickle cell anaemia with AIDS, which is understandable. However, he does this by contrasting Rodney's nuanced approach to his own illness, which he used as a metaphor for the diseases of racism, apartheid and police brutality, with what he calls the 'declared and overstated victimology' of artists with AIDS.[12] This not only flattens and dismisses artistic responses to AIDS, but it also denies what are potentially productive, though admittedly complex, connections between Black and queer experience in the 1980s and beyond.

These wider examples from Rodney's practice reveal instances of quiet engagement with the work of queer artists, critical appropriation of their themes, and broad overlaps in their subject matter. Rodney's appropriation of Hockney, arguably continues in this vein. The *Untitled* drawing is a shifting combination of colonial and racial power, popular culture, interracial desire and queer intimacy. It allows power, coercion and closeness to sit, together, on its surface. Rodney spoke of his desire to make work that found a place for himself and other Black people in history, but he also spoke of his awareness of the way that history had been and could be distorted. His response in the *Untitled* drawing is not to create his own wilful distortion, but to create an appropriated image that forms unexpected connections between Black, colonial and queer histories – that links them, through this image, and, in the process, rethinks and recalibrates them. The effect is to at once restate the damaging history and endurance of the figures of the cowboy and Native American, to unsettle that history and its power by inserting elements of interracial, homoerotic desire, and to create unexpected links between the Black community and the queer community at a moment of mutual suffering in the 1980s in Britain and around the world.

Rodney's *Untitled* drawing extends and complicates his approaches to a subject he returned to frequently: Black masculinity. His 1990 work *Self-Portrait: Black Men Public Enemy* was made up of a series of five portraits: two were police mugshots, two were images of a man, handcuffed with his head bowed and one was an 'identikit' composite image of a Black man, used frequently at this point by the media when the police were seeking suspected criminals. Each of the men's eyes, aside from those of the identikit figure, have been obscured by black rectangles, taking away their individuality. In this work, Rodney produced a self-portrait built out of stereotypical images of Black men where they are framed 'as the enemy within the body politic', highlighting the way in which Black male selfhood is inevitably affected by such negative representations.[13] Similarly, *Doublethink* (1992, p. 96–97), brought together a series of sporting trophies that were engraved with stereotypes about Black people; the male football players and athletes caught in motion on top of many of the trophies, spoke to stereotypes of sporting prowess that both offered possibilities to young Black men while also limiting and trapping them. The *Untitled* drawing, however, is a less direct engagement with the question of masculinity. To unpack its relationship to masculinity, I want to place it in conversation with another work of art from Wolverhampton Art Gallery's collection by Keith Piper. Rodney and Piper were both founder members in 1982 of the Blk Art Group, alongside Marlene Smith and Eddie Chambers, and they exhibited and worked together throughout the 1980s.

Like Rodney, Keith Piper's short film, *Go West Young Man*, from 1996, brings together Black history with the history of American expansionism and places the question of Black masculinity at the heart of their intertwining. It is just one iteration of the merging of these themes that first appeared in Piper's student work in the late 1970s, when he combined the engraved plan of the English slave ship *The Brookes*, first published in 1788, with Horace Greeley's call – 'Go West young man' – for white male settlement of the American West. Piper has described how he was 'struck by the ironic tension generated between this optimistic invocation to embrace the 'west' and all that it offered, and the harsh realities of the forced transportation of African peoples into the western hemisphere via the terrors of the 'middle passage'.[14]

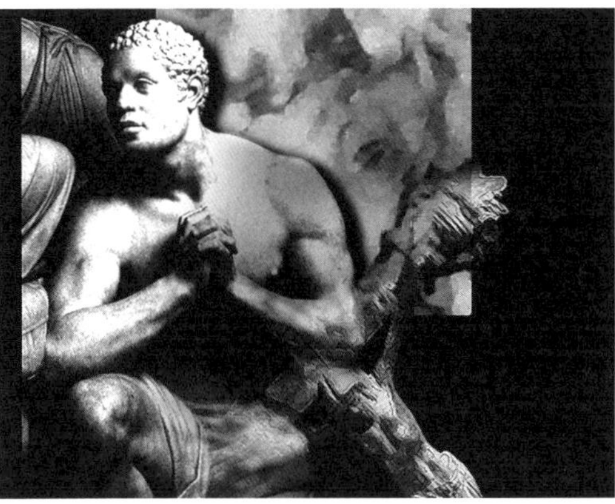

Keith Piper, still from *Go West Young Man*, 1996, animated film, 3:50 mins

                    Intertwining Histories

He returned to this theme – and the specific juxtaposition of the slave ship and Greeley's words – throughout the 1980s and 1990s. This included the computer-animated film, produced on a Commodore Amiga, in the Wolverhampton collection. The film combines music, sounds and images of the ocean, historical material, photography, fragments of documentary, news and commercial film.

Over the top of this is a conversation between a son (Wilbert Johnson) and a father (Hayden Forde). Their words place the young Black male at the centre of a history of Black suffering and violence, from the middle passage, to colonialism, migration and contemporary racial prejudice. For our purposes, it is important that Piper forms a link between American expansionism and the history of slavery; the call of 'go west young man' becomes both a rallying cry of possibility for some and a condemnation to forced enslavement for others. Piper's *Go West Young Man* frames Black masculinity as the focus of a long history of injustices. Early on, the father comments:

'All of us have done some hard times down here, I mean irrespective of age, irrespective of sex, man, woman, youth or elder, we've all been catching hell for centuries. But you: young, black and male, looks like they've reserved your prime spot, filed right up there amongst their worst nightmares.'

Rodney, as we have seen in *Self Portrait: Black Men Public Enemy* and *Doublethink*, was conscious of a similar idea and actively exploring it in his artworks. The *Untitled* drawing is rooted in questions of masculinity too, though Rodney's response to the 'Go West' call here is to move into a space of ambiguity, where masculinity is both coerced and caressed and its certainties begin to disintegrate. In this space, the oppressive histories of racism and slavery and the ever-present ideals of masculinity that reproduce these histories are present in the figures of the cowboy and Native American. But they are undermined and troubled by the presence of desire and traces of queerness. If Piper illuminated histories of Black masculinity to explain its present dilemma in 1980s Britain, then Rodney momentarily appears to have sought to undermine the histories and representations that sought to fix Black masculinity and, more widely, institutions of racism, classism and even heterosexuality in place. The clinging cowboy and Native American of Rodney's *Untitled* drawing are an intentionally ambiguous, imaginative response to the tropes and histories that appeared to divide and limit society in 1980s Britain.

First published in *Midlands Art Papers*, 2 (2018/19) 1–12.

1   For a study that gives an account of the violent history of the displacement of Native Americans, see Ned Blackhawk, *Violence Over the Land: Indians and Empires in the Early American West* (Cambridge, MA: Harvard University Press, 2008).

2   The work is reproduced in Richard Hylton (ed.), *Donald Rodney: Doublethink* (London: Autograph, 2003) 48.

3   Variations occur, for example, in Donald Rodney, *Sketchbook 22*, 1988, Tate Archive, TGA 200321/3/22, http://www.tate.org.uk/art/archive/items/tga-200321-3-22/rodney-sketchbook-number-22/121; and Donald Rodney, *Sketchbook 23*, 1988, Tate Archive, TGA 200321/3/23 http://www.tate.org.uk/art/archive/items/tga-200321-3-23/rodney-sketchbook-number-23/41.

4   Donald Rodney, Sketchbook 24, 1988, Tate Archive, TGA 200321/3/24 http://www.tate.org.uk/art/archive/items/tga-200321-3-24/rodney-sketchbook-number-24/67.

5   Eddie Chambers, 'Who'd a Thought It?': Exploring the Interplay Between the Work of Frida Kahlo and Donald Rodney' *Wasafiri*, vol. 27, no. 23, (September 2012) 23. (Reprinted in this volume, pp. 50–64)

6   Eddie Chambers, 'Remembering the Crack of the Whip: African-Caribbean Artists in the UK Visualise Slavery', *Slavery & Abolition*, 34.2 (2013) 298–99.

7   Donald Rodney, *Sketchbook 23,* 1988, Tate Archive, TGA 200321/3/23, http://www.tate.org.uk/art/archive/items/tga-200321-3-23/rodney-sketchbook-number-23/111; and http://www.tate.org.uk/art/archive/items/tga-200321-3-23/rodney-sketchbook-number-23/67. On Warhol's homoerotic relationship to Dick Tracy, see Bradford R. Collins, 'Dick Tracy and the Case of Warhol's Closet: A Psychoanalytic Detective Story', *American Art*, 15.3 (2001) 56.

8   Donald Rodney, *Sketchbook 31*, 1988–89, Tate Archive TGA 2000321/3/31 http://www.tate.org.uk/art/archive/items/tga-200321-3-31/rodney-sketchbook-number-31/87.

9   Steven Dubin, 'David Wojnarowicz: Against His Vanishing', *Art Journal Open*, 25 March 2011, DOI: http://artjournal.collegeart.org/?p=1360.

10 Eddie Chambers, 'The Art of Donald Rodney', in *Donald Rodney: Doublethink,* ed. Hylton, 30.

11 Amanda Sebestyen, 'Different Diasporas', *New Statesman & Society,* 3 February 1989, 49.

12 Chambers, 'The Art of Donald Rodney', in *Donald Rodney: Doublethink,* ed. Hylton, 31.

13 Quoted in Chambers, 'The Art of Donald Rodney', in *Donald Rodney: Doublethink,* ed. Hylton, 34.

14 Keith Piper, 'Go West Young Man: Project History', http://keithpiper.info/gowestintro.html.

In the House of My Father: Fragments of Body and Time

Diane Symons

In the House of My Father is a large-scale colour photograph measuring 123 × 153 cm that was produced by the artist Donald Rodney in 1997 (p. 102). The image shows the open hand of the artist, and in the palm of his hand is a sculpture of a house made from sections of his own skin held together with dressmaker's pins.

The photograph was produced in an edition of three and is now in the collections of the Arts Council of Great Britain, the National Museums and Galleries of Wales and Tate. The work's inclusion within these collections, and their accompanying publicity, exhibition catalogues and educational materials result in the image's increased visibility exponentially. A paragraph about the artist's work is often written alongside the image. While acknowledging the difficulty of writing a 100-word summary, the continued condensing and reducing of the work, as a consequence, has closed down meaning into a few key word fragments.

> 'Rodney uses autobiography to address larger social and political issues from the perspective of a black British man. He also deals with more personal issues of identity, family and home. This small house has been seen as symbolising "the fragility and the near-futility of Rodney having to live within a structure hopelessly unable to sustain itself".'[1]

As an arts educator, it is a reminder, that display panels and exhibition catalogues can reduce the meanings in work to 'sound' or 'text' bites. One can get caught up in this reduction all too easily and replace the complexity of meanings – its ambiguity and fluidity – with fixed, oversimplified definitions. In many ways this essay is an attempt to free up some of the 'fixed' meanings, to find other ways to come to understand the work, its production and reception without reducing it to a single narrative.

In The House of My Father is often viewed through postcolonial discourses and cultural theory. However, in limiting the reading of the work other important readings are neglected or missed altogether. David A. Bailey and Stuart Hall have argued that, 'ultimately, there has to be a wide, active dialogic community which is interrogating, evaluating, reconstructing histories, putting back in place the invisible discursive conditions which makes new texts possible'.[2] Jean Fisher echoes these sentiments in her essay, 'The work between us':

> 'Art has been absorbed into discussions of cultural context that treat it and the artist, as a subcategory of social anthropology. Regarding its international context, art is currently ensnared in debates of cultural difference and identity that are noticeably lacking in critical discussion about the work itself. Thus, what remains underdeveloped are transcultural studies of aesthetic practice that would extend our understanding of the art of others beyond ethnic typology.'[3]

Significantly, Rodney's solo exhibition '9 Night In Eldorado' at the South London Gallery, in which *In The House of My Father* was first shown, was conceived as a narrative; the life story of the artist and his father. While the work is often read in terms of racial identity, little reference has been made to the relationship between father and son.

Virginia Nimarkoh notes how 'in the mid 1990s through "art and science" type exhibitions, Donald Rodney found himself in the realm of what is benignly referred to as body art'.[4] Indeed, he certainly identified with a diverse range of artists working with notions of 'the Body' – from Fanko B, Zarina Bhimji and Helen Chadwick to Mona Hatoum and Andres Serrano. Nimarkoh, suggests that 'the imperative that drove his later practice was more than aesthetic, conceptual or even political.'[5] The period in which the work was produced coincided with the deterioration in Rodney's health, surgery was more radical and more and more time was spent in hospital. Again, Nimarkoh comments, 'For Donald Rodney, his art was indeed a testament to his having survived thus far. It was also a tool of self-empowerment – a means of retaining an identity, a survival strategy.'[6]

The survival strategy was inherent in the show '9 Night in Eldorado', the story of his father's journey to England from Jamaica, his hopes and aspirations for himself and for his son. It was a 'portrait' of the artist's journey as a young man.

Fragments of Body and Time

All photographs have the potential of being about time, the moment captured and frozen forever. The photographic medium has the potential to imprint the real:

In the House of My Father

'Unlike painting or language, photography can never deny its past, that the thing existed and was there in front of the camera, but that real is lost the moment the photograph comes into being. And it is this very essence of photography – its noeme, that is to say, its 'that-has-been' or its intractability.'[7]

I would suggest that *In The House of My Father*, like Sean Homer suggests, is haunted by this encounter with the real, 'the encounter with the "that-has-been" essence of photography, the intractability of the real and of grasping one's own mortality'.[8]

If the photograph is received as a form of testament, then the small skin-house placed on the artist's hand can be experienced as an artefact within an artefact. There is a sense of doubling and folding in this work, the living skin of the hand and dead skin of the house, both the hand and house act as containers. The title, alludes to the relationship between father and son, through the image of the male hand and the reference to 'My Father.'

In an interview with the photographer Andra Nelki, who took the image, she recalls how there were several photographs taken of the house with the hand in varying degrees of openness.

She describes the final image as open and yet protective, 'the intimacy and vulnerability of looking down at a person lying in a hospital bed and the photograph taken with a closeness that has a familial touch.'[9] She describes it as the 'artist's swan song'. The photographer's own son had died of AIDs a few years earlier and the choice to frame and light the house in this way is as much about her reaction to the frailty of Rodney's situation in hospital, as it is about the artist's intentions.

The colours and overall tonal qualities are soft and muted; there is an air of melancholia. The close-up, concentrated shot and sharp focus of the hand, allow the viewer to see the pores in the skin, the individual strands of hair, the lines and creases on the palm. At 123cm × 153cm, the image becomes monumental. Although there is a close personal distance, the scale of the work prevents the viewer from reaching out to take the artist's hand.

The deliberate staging and extreme close cropping of the image gives the appearance of amputation, the body is broken and lies in pieces. The house sits at the intersection of the lines on the palm of the hand, as if offered to the viewer for a palm reading. To the left of the frame, a glimpse of the inside of the artist's wrist, the vulnerability of the wrist inviting the viewer to simultaneously trust and protect. It is a site of the pulse and a measure of life. By laying the hand out on a horizontal surface, it becomes an object rather than part of a subject. Art historian, Landa Nochlin, uses the term 'body/in/pieces'[10] to describe the works of Cindy Sherman, Louise Bourgeois and some of the fragmented photographs of Robert Mapplethorpe. Here we see Rodney's 'body/in/pieces', with skin from one part of the body now in the palm of his hand.

Knowing the provenance of the skin-house evokes an emotional response, this is the artist's own skin, he has in effect, 'made something of himself'. By only showing the hand, we are left with the absence of the whole person, a fractured body, and for Christian Metz this 'character' who is off-frame in the photograph will, 'never come into the frame, will never be heard – again a death, another form of death.'[11] Metz also understands the encounter with the work as a dialogue, depending as much on the viewer as with the photograph itself: 'The spectator has no empirical knowledge of the contents of the off-frame, but at the same time cannot help imagining some off-frame, hallucinating it, dreaming the shape of this emptiness.'[12] The small skin-house is viewed from the outside. It has the appearance of an abandoned house, pinned together. It evokes the sentiment 'keeping body and soul together'.

The Real, The Symbolic and the Imaginary

By giving the work the title *In the House of My Father*, the artist recreates the symbolic 'In the Name of the Father' and the invisible laws of the fathers. Using this Oedipal metaphor, the work can also be seen as a suggestion of male inheritance as a natural and logical progression. Acquired by the collections of national museums and galleries, this 'receiving into the canon of art' can also be read in terms of what Pen Dalton observes as 'Oedipal male inheritance providing a "logical" process for the reproduction and transmission of knowledge and culture':[13]

'Historicist accounts of art, for instance, suggest that change is brought about by the struggles of power between the established Old Masters – the fathers – who are threatened by the radical arts of the "young Turks", their murdering sons.'[14]

There is a sense of disruption or crumbling in the photograph, the walls of the house are thin, almost translucent and the edges are torn. Perhaps the old patriarchal system is disintegrating.

Abjection, Fetishes and Fossils

Rosemary Betterton, in her book *An Intimate Distance*, draws on Julia Kristeva's essay, *Powers of Horror* for her definition of abjection, she writes the abject as the place where meaning collapses. Betterton sees it as the 'borderline, that which defines what is fully human from that which is not. The most significant borderline is that which separates the inside from the outside of the body, the self from its Other.'[15]

                    In the House of My Father

I would like to posit the idea that *In The House of My Father* is about abjection, in the shedding of the skin, as a shedding of the body's physicality. Both the skin of the artist's hand and the skin structure of the house appear dry, ebbed of internal flow and energy. The skin-house has separated from the body and become what Mary Douglas refers to as 'matter out of place'.[16] Without a blood supply the flayed skin has become parchment.

In The House of My Father has been displayed once in the artist's lifetime. I suggest the audience, knowing that the work was produced only a few months before his death, approach the work as if they are already looking at a corpse. The photograph captures a transformative process a 'shedding', the skin as a house still functions as a container, not for the body, but for the soul.

In 2001, both *In The House of My Father* and *My Mother. My Father. My Sister. My Brother* (1987), formed part of the exhibition 'Homes for the Soul: Micro-architecture in Medieval and Contemporary Art' at the Henry Moore Institute in Leeds. In this exhibition, both medieval and contemporary works expressed ideas about ideal and real space, relationships between body and soul and according to the exhibition publicity, 'associations between domestic and ecclesiastical architecture'.

Gen Doy writes about the photograph as suggesting 'religious veneration, protection, belonging and inheritance'.[17] This wasn't the first time that the idea of religious veneration has been alluded to, in a review Sarah Kent commented:

> 'The fragile structure becomes an icon of pain as well as belonging – a paper-thin dwelling not robust enough to protect its inhabitants. A photograph (*In the House of My Father*) shows the artist holding it in the palm of his hand as though, like the wheel held by St Catherine or the severed breasts offered to St Agatha, this little structure stuck with pins were an attribute to martyrdom.'[18]

As a biblical reference point, the pins piercing through the skin-house can also refer to stigmata. The dressmaker's pins can refer both to the Christian symbolism of the nails through the hands of Christ and to the use of nails as a fetishising practice:

> 'The fragility and delicacy of the skin, the pain suggested by the pins, the ritual and magic aura of such a construction, are connected by the artist to his religious and family background, as well as larger social and political issues.'[19]

My Mother. My Father. My Sister. My Brother can be seen as a fetish. In an attempt to 'build a recuperative notion' of fetishism for her discussion on intercultural cinema, Laura U. Marks develops an interesting framework in which one can also respond to the popularity of both the skin-house and the photograph. She recognises that 'an oppressive kind of fetishism is at work in postcolonial relations. Fetishism aptly describes the violent colonialist impulse to freeze living cultures and suspend them out of time.'[20] However, in claiming other meanings of fetishism, Marks believes that fetish objects can give voice to buried knowledge as an expression that is 'specific to intercultural encounters':[21]

> 'Fetishism, then, originated as a term used to separate the ruling Protestant, proto-capitalist groups from others both outside and within the culture. The early use of "fetishism" to describe the practices of both European peasants and West Africans reaffirmed the emerging European powers' belief that, unlike themselves these groups were irrational, incapable of abstraction and mired in the body.'[22]

However, there are wider issues literally embedded within Rodney's body. As a Black male whose parents and ancestors were from Jamaica, contained within the bloodlines of inheritance are the genes responsible for the artist's illness, sickle cell anaemia, and the legacies of the slave trade. Houses and wealth were built off the bodies and souls of his ancestors. This skin-house also presents a personal memorial, the result of personal and historical trauma. The house as fetish is simultaneously jettisoned and reclaimed by the artist. By transforming his own skin, the artist's body has become the witness to a personal history and the photograph re-inscribes another level of witnessing.

Conclusion

Eddie Chambers cautions those commentators who would seek to 'over racialise the motivations, the influences and the practice of Black artists':

> 'In scanning Black artists' press coverage of the 1980s and 1990s, we see that much of what was written was superficial and reductive, with meaning in the work being ignored or closed down too quickly and too easily. Rodney's work (as much as that of other Black artists) suffered from this stunted attention from critics.'[23]

In attempting to use psychoanalysis and critical discourse to open up fixed meanings within the work. It has been difficult not to be continually redrawn into the discourses of cultural theory. During the 1980s and 1990s Rodney's work was usually framed under 'identity', thus as Chambers, Fisher, Bailey

In the House of My Father

and Hall have all pointed out, this reduction of the work's meaning has meant that Black artists like Rodney were 'essentially' positioned:

> 'To be locked into the frame of ethnicity is also to be locked out of a rigorous philosophical and historical debate that risks crippling the work's intellectual development and excluding it from the global circuit of ideas where it rightfully belongs.'[24]

Psychoanalysis offers a way to describe the fluidity and sometimes 'slippery' glimpses of meaning that appear in the work, it has some advantages in being able to open up the work through multiple viewpoints.

Undertaking this writing has been a very personal journey, a dialogue with the work that reflects on its production and continued reception in museums and galleries. In a wider context, I hope it will urge other writers to question the 'fixed' frameworks in which Donald Rodney's work and that of other Black artists can be bound.

First published in Sonia Boyce (ed.), 'An Archive, Some Art Works, A Legacy: Returning to the Blk Art Group', *PAPER*, issue 1 (October 2012) n.p.

1   Tate Display, 004.

2   David A Barley and Stuart Hall, 'Critical Decade: Black British Photography in the 1980s', Ten.8. vol 2/3 (1992).

3   Jean Fisher, Vampire in the Text: Narratives of Contemporary Art, (London: Iniva, 2003).

4   Virginia Nimarkoh, 'Image of Pain: Physicality in the Art of Donald Rodney' in *Donald Rodney: Doublethink* ed. Richard Hylton (London: Autograph, 2003). (Reprinted in this volume, pp. 38–49)

5   Ibid.

6   Ibid.

7   Sean Homer, *Jacques Lacan* (London: Routledge, 2005).

8   Ibid.

9   Interview with Andra Nelki, 2 December 2005.

10 Linda Nochlin, *The Body in Pieces: The Fragment as Metaphor of Modernity* (London: Thames & Hudson, 2001).

11 Christian Metz, Photography and Fetish, *October*, vol. 34 (Autumn 1985).

12 Ibid.

13 Pen Dalton, *The Gendering of Art Education: Modernity, Identity and Critical Feminism* (Buckingham: Open University Press, 2001).

14 Ibid.

15 Rosemary Betterton, *An Intimate Distance: Women Artists and the Body* (London: Routledge 1996).

16 Mary Douglas, Purity and Danger: An Analysis of Concepts of Pollution and Taboo (London: Routledge, 1992).

17 Gen Doy, *Black Visual Culture: Modernity and Postmodernity* (London: I.B. Taurus, 2000).

18 Sarah Kent, review of the exhibition 'Homes for the Soul: Micro-architecture in Medieval and Contemporary Art', *Time Out*, 19 September 1997.

19 Doy, *Black Visual Culture*.

20 Laura U. Marks, *The Skin of the Film Intercultural Cinema, Embodiment, and the Senses* (Durham, NC: Duke University Press, 2000).

21 Ibid.

22 Ibid.

23 Eddie Chambers in *Donald Rodney: Doublethink*, ed. Richard Hylton (London: Autograph, 2003).

24 Jean Fisher 'The Syncretic Turn: Cross-Cultural Practices in the age of Multiculturalism', in *Theory in Art Since 1985* eds. Zoya Kocur & Simon Leung (Oxford: Blackwell, 2004).

In the House of My Father

Donald Rodney: Autoicon

Richard Birkett

The Hardware

USER Hello

AUTOICON [text]: how are you?

USER I'm ok. How are you?

AUTOICON [sound file, recording of Donald Rodney]: '… pain, is there constantly …'

USER Where do you feel pain?

AUTOICON [sound file, recording of Donald Rodney]: '… it's slow necrosis of the joints, and the necrosis means that the joints are slowing breaking down, slowly corroding …'

USER How did your illness impact on your work as an artist?

AUTOICON [sound file, recording of Donald Rodney]: '… simply calling our work propaganda, I think people should go and look at art that has been produced by so-called Western artists. Each piece of work has been set up to propagate their own lifestyles or their money, their wealth …'

USER Was your art seen as too political by some people?

AUTOICON [text]: I was actually thinking that yes, this is a career. And by that time I knew of other Black artists. Not that many, but I knew of Rasheed and I knew of Eddie, and the Black Audio Film Collective. Because we'd had the conference in Wolverhampton – the first National Black Art Conference – just think of the sheer arrogance of students organising the first conference on Black arts – the sheer arrogance of it (self-mocking/ laughing). It was attended by the Black Audio Film Collective, and Sonia Boyce who I'd never met before and people who would then go on to open the Black Art Gallery.

USER Did dialogue with other black artists change your work?

AUTOICON [video, image heavily blurred, slow zoom towards the head and shoulders of Rodney set against a pale-yellow background]: '… just to put on exhibitions, and to discuss amongst ourselves what type of, um, issues we raise in our work. But we don't operate as a group, um, to tell each other what type of work to produce, we're collective, we're, we're free …'

USER What does freedom mean to you?

AUTOICON [sound file, recording of Donald Rodney]: 'Like, I'm trying to be an artist.'

USER Is *Autoicon* an artist?

    AUTOICON [text]: MESSAGE STARTS …
DAVE VISITS DONALD IN HOSPITAL. STOP. DONALD TELLS
DAVE PLAN TO MAKE FILM WITH CINE-CAMERA. STOP. DAVE
SEES 8MM SEGMENT IN BLACK-AUDIO FILM COLLECTIVE
DOCUMENTARY. STOP. LIGHT, ANGLE, MUTED COLOUR,
HUMAN SHAPES, RESONANCE, FEEL. STOP. DAVE SAYS 'NOW
THAT BOY'S AN ARTIST!' STOP. DAVE LEWIS. MESSAGE ENDS

USER This makes me think of your use of X-rays in your work …

    AUTOICON [image, X-ray of human hand]

USER Did you feel reduced to medical data as you spent longer periods in
hospital?

    AUTOICON [video, reddish-pink abstract image with darker lines
suggesting view through microscope of blood cells]

USER *Autoicon* references Jeremy Bentham. What do you think of his ideas?

    AUTOICON [image, blurred Auto-Icon of Jeremy Bentham with overlaid
text]: 'How little service so ever it may have been in my power to render
to mankind during my lifetime, I shall at least be not altogether useless
after my death.' – Jeremy Bentham

USER He seemed interested in his legacy, his intellectual property, after death …

    AUTOICON *Autoicon* [text]: That is a hair and we don't know whose hair
it is. I don't know if it's mine or hers. It's intriguing isn't it?

    — Conversation between the author and *Autoicon*, July 2021[1]

Launching the *Autoicon* CD-ROM lands the user in an ascetic digital
platform-space (pp. 118–119). A predominantly greyish-white screen bears a
full-bleed backdrop of faint-grey vertical stacks, the familiar representation of
a DNA test. The visual product of chromosomes stained and viewed under a
microscope, then organised into graph-like tabulation, the sequence of light
and dark bands portrays and indexes parts of a person's genetic code – in this
case, that of Donald Rodney. Over this background, a loading script populates
the lower left-hand corner of the screen, with *Autoicon*'s menu bar running
across the top edge offering minimal options: 'File', 'Activities' and 'Help'.
In the centre of the screen a stylised font states 'autoicon/chat' above an
empty white rectangle, appearing like a window through the chromosomal
stacks. A blinking text cursor within the window provides a call to action.

It is a key ontological condition of net art and the format of the
interactive CD-ROM that they exist through multiple and unlimited
interactions. *Autoicon* is no different. Yet in its 'Simulation' of an afterlife,

Donald Rodney: Autoicon

as much as in its enactment of a 'before', *Autoicon* requires an engagement
not only with its past, present and future activations, but with the temporal
anteriority of Rodney's biography. As the name suggests, *Autoicon* is a self-
likeness. lts conception therefore encompasses Rodney's artistic life and
actions: from his body of work produced from the early 1980s on, to his
methodologies, discursive relations and influences – notably, his formative
involvement in collective organising and exchange with other black artists
in Britain,[2] including as part of The Blk Art Group between 1982 and 1984[3]
– his aesthetic and political concerns, and his personal and familial history –
particularly, his parents' move from Jamaica to Birmingham in 1958, before
Rodney's birth in 1961. It is necessary therefore to add a fourth temporality
to the mix when addressing the work, one perhaps best captured by the
past perfect continuous: the tense of *Autoicon* in its extended conception
by Rodney, as opposed to, but relative to, its moment of completion. Early
conversations between Rodney and his friend Mike Phillips that would
eventually feed into *Autoicon* had taken place while both were studying
at the Slade School of Fine Art between 1985 and 1987, inspired by the
presence of nineteenth-century philosopher Jeremy Bentham's Auto-Icon
in the main cloisters of University College London. Returning to these
conversations, Rodney further developed *Autoicon* during a period of frequent
hospitalisations in the mid-1990s that nonetheless yielded many concepts
for new works, a number of which were realised with the support of Phillips,
Rodney's partner Diane Symons and other collaborators – a group that
became an informal collective of care and facilitation. *Autoicon* had been a
spectral, background presence in this period, an idea now inseparable from
other lines of thought and possible projects, including a work utilising
computer game technology to be developed with Gary Stewart, the head
of multimedia at Iniva; a 'digital studio' conceived with artist Virginia
Nimarkoh; and most significantly, the body of ideas and work eventually
distilled into Rodney's extraordinary 1997 solo exhibition '9 Night in
Eldorado' at South London Gallery.

In 1997, Rodney and Phillips completed an application to Arts Council
England for funds to produce *Autoicon*. In March 1998, the day the award
letter from the Arts Council was received, Rodney died from complications
surrounding sickle cell anaemia, a disease he was diagnosed with as a
child. *Autoicon* was completed two years later, overseen by Phillips and his
colleagues Adrian Ward and Geoff Cox at Science Technology Arts Research
(STAR) at the University of Plymouth, alongside a number of Rodney's
past collaborators and interlocutors working under the ironic name Donald
Rodney plc, including Symons, Stewart, Nimarkoh, Eddie Chambers, Richard
Hylton and Keith Piper.

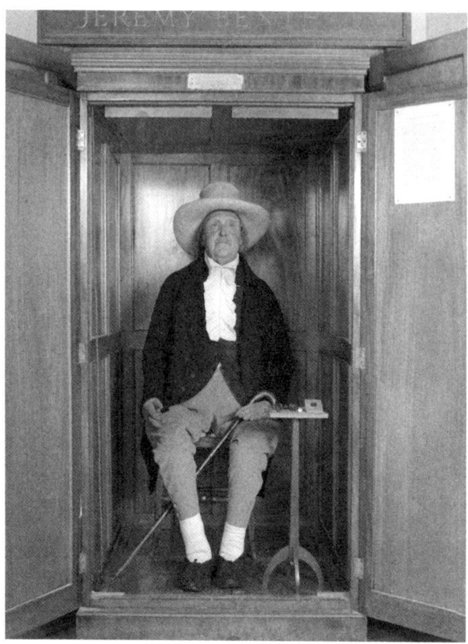

Jeremy Bentham's Auto-Icon, 1833

Autoicon is in fact predicated on Rodney's death. The death of the author was to be followed by a reanimation in the hands of a 'company' of friends and co-authors, echoing Michel Foucault's proclamation that in 'the author's disappearance ... we should attentively examine, along its gaps and fault lines, its new demarcations, and the reapportionment of this void; we should await the fluid functions released by this disappearance'.[4] The Arts Council application itself refers to an incident in 1988, when a review of a group exhibition in the magazine *20/20* inaccurately pronounced: 'Rodney, who suffered from a rare blood disease, did not live to see his work in this show'.[5] From this premature announcement of death, the application lays out a vision for *Autoicon*: for the assembly of a 'virtual body' fashioned from Rodney's biomedical 'data trail of information: photographs, X-ray's, scans, measurements, data, scars, and imprints'; the endowment of this 'avatar' with 'Rodney's memories and experiences, fleeting images of the past, captured in a dynamic digital album of live "media"'; and the inclusion of an artificial intelligence [to] allow visitors to enter into conversation and discuss the development of new ideas and projects, that can evolve and be maintained in the organic Rodney's absence'. The application details how, through this avatar, 'like Jeremy Bentham, whose embalmed body still sits in the corridor

                    Donald Rodney: Autoicon

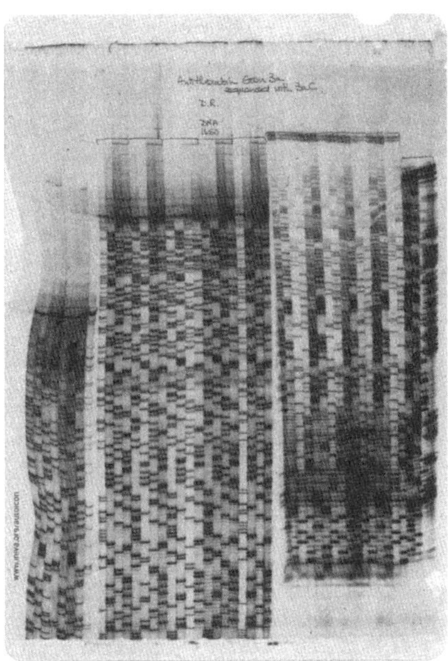

Invitation to launch of 'Donald Rodney: Autoicon', Web version,
Institute of International Visual Arts (Iniva), London, 10 June 2000

of University College London, ... Rodney will join the distinguished club of
the un-dead'.[6]

This conception of *Autoicon* as part repository, part continuance of
consciousness and creative production beyond death, marks the auto-
institutional exigency of the work. Intrinsically bound to the physical,
intellectual and social necessities of the final years of Rodney's life, when
he was confined for longer periods to a hospital bed, *Autoicon* explores the
implications, in Sylvia Wynter's words, of 'our having been, from our species
origin, hybridly (skins/masks, phylogeny/ontogeny/sociogeny, bios/mythoi,
and thereby always hitherto, relatively) human'.[7] At its core, *Autoicon* is
composed around the remnants of Rodney's life, from his artworks, to traces
of his body, to audio and video recordings of him speaking; and around the
acts of collectivity, aggregation and care undertaken by Donald Rodney
plc to realise the work. In engaging with *Autoicon*, the user is not simply an
observer, a witness to the life/body that these remnants partially document,
but is called to enter into its interstices, to engage in writing and rewriting a
state of being that is simultaneously biological, cultural and affectable – or in
Wynter's articulation, a 'hybridly organic' and 'languaging existence'.[8]

Encounter, engage, affect

'The degrees of "understanding" and "misunderstanding" in the
communicative exchange depend *both* on the degrees of symmetry/a-
symmetry between the position of encoder-producer and that of the
decoder-receiver: and *also* on the degrees of identity/non-identity
between the codes which perfectly or imperfectly transmit, interrupt or
systematically distort what has been transmitted.'
— Stuart Hall, 'Encoding and Decoding in the Television Discourse'[9]

Such a process of encoding and decoding is exemplified in the ebb and flow
of an exchange with *Autoicon*, where the latter's particular coding results
in an antiphony full of gaps and deviation. Typing into the chat box and
hitting return prompts the text to be logged above. Rather than a response
appearing in the same box, the entry generates a pop-up window in a random
location on the screen, titled with a single keyword related to the statement
or question submitted. The response can take the form of a text, or an image,
sound or video file; a segment of a transcription, of Donald Rodney speaking,
or a recording; a medical X-ray, scan or microscopic image; a hypertext link
to another website; or a seemingly random gif or jpeg of late-1990s internet
iconography. Incrementally, the programmatic pattern of pop-up titles
and responses reveals an internal logic of trigger words, at times distinctive
(for instance, 'Bentham') and at others less so (the adverb 'how' generates
multiple different responses). The premise of talking with Rodney is largely
delimited by the extant media archive of recorded or written interviews with
the artist, including three vital audio-visual documents: Channel 4's *State
of the Art: Ideas and Images of the 1980s* (1987); Valerie Thomas and Ceddo
Workshop's *The Flame of the Soul* (1990); and Eddie George and Trevor
Mathison of Black Audio Film Collective's *Three Songs of Pain, Time and Light*
(1996).[10] The clips from these videos that appear in the chat have often been
cropped and layered with digital effects, in many cases to the point of visual
abstraction. The dialogue is also extended through outer circles of associative
material, such as testimonies of friends, fellow artists and doctors, or spectral
medical images of Rodney's body. Despite *Autoicon*'s governing limits and
rules, and its transparent artifice of conversation, throughout any exchange
there are moments of profound and seemingly unprescribed confluence. In
the exchange transcribed above, the question 'How did your illness impact
on your work as an artist?' generates a recording of Rodney addressing the
dismissal of his work and that of other members of The Blk Art Group as
'propaganda'.[11] The response seems non-sequitous, yet could also be read as a
resistance to the possessive 'your illness' as a presupposed formative condition

          Donald Rodney: Autoicon

for Rodney's art production, instead implicating the propagation of lifestyle
and wealth in the work of 'so-called Western artists' – a gesture towards
the endemic disease of racial capitalism. The unpredictability of *Autoicon*'s
responses is not driven by the game of simulating human thought, but instead
draws on a life lived with and through others.[12] The user is confronted with
the ongoing entanglement of identity and alterity.

As described in the CD-ROM's sleeve notes, *Autoicon*'s auto generative
montage machine actively pulls material from a computer's hard drive,
trawling libraries and databases for suitable graphics based on keywords from
the chat, along with those that exist in the CD-ROM's own database; or, in
the case of the original online version, it drew from the incessantly expanding
image bank of the internet. Seemingly hardwired into this montage system
is the exploitation of error, the faulty transposition and splicing of the digital
code that makes up images, graphics or text, fragmenting their appearance
and causing the emergence of background file names and html.

Eddie Chambers, in his biographical text that can be accessed through
the 'View Biography' function in *Autoicon*'s 'Activities' drop-down menu,
indicates the basis of *Autoicon* as a collective project of inquiry, memory,
celebration and critical speculation in the particular conditions of Rodney's
life: 'By the mid 1990s Donald had, with the help of his partner Diane Symons
and close friends and fellow artists such as Virginia Nimarkoh, perfected his
ability to direct and produce a range of work from his hospital bed. ... *Autoicon*
marks the fulfilment of Donald's collaborative process.'[13]

As a 'machine which is productive in turn', produced under the signature
of Donald Rodney but with the knowledge of its realisation only in the
event of his disappearance, *Autoicon* can be seen as an extrapolation of
critical questions around legacy, presence, identity and history. In its very
proposition, *Autoicon* problematises the notion of individual identity tied
to artistic production, in that it sets itself up not as self-portrait, nor even
as portrait composed of remnants or artefacts of the self, but as the 'self'
preserved and re-actualised through a polyvocal endeavour – that of both
Donald Rodney plc and any user of the programme.

While less pored over than Jeremy Bentham's plans for the Panopticon, (a
hybrid architectural tool of incarceration and surveillance), the philosopher's
Auto-Icon serves as a parallel technological speculation on the biopolitical,
one that seeks to resolve the lingering problem of the sovereign self and
the forces it holds and is subject to, both internal and external to the body.
It belongs to what Michel Foucault described as 'technologies of the self':
techniques which 'permit individuals to effect by their own means or with the
help of others a certain number of operations on their own bodies and souls,
thoughts, conduct, and way of being ... in order to attain a certain state of

happiness, purity, wisdom, perfection, or immortality'.[14]

Rodney's reference to Bentham's Auto-Icon is more than a tipping-of-the-hat to a historical precursor. In his use of imagery and language – from his choice of titles to his text-heavy assemblages of the mid 1980s – Rodney's works often critically draw on the material and symbolic grammar of British colonial and imperial history, and its outgrowth from a theological rhetoric of family, home and body. In parallel, the construct of the reflexive self and its representation features prominently in his practice from the late 1980s on, in pointed lockstep with the coding of the body.[15] Seen within this wider context, the historical oddity of the Auto-Icon plays a dual role as the ground on which *Autoicon* is set. Firstly, it serves as a technological antecedent of the late-twentieth-century transhumanist promise of digital networks to surpass the mortal subject. In adopting Bentham's concept of extending personhood beyond death through the substance of 'his own self', rather than through mere representation, *Autoicon* functions as a palimpsest, a digital overwriting of Bentham's corporeal conception of auto-iconography. Secondly, connected to this lingering imperative to transcend the human body, the concept of auto-iconography acts as a prism through which to critically engage European modernity's writing of the self-determined, interior subject – a productive force that continues to define notions of humanity and conditions of globality. Even in the grammatical shift from the hyphenated neologism 'Auto-Icon' to its echo in the closed compound '*Autoicon*', which fictitiously suggests a familiarity of usage in the intervening 165 years, Rodney's work emphasises Bentham's gesture as genealogically bound to the discursive and material present. Through points of contact and dissent with Bentham's vision – from the body as both constituted and fragmented by scientific analysis, to interlocution as a paradoxical force of affirmation and dispersion of identity – *Autoicon* establishes a set of critical relations that refract across Rodney's wider practice.

* * * * *

'*me … not me … me again*'

For '9 Night in Eldorado', his 1997 exhibition at South London Gallery, Rodney walled off the rear section of the gallery, creating a long, dark corridor. At its end, he positioned *Pygmalion* (1997, pp. 116–117), his remake of a fairground automaton in a glass case (an attraction from the lineage of Roger Bacon's 'brazen head' and Bentham's Auto-Icon) illuminated only by internal lights.[16] Whereas the automaton would originally have taken a coin to activate movement, Rodney fitted *Pygmalion* with a sensor to respond to approaching viewers. The figure inside the case – whose torso,

                    Donald Rodney: Autoicon

arms and head jerk jarringly back and forth in the presence of a viewer – he customised with the unmistakeable Napoleonic military jacket, curly perm hair and single rhinestone glove of the popstar Michael Jackson. But rather than the face of the 'King of Pop', who achieved global renown in the 1980s and 1990s, the automaton's head is made-up in the blackface of minstrelsy. Rodney had long been interested in Jackson's treatment in the British press, and he collected newspaper clippings over many years. The theatrical horror of *Pygmalion* implicates the ways in which the musician's appearance and behaviour had been stigmatised in the mould of a Victorian sideshow. The assertion of constructions of race, gender and sexuality was central to this sustained tabloid narrative, a backlash against Jackson's perceived cultural and physiological mutability.

The work's title, *Pygmalion*, roots it in relation to a specific trajectory of Western classical thought. In Ovid's telling of Greek mythology, Pygmalion is a sculptor who, having sworn himself to celibacy after coming into contact with the libertine daughters of Propoetus, falls in love with his own statue of a girl. The goddess Venus grants Pygmalion's wish for the statue to become his bride, and she comes to life upon his kissing the ivory form. In 1913, George Bernard Shaw inverted the myth into a satire of social betterment and gender relations, as a man endeavours to turn a woman into an automaton of upper-class vocal mimicry.

In Rodney's *Pygmalion*, a similar inversion is performed as Jackson is rendered as crude automaton, his proficiency as dancer, singer and musician reduced to three silent, robotic upper-body movements. The use of blackface centres the contradictions and cultural pathologies of whiteness as they have played out in the mainstream reception of Jackson as an artist and celebrity. The horror of minstrelsy, with its roots in antebellum America, was still performed weekly on national television in the UK until the late 1970s.

A copy of *Frankenstein* is listed in Nimarkoh's 1997 inventory of the books, magazines, CDs, films and computer fames stored close to Rodney's hospital bed. Tellingly, Rodney's preparatory notes for *Pygmalion* include a series of transcribed passages from a 1996 Open University television documentary on *Frankenstein*:

> The creature is the other beyond and the outsider a monster without control of his identity; anger at the betrayal of the body ... the monster has appropriated he master's name ... it creates a debate about difference ... the exterior being not an indication of the interior.[17]

＊＊＊＊＊

In his work, Rodney related the diasporic experience to the displacements of the transatlantic slave trade; to his family history of migration; to the cultural and political identity of black British life; and, in the later years of his life, to the heterotopic possibilities held within the digital 'multiverse'. For philosopher and poet Édouard Glissant, the diasporic experience of translocation, resting on the moment of departure, is intrinsically linked to 'the passage from unity to multiplicity'. The departure that *Autoicon* signifies and comes into being around can similarly be understood, in Glissant's vastly resonant words, as a 'moment when one consents not to be a single being and attempts to be many beings at the same time'.[18] The notion of consent holds deep resonances when interacting with *Autoicon*, and when interpreting those interactions, built both on algorithmic artifice and artefacts. In an echo of Rodney's *Pygmalion*, hovering in the background of the user's interaction is always the spectre of whiteness and its constitution of a false unity of self through the 'indiscriminate use and possession of the black body' – a condition that Saidiya Hartman links to white conceptions of liberty.[19] On a more foundational level, the question of consent was intimately at play in the work undertaken by Donald Rodney plc. The group – whose nomenclature ironically evokes the corporate legal structure of limited liability, itself an invention of colonial and racial capitalism – by necessity wrestled with consensus, responsibility and multiplicity in progressing Rodney's conception of the work in his absence. Fundamentally, therefore, the work traces layers of labour, interdependency, exchange and memory, laying bare the entanglement of the production of things, services and subjects with the production of life.

Autoicon activates sites of personal, collective and cultural memory where what has passed before is mediated not through direct recall, but by imaginative investment and creation in the present and future. As an avatar, *Autoicon* sits in relation to Rodney's invocation of the ceremony of Nine Night in the exhibition '9 Night in Eldorado'. A gathering practiced in Jamaica and amongst the Caribbean diaspora at the death of a family member, Nine Night performatively marks and ensures – through celebratory remembrance, song, biblical texts, the making of food and domino playing – the moment of departure of a spirit from the physical world. Echoing the roots of this practice in acts of resistance against the violent displacements of the transatlantic slave trade, *Autoicon* is engaged in reconstruction in its double sense, what Toni Morrison called the exploration of 'two worlds – the actual and the possible'.[20]

*****

          Donald Rodney: Autoicon

'A Postmodern Postmortem'

First presented at Chisenhale Gallery in London and then at Graves Gallery in Sheffield, Donald Rodney's 1989 solo exhibition 'Crisis' featured multimedia works that made extensive use of X-ray plates arranged in grids or cut into silhouettes.[21] The periods Rodney had spent in hospital because of his sickle cell anaemia gave him access to used plates otherwise destined to be destroyed, along with X-ray images of his own body. Used en masse, the plates appeared as large-scale fragmented grounds over which Rodney applied oil pastel and paint to render figurative scenes, stencilled text and glyphs. Authored by Rodney, the Graves Gallery press release states:

> 'Sickle cell affects only black and some mediterranean people. Within the society blacks are perceived widely as the disease within the body politic of Britain. The illness metaphor is the key to decode the visuals. The titles should be taken as a running commentary on real events within recent history.'[22]

The exhibition marks individual instances of violence and premature death perpetrated by the state on black people in Britain in the 1980s, as well as those committed under apartheid rule in South Africa, while locating these events within wider structures of physical, cultural and political evisceration. To a degree, the works in 'Crisis' took on the form of history painting – a register of events that, revisited a few years after their happening, are made manifest as both mnemic haunting and material trace.

The presence of the X-ray plates in Rodney's work was constituted by his interactions with hospital environments; by the social symbolism of multiple bodies receiving medical assessment; and by the economic conditions that led to the availability of used plates (one review of 'Crisis' reported that Rodney purchased X-rays for '£1 per kilo from hard-up hospitals'[23]). As bodily and technical organs and social organisations coalesced in Rodney's methodological and formal approach, his use of X-ray plates in *Crisis* prefigured a scenario that was to culminate in *Autoicon*'s digital form, in which 'living' memory and 'dead' memory 'compose without end'.[24]

* * * * *

Digital Diaspora

Rodney's *Autoicon* emerged out of a distinctive set of conceptual and organisational formations that carried forward the late-1980s discourse around the diasporic into the sphere of the digital. These formations specifically marked out the shifting ground of technological image production

– from photography to moving-image and digital media – as possible sites of counter-modernity and intertextuality. Keith Piper and Gary Stewart, future members of Donald Rodney plc, were central to these developments.

The formation of Iniva's X-Space [a platform for online and digital media-based commissions, curated by Gary Stewart] and the work of Digital Diaspora / Displaced Data [a shifting collective of artists and curators of colour including Derek Richards, Marc Boothe, Janice Cheddie, Roshini Kempadoo and Keith Piper, working with digital media in the mid-1990s] collectively point to the critical socio-technological juncture at which *Autoicon* was conceived. The development and diffusion of 'home' digital devices, information processing tools and learning algorithms in the 1990s exacerbated the technological mediation and mapping of everyday life. The organising of data into discrete spatio-temporal classifications serves only to amplify the existing epistemic processes by which a racial imaginary becomes possible – a process that the notion of 'digital diaspora' troubles and subverts. The resistant digital environment that Piper has articulated in his research into the work of Jamaican-American computer scientist John Henry Thompson, and his foundational late 1980s scripting language Lingo, reflects Sylvia Wynter's framing of blackness in relation to 'tactics both of metamorphosis and of marronage (escape)'.[25] It is telling that in his sketchbook notes Rodney imagined a computer game work placed at the intersection between narrative and the 'cocooning' of the black body. As a work of 'displaced data', in turn inspired by the ceremony of Nine Night in its aim to surpass corporeal, spatial and temporal bounds, *Autoicon* is invested in both narrative (re)invention through the navigation of memory fragments and media artefacts, and the resistance to states of physical capture reproduced by technology.

> 'What is culture and how is it housed? Within Black culture in the West we diaspora we contain Black culture we house our own culture since so much else has been taken away and housed inside other bodies as part of British colonial past. . . Home as sanctuary as body in a state of siege.'[26]
> — Donald Rodney, Sketchbook No.28, 1989

* * * * *

Included in the database of materials composing *Autoicon* is a video of the opening night of '9 Night in Eldorado' at South London Gallery, an occasion that Donald Rodney was unable to attend. The video is in many ways a neat analogy for *Autoicon* itself, showing a convivial gathering in the absence of its central subject, but in the presence of his work and collaborators. The

                    Donald Rodney: Autoicon

footage records a familiar scene of congregating friends, drinks in hand, with some peeling off to view the exhibition. The videographer focusses in on another active presence in the space: the work *Psalms* (1997, pp. 114–115), a motorised wheelchair that of its own accord plots a route around the gallery. Occasionally the wheelchair can be seen encountering an obstacle in the form of a person deep in conversation, stopping for several seconds then changing its orientation and continuing its journey. The wheelchair seems to haunt the room, silently approaching groups of people chatting and drinking. It is hard not to read *Psalms* as a surrogate for Rodney, the wheelchair's interactions gesturing towards the expected bodily and social labour of artistic mediation, underscoring its notable absence and the artist's presence elsewhere.

Rodney's *Psalms* offers an opportunity to reflect upon presence as a reminder of particular absences. The work, in its binding of narratives of journey and desire to a surrogate technological body, animates 'the relational, intra personal, asymmetrical, non-reciprocal, non-recuperable parts of life', an operative quality that is carried forward as a formative aspect of *Autoicon*.[27] On its surface, *Autoicon* is a project of recuperation and preservation: of the body through biomedical data, and of Rodney's persona through documents of his life and work. Yet, in engaging with the work and the circumstances of its production, the user is confronted with a complex understanding of presence, its interdependencies and vulnerabilities.

It is perhaps telling that the rapidity of technological obsolescence in the twenty-first century led to the inoperability of *Autoicon* as an online space within a matter of years, in that it proposed an openness to absorption from and impact by its environment and users that has been largely corporatised and monetised within today's Internet ecosystem. Perhaps, *Autoicon* was conceived and produced in awareness of its own dissolution, less interested in reproducing its terms of creation and sustenance than in what might alter its conditions of emergence.[28]

Autoicon is 'alive', not because of its technological competency in simulating 'liveness' or in circumventing finitude, but because of its opacity, its gesturing always beyond itself to events past and yet to come. It is above all an articulation of un-measurable ways of being that exceed the body politic; an embodied voice – incisive, humorous, confrontational, mischievous, testing, critical, speculative – and its morphing into multiplicity through the intimacy, care and mutability of affective meeting.

Extracts from Richard Birkett, *Donald Rodney: Autoicon* (London: Afterall Books, 2023).

1   This 'conversation' took place through the CD-ROM *donald.rodney:autoicon v1.0*.

2   Stuart Hall's 1988 text 'New Ethnicities' addresses the use of the term 'black' as referencing 'the common experience of racism and marginalisation in Britain, which came to provide the category of a new politics of resistance among groups and communities with, in fact, very different histories, traditions and ethnic identities'. Stuart Hall, *Critical Dialogues in Cultural Studies,* eds. Kuan-Hsing Chen & David Morley (London: Routledge, 1996) 441. This conception of 'political blackness', with roots in the trade union and anti-racism movements, served as a vital ground for postwar solidarity amongst people of African, Caribbean and South Asian descent experiencing racial discrimination in the UK. In parallel, in 1980s Britain the capitalised 'Black' was used in the context of cultural organising and beyond to mark the unified political struggle of an African diaspora. Across Rodney's work and writings, he used both uppercase and lowercase, seemingly without any consistent intent to signify either usage differently. In a number of works, he also used the words 'Blk' and 'Blak' in particular reference to a Pan-African political identity. In this book, I have retained the original use or non-use of capitalisation when citing a particular source, and elsewhere chosen to use the lowercase 'black' in reflection of the term's mutability in different social and historical contexts, and in awareness of blackness as, in La Marr Jurelle Bruce's words, 'ever unfurling rather than rigidly fixed'. L. J. Bruce, *How To Go Mad Without Losing Your Mind: Madness and Black Radical Creativity* (Durham, NC: Duke University Press, 2021) 6.

3   Rodney studied art from 1981–85 at Trent Polytechnic in Nottingham and then from 1985–87 at the Slade School of Fine Art in London. Participating in the open exhibition organised alongside the First National Black Art Convention in Wolverhampton in 1982, he became a member of a group of artists known as The Blk Art Group, which included Eddie Chambers, Claudette Johnson, Keith Piper, Marlene Smith and others.

Between 1982 and 1983 the group held a number of exhibitions, with a changing lineup of artists, under the title 'The Pan-Afrikan Connection'. Clarifying the multiplicity of groupings and collective organising occurring amongst black artists in the early 1980s, and challenging the present tendency to conflate these under the banner of The Blk Art Group, Chambers has stated: 'One of the most irksome and tiresome consequences of the conflation of multiple iterations of the loose group (which at different times during its existence was variously known as Wolverhampton Young Black Artists, the Pan African/Afrikan Connection, Art for Uhuzu and, in its final stages, The Blk Art Group) is the problem of omission. The Blk Art Group has become increasingly identified with only a very limited number of artists, primarily Piper, Rodney, Smith and Johnson. Conspicuous by their absence from pretty much all 1980s-related attention are the likes of [Janet] Vernon, Dominic Dawes, Ian Palmer, Andrew Hazel and Wenda Leslie, all of whom have as much right to be recalled and cited as anyone else.' Eddie Chambers, 'Black Artists and the Fetishization of the 1980s', in *World is Africa: Writings on Diaspora Art* (London: Bloomsbury, 2021) 13–36.

4   Michel Foucault, 'What is an Author?', trans. Donald F. Bouchard & Sherry Simon, in *Language, Counter-Memory, Practice: Selected Essays and Interviews*, ed. Donald F. Bouchard (Ithaca, NY: Cornell University Press, 1977) 121.

5   Emmanuel Cooper, 'Helen Robertson, Maurice Hobson, Helen Underwood, Donald Rodney', *20/20*, (August 1990).

6   'Donald Rodney: *Autoicon*', Arts Council application, December 1997, in Donald Rodney Papers, TGA 200321, series 1, item 27, Tate Archive, Tate Britain, London.

7   Sylvia Wynter & Katherine McKittrick, 'Unparalleled Catastrophe for Our Species? Or, to Give Humanness a Different Future: Conversations', in *Sylvia Wynter: On Being Human as Praxis,* ed. K. McKittrick (Durham, NC: Duke University Press, 2015).

8   Sylvia Wynter, '1492: A New World View', in *Race, Discourse, and the Origin of the Americas: A New World*

View, eds. Rex Nettleford & Vera Lawrence Hyatt (Washington DC: Smithsonian Institution Press, 1995) 7.

9   Stuart Hall, 'Encoding and Decoding on the Television Discourse', paper delivered for the Council of Europe Colloquy on 'Training in the Critical Reading of Television Language' (Birmingham: Centre for Contemporary Cultural Studies, University of Birmingham, 1973) 4. Emphasis in the original.

10 Other video materials include an interview with The Black Art Group on *Ebony*, broadcast on BBC2 in 1984, and interviews with Rodney on late-night culture shows on BBC2 and CNN from 1991 to 1992.

11 Interview with The Blk Art Group on *Ebony*, BBC2, 1984.

12 The Turing Test, originally called the 'imitation game' by mathematician Alan Turing in 1950, has become a cultural signifier of the ultimate proof of artificial intelligence (AI) equivalent to that of human intelligence.

13 Eddie Chambers, 'Biography', December 1999, in *donald.rodney:autoicon v1.0*, (see note 1).

14 Michel Foucault, 'Technologies of the Self', in *Technologies of the Self: A Seminar with Michel Foucault* eds. Luther H. Martin, Huck Gutman and Patrick H. Hutton, (London: Tavistock Publications, 1988) 18.

15 See, for example, Rodney's *Blood In My Eye* (1986, pp. 68–69), *The House that Jack Built* (1987, p. 74) and *Self-Portrait: Black Men Public Enemy* (1990, p. 92).

16 Bentham adds a note to his 'Auto-Icon' text detailing a 'utilitarian' example of an automaton: 'The skeleton of Corder, the murderer, has been placed in a recess of the museum of the Suffolk Infirmary, Bury St Edmund's. It is covered with a glass case, beneath which is a box to receive contributions. . . . By an ingeniously constructed spring, the art of the skeleton points towards the box as soon as the visitors approach it. The receipts are said to reach £50 per annum.' Fairground automata such as fortune tellers and 'the laughing police man' were popular in Britain from the Victorian era through to the mid twentieth century. In relation to Rodney's *Pygmalion*, a notable example is 'Jolson Sings', an accompanied automated ventriloquist's dummy of the popular purveyor of minstrelsy Al Jolson.

17 D. Rodney, *Sketchbook No.44*, 1996. The Tate Archive and Public Records Catalogue holds 48 of Rodney's sketchbooks; digitised versions are accessible on Tate Archive's website.

18 'One World in Relation: Edouard Glissant in Conversation with Manthia Diawara', *Nka Journal of Contemporary African Art*, vol. 3, no. 28 (March 2011) 5.

19 Saidiya V. Hartman, *Scenes of Subjection: Terror; Slavery, and Self-Making in Nineteenth-Century America*, (New York: Oxford University Press, 1997) 32.

20 Toni Morrison, 'The Site of Memory', in *Out There: Marginalization and Contemporary Cultures*, eds. Russell Ferguson, Martha Gever, Trinh T. Minh-ha and Cornel West (Cambridge, MA: MIT Press, 1990) 304.

21 The exhibition was principally produced while Rodney was on the artist's placement at The Hub, a black community centre in Sheffield.

22 Press release for 'Donald Rodney: Crisis', Graves Art Gallery, 1989. Available at https://diaspora-artists.net/display_item.php?id=63&table=artefacts.

23 Adeola Solanke, 'Donald Rodney', *Art Monthly*, issue 124, (1 March 1989) 13.

24 Bernard Stiegler, 'Anamnesis and Hypomnesis: Plato as the first thinker of the proletarianisation', *Ars Industrialis* (2010), available at https://arsindustrialis.org/anamnesis-and-hypomnesis.

25 Sylvia Wynter, *Black Metamorphosis: New Natives in a New World,* unpublished manuscript, n.d., p. 116.

26 Donald Rodney, *Sketchbook No. 28*, 1989.

27 Park McArthur, 'Sort of Like a Hug: Notes on Collectivity, Conviviality, and Care', *The Happy Hypocrite*, no. 7, 'Heat Island', ed. Mason Leaver-Yap (London: Book Works, 2014) 51.

28 Jasbir Puar writes of conviviality in similar terms, as an ethical orientation open to destablisation, 'an openness to something other than what we might have hoped for'. Jasbir K. Puar, 'Prognosis time: Towards a geopolitics of affect, debility and capacity', *Women & Performance*, vol.19, issue 2 (2009) 169.

Things Arrive Together as Suffused and Inseparable

Jareh Das, Carolyn Lazard and Robert Leckie in conversation

Donald Rodney (1961–98) was a pivotal figure in the Blk Art Group, a collective of Black artists that emerged in the United Kingdom in the 1980s. He developed a diverse practice that eschewed the mainstream art-world norms of the period by addressing issues related to race, representation and identity politics through an engagement with Caribbean diasporic experiences in Thatcher's Britain, cultural histories, as well as physicality and subjectivity. Throughout his life, Rodney grappled with challenges posed by sickle cell anaemia, a genetic disorder that mainly affects people of African, Mediterranean, Middle-Eastern and Indian descent. This condition significantly impacted his work and became a recurring theme in his art, which engaged with the intricate relationship between the body, medical science and the societal and racial implications of illness. In the following discussion, Jareh Das, Carolyn Lazard and Robert Leckie consider Rodney's artistic explorations against broader conversations about the politics of sickness and racialised individuals; complex interconnections between care and constraint; Rodney's ability to merge personal stories with wider sociopolitical themes, which resulted in work both deeply intimate and universally relevant; and how Rodney's contributions and legacy may reverberate among younger generations of artists.

JAREH DAS I grew up in Nigeria, and so Black British artists of the 1980s and 1990s didn't enter into my consciousness until later. In the case of Donald Rodney, I discovered the work in 2009 as an MA student. I am very familiar with the illness he had, sickle cell anaemia, as it has affected a sibling of mine. I began asking myself, what happens when illness is entwined in a conversation about contemporary art? This influences the artists, the kinds of work they're making, the spaces in which they make work, some of the strategies of resistance that come into the work at the intersection of art and illness, the duality of being an artist and being a patient, and how certain spaces are reconfigured as creative spaces. Then also, thinking within the histories of

Black British art: Who's more prominent, and who don't we hear about? Rodney was extremely prolific – he was exhibiting, writing, doing so many different things during his short life span, and I've interrogated the systems of support and the network that fostered that.

CAROLYN LAZARD I first encountered Rodney's art in a 2019 London group exhibition in which my work was also included. Like you, Jareh, not working in a British context, it took longer for me to come to it. *Psalms* (1997, pp. 114–115) is the only work by Rodney I've ever seen in person, so almost my entire understanding of his oeuvre has been from a distance.

ROBERT LECKIE There's a generation of people in the United Kingdom who will have seen many of Rodney's works in the flesh thanks to his solo exhibitions '9 Night in Eldorado' at South London Gallery in 1997, and 'Donald Rodney, In Retrospect' at Iniva, London, in 2008. But a lot of people of my generation haven't, and for them Rodney occupies this semi-mythical status – he's someone they've read about, and whose work they've seen in books or on the internet but not in real life. It's so different when you experience it in person. Recently, one of my favourite works, *Visceral Canker* (1990, pp. 62, 90–91), was installed in the Tate Britain collection rehang 'No Such Things as Society: 1980–1990'. It's so much bigger than it looks on the page, and you appreciate the materiality and ingenuity more when you see it in the flesh.

CL Indeed, an integral part of the work is about being at a remove from what we assume to be the site of art, how art is usually encountered. It's noteworthy that in this moment, with changes in technology, there's a continuation of this relationship of distance, separation and absence that he was intimate with. For me, Rodney's work is very much about his positionality as an artist in regard to art making and production, and his relationship to spaces of art. Yet those are critical things that tend to be left out in conversations around him.

RL In my own research on Rodney's work and legacy, it's been curious to encounter many different, passionate perspectives that often don't align. But in talking to Diane Symons, Rodney's widow (and tireless advocate), it's become clear to me that this multiplicity of opinions is not necessarily about disagreement; it's more a demonstration of people's willingness to engage with the work from different perspectives at once. According to Diane, it's just a continuation of what it was like when his friends were all gathered around his hospital bed. There was always an active, dynamic conversation happening, and of course people didn't always agree.

The question of what point we enter or engage with the work is challenging to grapple with. On the one hand, a lot of artists today are interested in and inspired by Rodney's practice, but not necessarily for the same reasons that have been discussed up until now by the people who were closest to him. What happens when the work comes to occupy a fixed historical position? Surely we need to take account of the kinds of conversations that have happened over the past twenty-five years, since his death.

JD Different people come to the work and take up aspects of a line they want to follow, whether it's illness, or race, or identity politics or Black masculinity and ideas around representation. There is also a technological element in his work that was way ahead of its time and was speaking, especially in the later works, to the language and the equipment around him.

RL To me, the work alternately resists and anticipates the future. One concrete example of its tendency to resist the future is the series *Britannia Hospital* (1988, pp. 75–77) which is made up of grids of oil pastel paintings on X-rays – apparently a conservator's worst nightmare. I understand Rodney was told that it was a bad idea because the work would so easily erode over time, but there's something wonderful about the fact that he just went ahead and did it anyway. Then you have more future-oriented works like *Psalms* (1997) and *Autoicon* (1997–2000, pp. 118–119). *Psalms*, a motorised wheelchair fitted with proximity detectors, was made for Rodney's South London Gallery show, to represent him when he couldn't be there physically. *Autoicon*, on the other hand, engages users in a digital, text-based 'chat' with Rodney. It embeds him in the future through technology, and was completed by a close-knit group of friends after his death.

CL I see *Psalms* as a critique of the positionality of the artist, the preconceived conditions of being an artist and art making. I don't read the conditions of his life as a constraint, but rather, that he pulled the art context to himself, to his situation, to reframe art and art production. Some people talk about his illness, or how he used his experiences of medicalisation as a metaphor for racial violence. I have a hard time with that. Would we look at some other artist who is multiply marginalised and say, for instance, 'Oh, that person was engaging their gender as a metaphor for their queerness'?

In the case of *Britannia Hospital*, the very materiality of the work prevents such a reading. The X-rays are the surface and the foundation of these scenes of medical and racial violence. Here we might invoke Hortense Spillers' conception of 'flesh' in Rodney's collapsing of the figure and ground of racial violence. In his work, those things arrive together as suffused and inseparable.

　　　　　　　　　　　Things Arrive Together

JD Rodney was the son of immigrants who came to the United Kingdom and discovered that things weren't quite as 'promised land' as they'd expected, and so he spent time thinking about his own biography. But this can also be removed from the personal and broadened to speak to the oppression of Black people around the globe, particularly in South Africa under Apartheid, and showing solidarity with that. My understanding was that he was very interested, especially in the early work, in global struggles of Black people and the ways in which that impacted representations of the Black body – the Black male body and Black masculinity in particular. I believe he used illness as an expression of autobiographical struggle that in turn spoke to, became a metaphor for, universal struggles.

CL All of those things certainly occur at the same time in the work; Rodney's conception of himself was intimately connected with history and ongoing struggles. One particular piece that comes to mind is *Flesh of My Flesh* (1996, pp. 100–101) in which his experience of medical racism is an extension of a global struggle against antiBlackness. I also keep wanting to do a more materialist reading of the work because Rodney was so interested in the ephemera related to medicalisation. Medicalisation is an intensely private experience, and by turning the hospital into a studio, bringing people in socially, professionally, he broke that open. He was an artist, so he immediately took up these very specific practices of visuality from within the field of medicine. As an artist, he couldn't not think about the fact that his body was constantly being imaged. So he brought those images into the work, thinking about the relationship between race and visuality, the limitations of visuality, the fact that so much of our understandings of difference are indexed through sight. The way imaging reveals something and nothing simultaneously comes through in his work a lot.

JD Yes, there is a negation of the boundaries between public and private space, also public and private property in relation to the medicalisation of the body, reclaiming the body in a direct and confrontational way. Even when the hospital becomes your studio, you still have to deal with the parameters of being in a hospital – you have to take your medications at certain times, eat at certain times, receive visitors at certain times. Carolyn, you mentioned how all these different individuals were coming together in this space for him to implement an artistic vision. There are several layers of materiality in the resulting works – bodily fluids, objects left over from medical processes, skin from a surgical procedure becoming a sculpture that is then photographed. Taking a photograph of an artwork creates yet another, new artwork.

RL And he was in a shared hospital room, with other patients. So the binary of public and private is further complicated by the fact that there were strangers present. It's fascinating to imagine what they must have made of all his friends coming and going, the conversations they were having. Toward the end of Rodney's life, this group of friends formed a loose collective, or support network, which came to be known as 'Donald Rodney plc.' Though this was tongue-in-cheek, they took an active role in the work being made, constructed, produced and installed. That carries through in *Autoicon*, which was finalised after Rodney passed away.

CL Sickle cell anaemia is a Black illness. Where race and biology are uneasily brought together as fact. That goes against everything we've been taught through changes in civil rights discourse – Blackness as not a biological fact but something constructed through discourse, through the social, the conceptual, the material, the economic, etc. It generates, to my mind, a productive kind of anxiety, or ambiguity.

I'm also thinking about the impossibility of being a medicalised Black subject who speaks. We're talking about the social field that Rodney created in the hospital, and how radical it was to create artworks that were essentially a mode through which he spoke alongside the medical data that was produced about him and his body. *Autoicon* does that through a digital montage – the medical data is shown alongside footage of the work, images of friends. In the medical context, there's no subject but an anonymous, numbered collection of symptoms, body parts, compartmentalised discourses. Things that don't really add up to a person. Medical subjects don't speak, they are spoken for. For me, the social field alongside the work is doing that, but it's hard to talk about this because I don't want to put words in his mouth. There's something in his practice that is metaphorical, and there's also something in his practice about being a self. How a self is constituted, and how a self might speak back to its external constitution – not reject it but incorporate it, pull it in, recontextualise it.

JD Do you know 'Care and Control', which happened at Hackney Hospital in 1995? I thought it was interesting that the hospital in this case was a site not only for artistic practice, but also for exhibition making. The year-long exhibition was organised by Rear Window, an independent London-based art organisation, and took place at Hackney Hospital, a ten-acre abandoned Victorian site that was later demolished. It brought together an archive celebrating 270 years of local service on the site, including art by service users and artists such as Jordan Baseman, Jason Coburn, Smadar Dreyfus, Lyn French, Derek Jarman, Michael Lewis, Olivia Lloyd, Virginia Nimarkoh,

                    Things Arrive Together

Jane Roberts, Donald Rodney in collaboration with Graham Plumb, Kate Smith, Terry Smith, Jo Spence & Terry Dennett and Catherine Yass. Artists responded to the hospital's past and present histories, and Rodney's monumental installation *Othello* (1995, p. 198), consisting of twenty stacked mattresses, referenced the popular children's fairytale 'The Princess and the Pea', ideas of contamination and purity.

RL Yes, I am fascinated by the documentation I've seen of 'Care and Control', and I would love to be able to recreate it for the survey show I'm working on at Spike Island, but it's not possible, sadly. There are several archival images of the installation in the Doublethink book. In the preface, Stuart Hall describes constraint as one of the defining factors of Rodney's life and work. But Carolyn said something really interesting just now about not thinking about it as constraint per se, but more about productivity in relation to care. Rodney was cared for regularly and intensively: by Diane, by the people working in the hospital, by his friends. It was part of what enabled him to be so prolific. At the same time, his desire to overcome constraint is evident in how he creatively thought around certain physical challenges he faced, for example by collaging together lots of different smaller sheets of paper or X-rays in order to amplify the scale of his work, since he couldn't easily work on large canvases or rolls of paper.

CL I have some thoughts about the notion of care and constraint around Donald Rodney plc. His work was made with others when he was alive, and also after he passed. This dependency was a critical part of the work. The work in some ways destabilises questions around the singularity of his authorship. The conditions of his life allowed that to be troubled in an interesting way. My understanding of care is complex, as it's a beautiful thing but oftentimes arrives with abuse. You see that in his work, and you see it in terms of his experiences with medical malpractice. The people who loved him and were in his life took care of him, stewarded his work, coproduced the work and also provided its framing. But there's also a little bit of violence to that, which is hard to speak to, although we should.

A lot of the framing of his work, even by those who loved him, has been conditioned by cultural, social, societal understandings of illness and disability that are deeply embedded in ableism. We can look at the work and understand it according to its context, also understanding that that context is infused with certain beliefs. So our challenge, you might say, involves contextualising the contextualisation of his work. To say that this artist worked in this way despite his condition, even though the work says absolutely the opposite of that, is necessary because of the discourse insisting that the work was operating in spite of something. Looking at it retrospectively, we can ask what it means that in order to occupy the subject position of an artist, Rodney had to operate against his illness. In other words, there's a mismatch between what's actually happening in the work and the way the work is being talked about. It is more about a discursive constraint than an actual constraint in the life of Donald Rodney. Which is not to undermine the challenges of living with sickle cell anaemia.

RL It's pretty clear from this conversation that these things – meaning the materiality of the work, its pithiness and formal complexity, the conditions in which it was made, the broader social and political struggles with which Rodney sought to express his solidarity, etc. – needn't be mutually exclusive. Indeed, it seems vitally important to consider them together. It's not that Rodney was only making work about or because of his illness, or that he was only making work about the social and political conditions of his day. He was doing both in compelling and complex ways – this is what keeps the work as interesting and fascinating to people today as it was when it was made.

I'd like to pick up on something you said, Carolyn, namely the idea that, at least in the UK right now, many institutions are looking back and taking renewed interest in artists who have been 'overlooked', especially those associated with the British Black Arts movement. It can be difficult to find interpretations that permit these artists to be artists and just that. More often than not, they're treated somewhat one-dimensionally as artists who are overdetermined by their identity, only making social or political work in opposition to a white establishment mainstream. I think there is something profoundly radical in insisting on Rodney as an artist who made great art.

CL I agree entirely, and I think the context within which work circulates is so important. The deeply anti-Black context of art makes it impossible for artists to be artists making art, and also be Black.

JD Whenever I write about – or speak about, or frame, or contextualise – Rodney, it's always a conscious struggle between critical distance and personal experience. As you emphasised, Carolyn, sickle cell anaemia affects people of colour. It goes beyond the usual conversation around race and medicine because it operates in a space of biological fact. So we have an artist, a Black artist, who's dealing with this illness and moving between these medical, racial, social, political realms. But then the work still gets rooted right back into the medical.

                    Things Arrive Together

CL I think about Rodney's investment in unpacking Black masculinity, and how that's largely seen as separate from other concerns in his practice. From my perspective, the experience of illness itself queers gender, and so Rodney's incisive critiques of Black masculinity, which were arrived at through a particular perspective, cannot be conceived as separate. All the threads inform one another in substantive ways. So much of medicine as a practice was developed in and through and on Black bodies. Black bodies were basically the testing ground for modern medicine. The work helps us think about the deep entanglement between racial violence and modern medicine.

RL This makes me think about Rodney's lightbox works like *John Barnes* (1991, p. 94), which features an image of the British footballer back-heeling a banana off a football pitch in 1988. Or the installation *Cataract* (1991, p. 93), where he combined anthropological illustrations, medical photographs and self-portraits to explore the public image of Black males. Although images of athletic Black male bodies or photos that highlight prejudiced public perceptions of Black men as a threat are somewhat at odds with Rodney's experiences as a patient, you can nevertheless draw a straight line from these racist media representations to the medical violations that he was subjected to, as is documented so viscerally in *Flesh of My Flesh*.

JD I'm so curious as to the ways in which younger generations will engage with Rodney's practice and legacy. Will the next wave of scholarship focus just as much on the materiality of his practice? It's probably about time for a shift in direction.

CL Jareh, thank you for bringing that up, because I'm trying to relate to his work as a kind of lineage. It's especially important for a contemporary generation of artists who share some formal and topical interests with Rodney. It is hard because of this question of who is an artist and who can make work and how that has conditioned the kinds of practices that have been highlighted, supported and so on. I'm also curious to see new contextualisations. I think it's beautiful that a lot of artists around the world regard his work as a critical, important historical precedent. There's also something beautiful about the way his work resists that. We've spent this whole time talking about our feelings about it, what people have said, and also this weird thing about the work being made by him with others, which allows for a messy fluidity around the interpretation that might speak to an intentional opacity on his part. *Autoicon* is an encounter with the artist postmortem, but in all the descriptions I've read, it seems to arrive in this very diffuse way. Perhaps some of its strength is the fact that it's simultaneously incredibly particular and also opaque. It seems he was resisting the reading of the work, and resisting the reading of him. It's fascinating that we don't know his feelings about the work, directly. That's somewhat rare for an artist of his generation. I'm starting to suspect that he might have been insisting on opacity as his right as an artist. A kind of recuperation around the meaning of the work that has to do with maintaining its meaning as radically unstable, unpinnable, unknowable, which encourages us to still be here having these conversations.

First published in *Mousse Magazine*, issue 85 (Fall 2023) 49–54.

Things Arrive Together

Donald Rodney: Black Art with Cutting Edge

Kwesi Owusu

'Black Art is not just art produced by Black People. There is a necessary consciousness that goes with it.'
— D. Rodney

Black Art may well be at a crucial stage in its development. The vibrant upsurge of radical art produced by a new crop of Black artists is consolidating and paying off in many ways. When it asserted its presence in the late 1970s and early 1980s, as a movement, the 'ethnic tag' was still dominant and many artists were allowed to exhibit in 'multicultural' shows. Since then, the Black Art Gallery has opened and served as a much-needed facility and viewing space. Other galleries have complimented this; and even though the dominance of the Eurocentric tradition has kept the doors of the big galleries closed, what is interesting now is that there is the beginning of a new wave of interest on the fringes of the mainstream circuit. The ICA hosted 'The Thin Black Line' last year and a stream of exhibitions followed up and down the country. Whitechapel Gallery seems to make a definite statement on this trend with the 'From Two Worlds' exhibition.

New Wine – Old Bottles?

Response from Black artists to this new interest are varied. Most, naturally, welcome it. Some are bemused if not suspicious of it, conscious of 'trendy slots' and rapid shifts of fashionable concerns. After an intensive period of work and self-organisation most see the basis of collaboration as crucial. Are white galleries going to accept the ideo-political autonomy of Black experience or are we, on opening nights, going to simply drink new wine from old multicultural bottles? Whitechapel highlighted this by the negative 'non European' classification of the artists and the generally unfocused criteria of selection.

'There is also the emerging cult of the individual which is disturbing. Pieces of work are now being appropriated on the basis of elevated names. That is negative.' Said Donald Rodney, whose work is one of the latest expressions of the ideopolitical vibrancy of the Black arts movement. 'Some of us may have to start producing work under assumed names or anonymously.'

A Bitter Place

I met Donald Rodney after 'The Atrocity Exhibition and Other Empire Stories', which featured some of his most recent work, at the Black Art Gallery. The focus was on the historical experiences of Black people during the days of Empire and today. Personal reminiscences of mother, father, childhood are crystalised in collective experiences and complemented by some innovative use of media and technique. In a painting called *Edge of Darkness*, Mother emerges in contemplative pose over a prayer called 'Psalm 38': 'Dear, God – this is not as I wanted to believe, this place. This cold bitter land.' Mother's face told me all. The location was familiar and the realisation was commonplace in Black people's consciousness. In systems of slavery, the empire strikes back with a gun. Throughout the exhibition Donald creates moments of encounter in which images and words come together not merely to confront our consciousness but to seek urgent responses from it. 'The era of the Liberals and intellect came and vanished with broken dreams and promises; all that's left is the Watchman of the State.'

Encounters

The choice of media and content underlines a conscious selection of interests and perspectives which aims to explore the Black experience beyond familiar dogmas of exoticism and irreverent art. I inquired. 'At art school we realised something was wrong. People were doing some of the most weirdest of things and getting away with it because they called it art. We wanted to create work relevant to our own experience and define the Black aesthetic – work that may probably upset a white or middle-class audience but appreciated for real.' This persistence for relevant practice reflects the work of the Black Art Group to which Donald belongs. In the early 1980s, it engineered some of the most abrasive if not effective encounters with the white art establishment with a touring exhibition called 'The Pan-Afrikan Connection' With artists like Claudette Johnson, Marlene Smith, Eddie Chambers and Keith Piper, the group gave cutting edge to the growing resistance of ethnic arts practice and racism.

Relevance

The influences were varied and it is illustrative to Black arts in general to point to the social and political events which provide unavoidable material for exploration in relevant practice. 'When I went to Trent Polytechnic in the summer of 1981, the riots had just happened and I just could not continue

                    Black Art with Cutting Edge

drawing flowers.' In the Black Art Group, the exploration went beyond the situation of Black people in Britain. 'It was exciting to read Eldridge Cleaver's "Soul on Ice; Malcolm X and the Black Panthers" and relate that whole Black renaissance to what was happening here. It was enjoyable because our work got all that power and vibrancy.'

Breaking Boundaries

The Pan-Afrikan Connection was a symbiotic cord of communication. At each point it registered not only mere ideo-political signals but also significant aesthetic breaks with western art. 'All the heroes of western art achieved fame principally as single media artists. None of us ever said we were painters, sculptors or film makers. That would be pigeon-holing ourselves. Black artists approach different issues, ideas and concerns with different media. At art school they try to mould you as a single media artist. We keep expanding and breaking down the imposed boundaries all the time.'

Sound and Vision

One of the interesting pieces at Whitechapel was Keith Piper's installation exploring vision and sound which would have been so effective at the entrance with its engaging messages. In *Memories of Childhood*, Donald more than complements this experimentation with sound and images posited uncomfortably with the icons of imperialism and anthropology.

Crucial Issues

'Sound is necessary. One thing which strikes you in a western gallery in how quiet is it. People don't expect to hear music, poetry or see a performance. We try to get away from this.' Exploring the work of an artists like Rodney brings to the fore our concerns – the breadth and depth of the challenge which Black artists pose to white institutions and the elements which should inform the basis of collaboration. If more galleries are opening their doors, it is not to say that Black arts has made it. For many Black artists, this may not even be an interesting ambition. 'The next few years should see the ironing out of a few crucial issues', prompted Donald. Whether Black artists would explore them, utilising the movement's dynamism and strength or fall under the paternalism of white art institutions is one of the major questions as the 1980s spin to a close.

First published in *Black Arts in London*, issue 64 (16–31 October 1986), 3–5

Theory and Practice

Keith Piper and Donald Rodney

On Theory

In Britain's art schools, where the mythology of individual self-expression
is held at a premium, collaborative activity is discouraged. Apart from
throwing a spanner into bureaucratic machinery geared to assess the virtuoso,
collaborative activities begin to counter many of the negative effects of
an individualism which leaves the art student isolated and vulnerable.
Supporting collaborative activity has therefore never been in the interest of
the art school hierarchy, as many students expressing an interest in working
collaboratively have learned to their cost.

Beyond the art schools, within the hallowed halls of the so-called
'mainstream', collaborative activity has to an extent been embraced, processed
and rendered commercially viable. Within celebrated associations such as
Gilbert & George and Komar & Melamid, white male artists collaborate in
order to indulge their racism and misogyny before an art world eager for
voyeuristic titillation. Thus the claim of Gilbert & George that 'We want our
art to speak across the barriers of knowledge directly to the people about
their life and not about the knowledge of art', is rendered hollow rhetoric.
Their slickly executed consumer durables which come complete with fascistic
inflections, are the stuff upon which the capitalist art marked thrives. Nothing
is challenged.

The radical potential of like-minded artists working collaboratively
has yet to effectively challenge the established canons of an art history and
practice founded upon the notions of the original genius, the 'old master'. The
fact that this concept is not only sexist ('master' is by definition male) but
also racist by dint of its unquestioned Eurocentrality, makes it all the more
imperative that Black artists oppose it by all means necessary.

It is widely acknowledged that it has only been through a decade of
concerted and united activity on the part of Black cultural activists that Black
Art has secured for itself a modicum of visibility from which to challenge
the racist assumptions of the mainstream. Piper & Rodney recognise that
whilst loose association around the lobbying for visibility was necessary when
the existence of 'Black Art' was often questioned, now, when many of our
one-time comrades in struggle have found themselves coaxed into the claws
of the capitalist art market through the private gallery system, a new level of

                    Theory and Practice

collaborative activity is called for. It is collectivity which roots itself at the very core of our practice, where work is conceived, researched and constructed.

Along with the tactical advantages of collaboration, come its technical advantages. An African proverb says that 'Many hands make light work', and in a similar fashion collaboration, through the fusion of technical and creative input, renders increasingly ambitious projects practicable. Our work therefore spans media, fusing elements of disparate origin and technically outstretching the formal limitations of conventional gallery-based practice.

On Practice

From the *Caribbean Times*, Friday March 13 1987:

'The near blizzard that descended on Wolverhampton last weekend could not have picked a worse Saturday to strike. But it failed to deter 2000 people from marching through the Midlands town to vent their anger, not only at the killing of Clinton McCurbin, but at the all too frequent state-licensed attacks on Black people by police throughout the country.

"Police murderers" was among the popular chants as the march followed a route from West Park through the city, past the pedestrian shopping precinct where the killing took place.

Clinton's aunt, Mrs Esther Mcvoy, laid a wreath outside the Next shop where her nephew was killed, but only after demonstrators persisted in the face of police objections.

There are several reliable eye-witness accounts as to what went on outside the Next store on Friday, and all conflict with the police reports.

Two teenagers had just come out from the nearby Macdonalds shop and were passing by the Next store on Friday when they saw McCurbin lying face down, one plainclothes policeman holding his legs, a uniformed policeman on his back holding his arms and another policeman with his arm around McCurbin's neck.

A Black woman went into the shop and shouted vehemently at a police officer, later identified as PC Michael Hobday, 'loose him back' because they were quite obviously hurting him.

PC Hobday continued to tug at McCurbin's neck, even though there was no movement in his body. The three policemen then got off the lifeless McCurbin to put handcuffs on his wrists.

They dragged McCurbin by the arms into the back of the store's woman's section on the first floor. They did not bother to apply first aid.'

The strong arm of the state: Clinton McCurbin, Cynthia Jarret, Cherry Groce, are just a few of the names that come readily to hand when creating a list of recent state atrocities. There is an African proverb that says 'an injury to one is an injury to all'; there is also, dear reader, another African proverb that reads 'no next time, no next time'.

First published in Zarina Bhimji, Chila Burman, Jennifer Comrie, Keith Piper, Donald Rodney and Allan de Souza (eds.), *The Devil's Feast* (exh. cat.) (London: Chelsea School of Art, 1987) 113–114

     Theory and Practice

Critical

Lubaina Himid, Donald Rodney and Maud Sulter

Lubaina Himid

As a curator I have observed the work of Donald Rodney develop, change, grow and most importantly continue to challenge the viewer, over a period of eight years. In that time he has experimented with materials and presentation, and tried to push the installation further along the road to monument and memorial. His work is constantly true to his beliefs and often an all too real reflection of his experience. I am not sure I took his early pieces seriously, feeling that they threw away their power in pursuit of an easy laugh. A decade later I sometimes miss his humour – the ability to make jokes about serious matters of racism and injustice. All through the 1980s Donald Rodney has been a driving force, often unrecognised, in the progress of Black creative expression. His contribution to the image and text debate – in his work they have been inextricably linked – will always need to be acknowledged. Many times I have been riveted to a spot in front of a work, held by the image and transfixed deciphering the text. The easy option of reading rather than looking was never there. His work in recent years has taken the audience by the scruff of the neck and spectacularly revealed a truth. His X-ray pictures, eerie in their secret visual codes, overlayed with bright sharp strong realism, are the perfect metaphor for the perfect metaphor of Britain as a sick nation.

And so, as a curator who has shown Donald's work in smaller and more idiosyncratic locations in the past, it is a great pleasure to showcase the commissioned new work, in the context of the previous work, at Rochdale Art Gallery.

Donald Rodney, *Depicting History*, 1987

$e = mc^2$ / Destruction, Oppression, State Violence and Hidden History constitute the principal themes governing my work. X-rays reveal in Biological terms . . . 'what lies beneath the surface'. I use this metaphor to construct pieces that show the inner workings of late-twentieth-century capitalism and the desiring and needing mind / The vast terrain of Black History is one that cannot easily be charted, but within the pieces, *Klose Encounters of the Kolonial Kind* (p. 71), *Deja Voodoo* (p. 73), and *Family Tree* . . ., I try to indicate a type of unease (or dis-ease) with the order of things. Marcus Garvey said of black history – 'A people with no history is like a tree with no roots.

I have used those words as the pivotal framework onto which the last part of my Black history trilogy *Family tree, Ancestral Home* was made / I do not create analytic critique but simply comment on what is after all common knowledge. The use of narrative in the manifest leaves little room for subtle interpretations of my prevailing themes, but creates a platform for further analysis. Go away and find out. History is like everything . . . relative / $E = MC^2$

Donald Rodney *Critical* 1990

My work since the mid 1980s took several shifts that now, in retrospect, make some sort of logical sense, but at the time looked and felt like venturing out into unknown and dangerous territories. I was a student at the Slade School of Art on the Mixed Media MA and felt that I needed to make a break away from painting, a discipline that I had begun to despair of, because of its complex cultural hierarchy. I wanted a new historical distance, a practice not laden with European Art History as Painting, but to pursue a media that is both rich in its allegory, deliberately visually provocative and holds an autobiographical thread throughout.

The hospital metaphor became important, having spent many a month in and out of hospital with a 'Black Disorder'; sickle cell anaemia. This disorder needed to be identified within the wider context of British society. The allegory of illness began to take shape after I read Susan Sontag's seminal essay *Illness as Metaphor* (1978). After reading it I began a collection of newspaper clippings to test out my ideas. Over a period of six months, I collected from *The Sun, The Guardian, Sunday Times, Observer,* etc. at least 150 separate quotes relating 'social' economics in medical terms; *Bitter Pill, Midas touch that became a Plague, A democracy clapped with leg irons.* And so the body politic and disease imagery can be read against social order, economics, political concerns.

Donald's Discourse was interrupted at this stage by admittance to hospital – the work, however, takes up the chorus . . .

Maud Sulter

A hospital sheet moved almost imperceptibly. It hung in a radical Black Art Space. The Elbow Room.

The year was 1986. The sheet was placed there by an artist, Donald Rodney. It is part of a group exhibition, 'Unrecorded Truths'. I stand before it, the black paint outlines recurring motifs in Donald Rodney's work, that of The Slave Ship. Its subject crosses the border between the economics of slavery, in this case the sugar trade, and is critical of our contemporary situation – what health? what wealth? what happiness?

As a Black artist situated within a global Arts Movement any reading of the artist's work must recognise the significance of his contribution to the development of a radical practice within Britain. Sadly, some of his peers have been co-opted into Thatcherite arts administration while the Elbow Room was unable to continue operating as a bona fide gallery space due to imperialistic funding criteria and the current penchant of the funders for the bland, the safe, the controllable.

His media was to evolve from sheeting to X-ray. The potency of the X-ray as a metaphor evokes death, fragility, exposure, insight. So the layering of image and X-ray, the complementary use of oil pastel as a part of the surface, all evoke the body. A body politic. A site of struggle. The location of the transformation of power to action. A postmodern postmortem.

Turning on the video monitor I return to the Elbow Room captured in Channel 4's *The State of the Art*. The year is 1990. I see the artist's talking head. I hear his voice. I witness the art which at once rebukes notions of beauty and yet also itself becomes beautiful as it offers the viewer an understanding of a sick society and a potentiality for change.

Donald Rodney is an ironic Master of his craft. He needs no Slave to assert his power.

First published in *Critical* (exh. cat.) (Rochdale: Rochdale Art Gallery and Urban Fox Press, 1990) 1, 2, 8, 12

CATARACT [Progressive Opacity of Eye-Lens]: Light Box and Bronze Pieces

Donald Rodney

The *Cataract* installation and slide tape dealt with the stereotyping of black men as traitors, rapists, criminals and national heroes.

The black sportsman can move from the arena of criminal to hero and role model back to criminal in a matter of years. The work took place in November–December 1990, and was Shown at Camerawork Photo Gallery in 1991.

In many ways it dealt with issues that the Mike Tyson trial would voice later in the year. Black male sexuality as a violent threat.

Cataract featured four light boxes and two bronze castings of a Mr T doll. The bronze Mr Ts were placed next to two round light boxes, each containing a picture of a black male penis. (Mapplethorpe: *Man in Polyester Suit*)

Two large lightboxes featuring the image of black sportsmen who have represented their country on a world sporting stage and, in the eyes of the world, betrayed them.

One image is of Tommie Smith and John Carlos, runners in 1968 Mexico City Olympic Games. They bow their heads and raise their gloved hands in a Black Panther salute. For this act they were sent home and never ran for America again. Afterwards, Tommie Smith said of the act: 'If I win I am an American, not a black American. But if I did something bad, then they would say [I am] a Negro.'

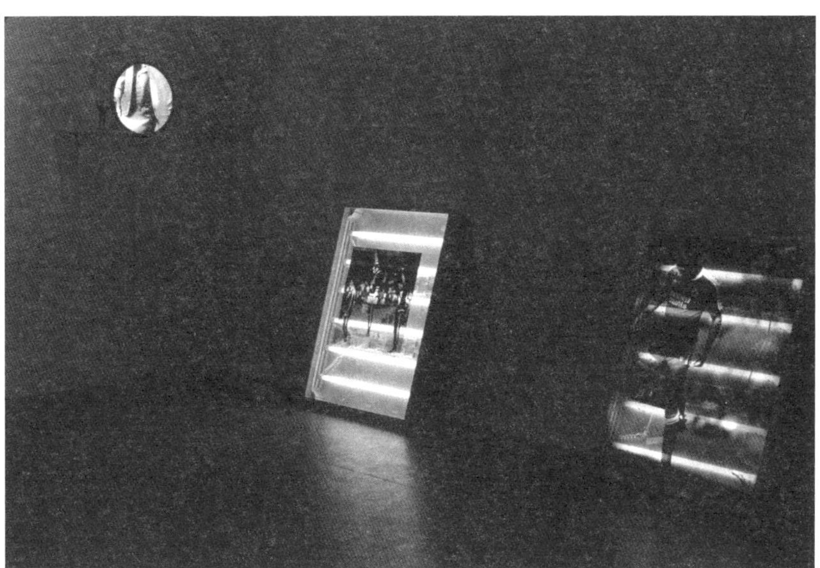

Installation view, 'Cataract', Camerawork, London, 1991

The next light box has an image of John Barnes, the black Liverpool and England footballer. It shows a banana being thrown at him at a soccer match in England. Black footballers are often greeted by boos and whistles when they have play of the ball; also darts are thrown and other objects. John Barnes is a world standard Footballer and played as part of the England team in 1990s World Cup. However, during the World Cup John Barnes played badly and not up to his usual standard. His loss of standard was greeted by the British press with hostility: 'Why Can't Barnes Play for his country?' The indication given was that John Barnes was unpatriotic by the fact of being black.

The slide tape featured several hundred images of black male faces constructed from composites. Making a generic black male face a criminal, a public enemy. The models for the photographs were all prominent black male artists, each allowing their image to be criminalised by the police photofit as they would be in day-to-day interactions within the public view.

Unpublished notes for *Cataract* exhibition, Camerawork, London, 1991

Chronology

Carolina Jozami

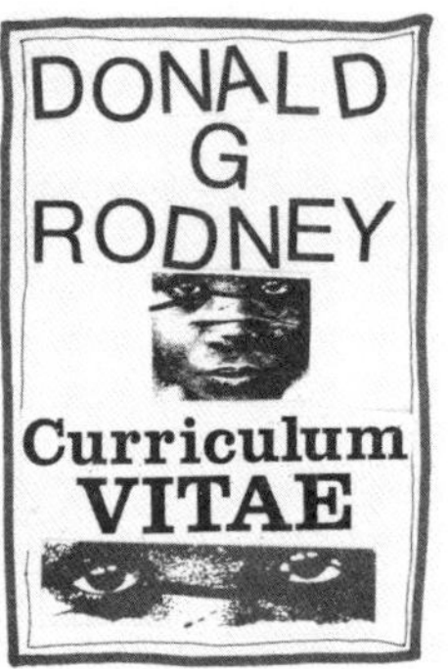

Donald G Rodney, *Curriculum Vitae*, 1985, Photocopy on paper

1961

Donald Rodney was born in Birmingham, England, on 18 May. The son of Jamaican parents, Rodney lived with his family in Smethwick, West Midlands, an area which became a centre of racial tensions in the 1960s. As the youngest of twelve siblings, who were split between Smethwick and Jamaica, he was raised in the rich traditions of Jamaican Pentecostalism. Since his childhood, Rodney lived with sickle cell anaemia, an inherited disease more common in people of African or Caribbean descent.

1981

Rodney studied Fine Art at Trent Polytechnic, Nottingham, from 1981 to 1985, where he graduated with honours. His Art History thesis was titled 'Black Independent Film as part of the Black Art Movement'. At Trent, Rodney met the artist Keith Piper, also a student on the Fine Art course, and who would be his lifelong friend. Piper introduced Rodney to the artist, curator, writer and critic Eddie Chambers, who was from Wolverhampton but at the time studying Fine Art at Sunderland Polytechnic. By

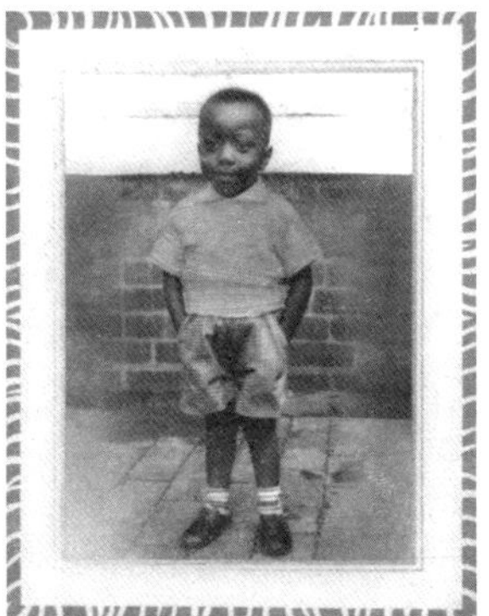

Donald Rodney as a young boy, n.d.

then, Chambers had gathered a group of young artists and friends who were children of Caribbean migrants and raised in the West Midlands. The group was first known as 'Wolverhampton Young Black Artist Group' and later re-named 'Blk Art Group'. During this period, Donald joined the group which, over the years, would include artists such as Dominic Dawes, Claudette Johnson, Janet Vernon, Wenda Leslie, Ian Palmer, Keith Piper and Marlene Smith, among others.

1982

The Blk Art Group organised 'The First National Black Art Convention', which was held on 28 October, and the 'Open Exhibition of Black Art' at The Gallery, in the Faculty of Art and Design at Wolverhampton Polytechnic. The group also carried out the first of the series of exhibitions under the title 'The Pan Afrikan Connection', in this case: 'The Pan Afrikan Connection: An Exhibition by Young Black Artists, Good Ideals' at 35 King Street Gallery, Bristol, in which Rodney took part. From this year and until his death, Rodney started using sketchbooks to explore ideas for artworks, writings and his memories of past exhibitions.

1983

The Blk Art Group organised three exhibitions under the title 'The Pan-Afrikan Connection' in different spaces: The Midland Group, Nottingham;

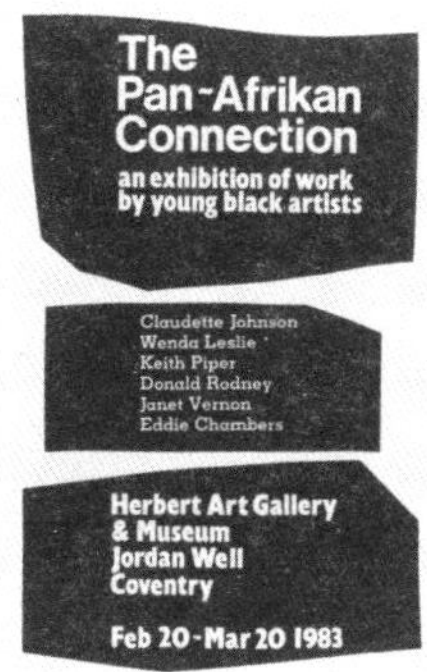

The Pan-Afrikan Connection: an exhibition of work by young black artists, 1983

Herbert Art Gallery & Museum, Coventry; and in The Africa Centre, London. Also this year, the group organised the show 'Beyond the Pan-Afrikan Connection' in the Midland Art Centre, Birmingham. Around this time, Rodney had his first hip replacement and sometimes had to interrupt his activities due to sickle cell crises.

1984

The group exhibitions continued with 'An Exhibition of Radical Black Art, The Blk Art Group' at Battersea Arts Centre, London and at Winterbourne House, University of Birmingham, Birmingham. On 28 March, Rodney participated in 'Radical Black Art: A Working Convention' at the Ukaidi Centre, Nottingham. The event was described in the programme as 'an opportunity for those actively involved in the production of radical, Black art to meet together and discuss the form, function and future of their work.'

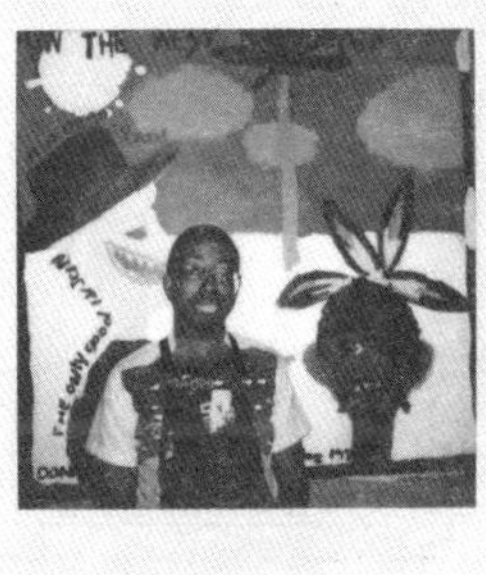

Donald Rodney with his painting *How the West was Won* (1984), at Trent Polytechnic, in Nottingham.

1985

At the end of his undergraduate studies, Rodney presented his works in his degree show at Trent Polytechnic. He also participated in the group show 'Heroes and Heroines' at The Black-Art Gallery, London, and began a postgraduate diploma at the Slade School of Fine Art, London.

On 9 December Rodney opened his first solo exhibition, 'The First White Christmas and Other Empire Stories', at Saltley Print and Media, Birmingham.

1986

Rodney's second solo exhibition opened at The Black-Art Gallery, London, under the title 'The Atrocity Exhibition & Other Empire Stories' (12 July – 12 August). The gallery, whose first director was the artist, poet and graphic designer Shakka Dedi, was the venue where many young artists had their first exhibitions, as was the case with Keith Piper. It was also well known for its exhibition posters, most of which were designed by Dedi. Exceptionally, Rodney designed the poster for his exhibition. It reproduced images and press cuttings that referred to the crime of Cherry Groce, a Black woman shot in her house by the police during a raid ten months before the exhibition took place.

Rodney also participated in three group exhibitions, 'Unrecorded Truths', The Elbow Room, London; 'Young, Black and Here', The Peoples Gallery, London; and 'State of the Art', Institute of Contemporary Arts, London. Rodney took part in the television documentary series *State of the Art*, written by Sandy Nairne, former Director of London's National Portrait Gallery. Rodney was interviewed for episode six, 'Identity', alongside other artists such as the Ramingining Performance Group, Nabuo Nakamura, the painter Michael Nelson Tjakamarra, Imants Tillers, Lubaina Himid, Chila Kumari Burman, Tam Joseph, Sonia Boyce, Sutapa Biswas and Shanti Panchal, in addition to Jean-Michel Basquiat and Andy Warhol.

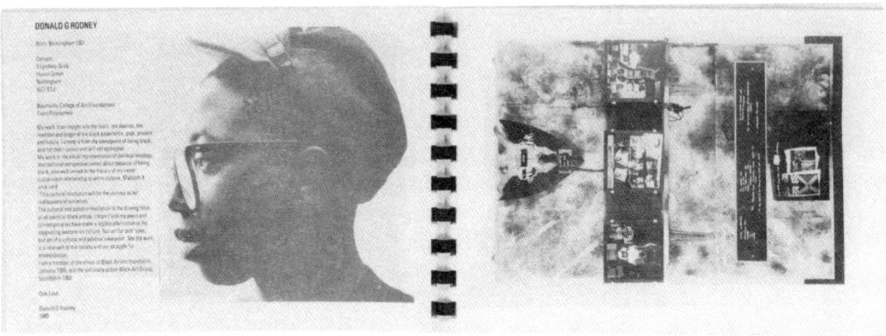

Artist's pages in the catalogue for Trent Polytechnic Fine Art Degree Show, 1985

1987

Rodney completed his degree at Slade School of Fine Art and took part in numerous group shows: 'The Devil's Feast', Chelsea School of Art, London; 'True Colours', Greenwich, London; 'The Image Employed', Cornerhouse, Manchester; 'Piper & Rodney', Prema Art Centre, Gloucestershire; 'Piper & Rodney, Adventures Close to Home', Pentonville Gallery, London; and 'Depicting History Today', Mappin Gallery, Sheffield.

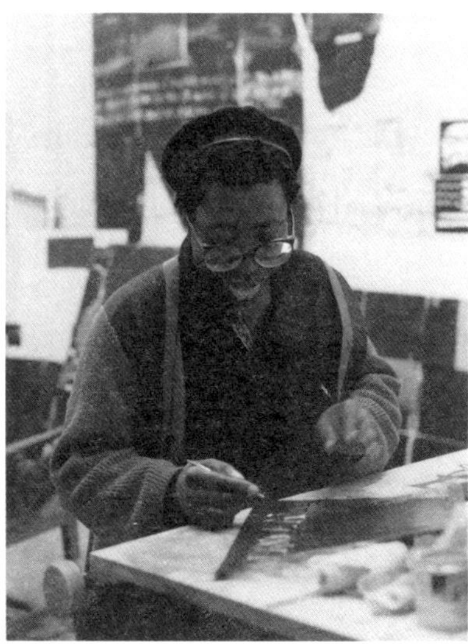

Donald Rodney preparing work to be included in his degree show at The Slade School of Fine Art, 1987

1989

Rodney's third solo show, 'Crisis' (18 January – 18 February), took place at Chisenhale Gallery, London. Rodney presented a series of works mainly made of collaged X-ray slides on which he added drawings and texts. He started using this unusual medium in the late 1980s, coinciding with the years in which his illness aggravated, and was compelled to spend considerable time in a hospital bed. Key works in this medium were included such as *The House That Jack Built* (1987, p. 74) and *Britannia Hospital 2* and *3* (1988, pp. 75–77).

Rodney also participated in the group shows 'Searchlight, Visibility/Surveillance/ Regard' at Ikon Gallery, Birmingham and in 'The Suitcase Show', a Film and Video Umbrella touring exhibition.

1990

Rodney began an Arts Council-funded traineeship in exhibition programming hosted by Ikon Gallery in Birmingham. He completed this in 1993.

Rodney's solo exhibition 'Critical' (19 May – 23 June), organised by the artist and curator Lubaina Himid, opened in Rochdale Art Gallery. The exhibition included both existing and newly commissioned works.

Rodney participated in 'TSWA Four Cities Project' (4 September – 29 October) at Mount Edgecombe Park, Plymouth,

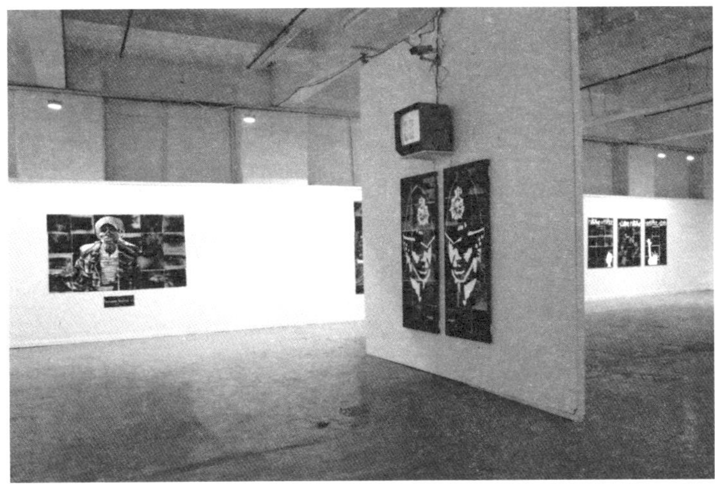

a project that allocated temporary installations in different cities, and for which he created the installation *Visceral Canker* (1990, pp. 62, 90–91).

Addressing the role of Britain in the Atlantic slave trade, Rodney included in this piece the coat of arms of John Hawkins, the first slave trader to sail from Plymouth, which he connected to that of Queen Elizabeth I with a system of medical tubes and pumps that circulated imitation blood. He originally intended to use his own blood, but the city council did not allow it.

Other group exhibitions that he participated in were 'Let the Canvas Come

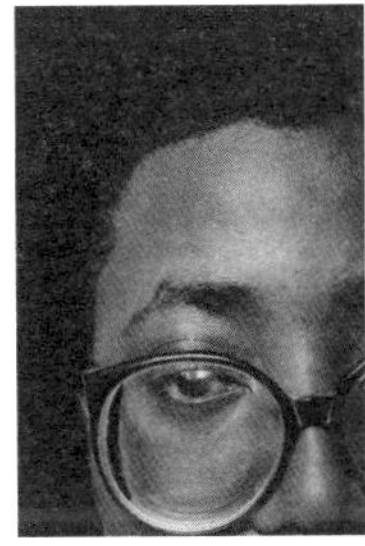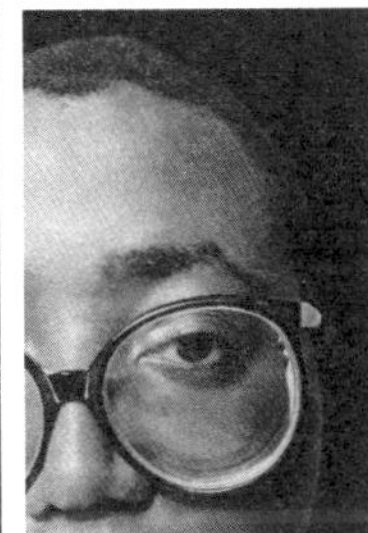

Photographs with hand tinted black background used to produce the slide tape work *Cataract* (1991, p. 93)

to Life with Dark Faces', at Herbert Gallery, Coventry; 'Black Markets', at Cornerhouse, Manchester; and 'Body', at Arnolfini, Bristol.

1991
For his fifth solo exhibition, 'Cataract' (13 February – 6 March), at Camerawork, London, Rodney included the work *Cataract* (p. 93) featuring a slide projector that projected fragmented portraits of Black men, including the artist, that composed an image similar to a police photofit.

Rodney also participated in the group exhibitions: 'Shocks to the System', a South Bank Touring exhibition; 'Interrogating Identity', Grey Art Centre Gallery & Study Center, New York (touring to: Museum of Fine Art, Boston; Walker Arts Center, Minneapolis; Madison Arts Center, Madison; Allen Memorial Art Museum, Oberlin); and 'Breaths: Art, Health and Empowerment', Rochdale Art Gallery, Rochdale.

1992
In the year of the quincentenary of Columbus's arrival in the 'New World', Keith Piper initiated 'Trophies of Empire' (August 1992 – January 93), a project that presented new commissions by numerous

artists and collectives, addressing the
legacies of colonialism and imperialism.
Curated by Brian Biggs, one edition of this
touring show took place at the Arnolfini
Gallery, Bristol, for which Rodney created
the installation *Doublethink* (1992,
p. 96–97). There, he displayed a large
number of cheap sporting trophies that
were assembled in vitrines and shelves,
each one of them carrying a racist phrase
engraved on a plaque.

As a contribution to the 'Sounds Like
Birmingham' festival, that celebrated
Birmingham's designation as City of Music,
Rodney was commissioned to curate the
show 'White Noise, Artists Working with
Sound' (8 August – 19 September) at
Ikon Gallery, Birmingham. The group
exhibition featured the artists Sonia Boyce,
Seán Hillen, Richard Hylton, Rita Keegan,
Pratibha Parmar and Andy Tipper. The
artists presented sound installations that
engaged with different musical traditions to
approach challenging issues and to present
music as a powerful medium for change.

1994
The artist Rose Finn-Kelcey invited
Rodney to present his works alongside
hers, in the exhibition 'Truth Dare,
Double Dare' (4 June – 16 July) at Ikon
Gallery, Birmingham. The exhibition
presented works that explored both
artists' affinities and common interests,
but also the difficulties that an artistic
collaboration implies. They also created a
sound installation comprising two speakers
displayed on opposite walls of an empty
room. Each speaker played a monologue
in parallel, one by Rodney and the other
by Finn-Kelcey, in which they referred
to themselves and to each other. The
catalogue featured a text by art critic, writer
and curator Guy Brett.

1995
Rodney's father died, and due to the
artist's worsening health condition, he
was not able to attend to his father's Nine
Night, a Jamaican mourning tradition that
follows the death of a loved one. Two years
later, Donald Rodney opened his last solo

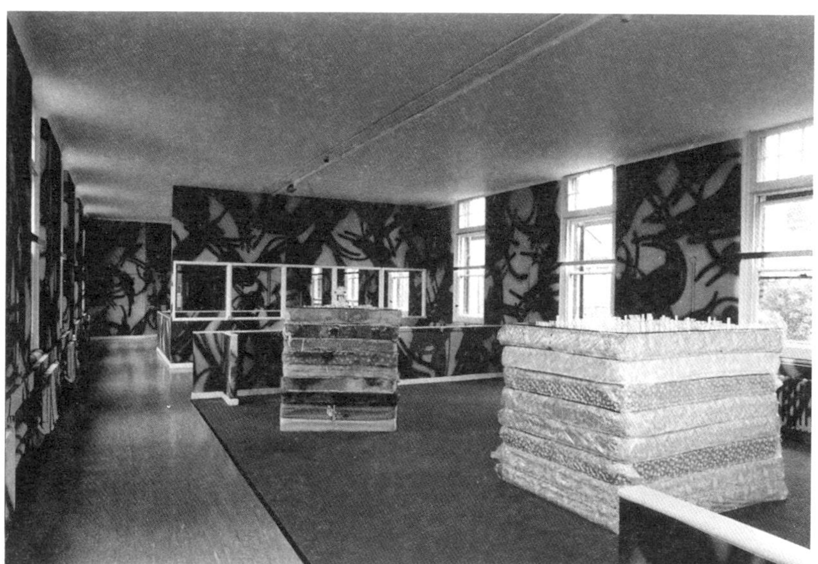

Installation view *Othello*, Donald Rodney in collaboration with Graham Plumb, 1995,
in the exhibition 'Care and Control', Hackney Hospital, London 1995

                    Chronology

exhibition at South London Gallery, which he chose to title '9 Night in Eldorado' in response to this experience.

Rodney contributed his work to the group exhibition 'Care & Control' (27 June – 5 August), held in a former workhouse building at Hackney Hospital, London. Rodney collaborated with the artist Graham Plumb for the piece *Othello* (1995), an installation comprising a wall painted in a camouflage pattern and a big wedding cake with the name Othello written on it. On top of the cake, he placed the traditional figures of a bride and a groom, in this case personified as O.J. Simpson and a white bride. The installation also presented a pile of mattresses, medical supplies and other elements relating to the subject of illness.

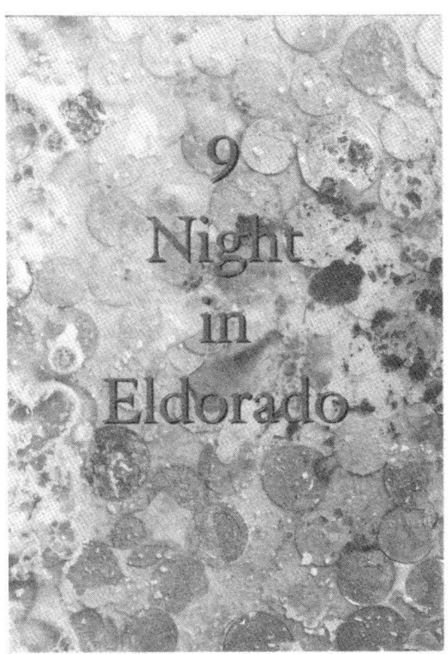

Invitation for the exhibition '9 Night in Eldorado', South London Gallery, 1997

1996

Rodney participated in two group exhibitions which explored connections between art, science, illness and the human body. For the exhibition 'Body Visual' (2 May – 27 May), Rodney presented works alongside the artists Helen Chadwick and Letizia Galli at Barbican Centre, London. Rodney's contribution was the large-scale colour photographic triptych *Flesh of My Flesh* (1996, pp. 100–101). The left and right panels featured knots of Rodney's and the artist Rose Finn-Kelcey's hair magnified under an electron microscope. The central panel shows a photograph of a scar from Rodney's own thigh, left after a hip operation.

The group exhibition 'The Invisible & The Visible: Representing the Body in Contemporary Art and Society' (21 September – 26 October) took place at The Wellcome Trust, London. Rodney exhibited with Vito Acconci, Sutapa Biswas, Louise Bourgeois, Tania Bruguera, Nancy Burson and David Kramlich, Maureen Connor, Brian Jenkins, Bruce Nauman, Virginia Nimarkoh, Yoko Ono, Jayne Parker, Doris Salcedo and Louis K Wilson.

Rodney received the Paul Hamlyn Foundation Award for Sculpture & Installation.

1997

Rodney's last solo exhibition, '9 Night in Eldorado', took place at South London Gallery (10 September – 12 October). It was his first solo show in London since 1989. The exhibition included works such as *My Mother. My Father. My Sister. My Brother* (1997), a tiny house made of his own skin retrieved after one of his numerous operations and *Psalms* (1997, pp. 114–115), a computer-programmed motorised wheelchair that navigated through the gallery, avoiding every obstacle that came in its way. The title of the exhibition referred to his father's favourite movie, *El Dorado*, a classic western from 1966, as well as to the Jamaican Nine Night mourning tradition.

Rodney successfully applied to the Digital Arts & Disabled People Scheme, set up by Arts Council of England and organised through the International Association of Visual Arts. The funding allowed him to take multimedia training to initiate one of his final projects, *Autoicon* (1997–2000, pp. 118–119).

1998

Donald Rodney died in London on 4 March at the age of 36.

Selected Bibliography

Aghedo, Nayaba 'I want to be John Barnes…', *City Life* (November 1990)

Aikens, Nick, & Elizabeth Kristiana Robles (eds.) *The Place Is Here: The Work of Black Artists in 1980s Britain* (Berlin, Germany: Sternberg Press, 2019)

Alison, Jane & Mary Ann Caws (eds.), *The Surreal House* (exh. cat.) (London & New Haven, CT: Barbican Art Gallery in association with Yale University Press, 2010)

Archer, Michael, 'Searchlight' *Art Monthly*, no.128 (July/August 1989)

Ascherson, Neal et al., *Shocks to the System: Social and Political Issues in Recent British Art from the Arts Council Collection* (exh. cat.) (London: Arts Council of Great Britain, 1991)

Bailey, David A. & Allison Thomson (eds.) *Liberation Begins in the Imagination: Writings on Caribbean-British Art* (London: Tate, 2021)

Bailey, David A., Zarina Bhimji, Sonia Boyce, Roshini Kempadoo, Keith Piper and Donald Rodney, *Black markets: Images of Black People in Advertising and Packaging 1880–1990* (exh. cat.) (Manchester: Cornerhouse, 1990)

Beauchamp-Byrd, Mora J. (ed.), Transforming the Crown: African, Asian and Caribbean Artists in Britain, 1966–1996 (exh. cat.) (New York: Caribbean Cultural Center, 1997)

Bernier, Celeste-Marie, '"X is for X Ray, X Slave, X Colony:" A "Lexicon of Liberation" versus "My Slave History" in the Paintings, Installations and Sketchbooks of Donald Rodney' in Celeste-Marie Bernier & Hannah Durkin (eds.), *Visualising Slavery: Art Across the African Diaspora* (Liverpool: Liverpool University Press, 2016) 218–48.

Bernier, Celeste-Marie, *Stick to the Skin: African American and Black British Art, 1965–2015*, (Oakland, California: University of California Press, 2018)

Bhimji, Zarina, Chila Burman, Jennifer Comrie, Keith Piper, Donald Rodney and Allan de Souza, The Devil's Feast (exh. cat.) (London: Chelsea School of Art, 1987)

Biggs, Bryan (ed.) 'Trophies of Empire' (exh. cat.) (Liverpool: Bluecoat Gallery and Liverpool John Moores University, 1994)

Birkett, Richard, *Donald Rodney: Autoicon* (London: Afterall Books, 2023)

Buck, Louisa, 'Moving The Goalpost', *New Statesman and Society* (21 September 1990)

Chambers, 'Who'd a Thought It? Exploring the Interplay Between the Work of Frida Kahlo and Donald Rodney', *Wasafiri: International Contemporary Writing*, issue 71 (Autumn 2012) 22–33.

Chambers, Eddie (ed.), *Let the Canvas Come to Life with Dark Faces* (exh. cat.) (Coventry: Herbert Art Gallery & Museum, 1990)

Chambers, Eddie, 'Breakthrough: Donald Rodney's X-Ray Vision', *Royal Academy of Arts Magazine,* no. 151 (Summer 2021)

Chambers, Eddie, 'His Catechism: The Art of Donald Rodney', *Third Text*, no. 44 (Autumn 1998) 43–54.

Chambers, Eddie, 'Liberator armed with paintbrush', *7 Days* (26 July 1986) n.p.

Chambers, Eddie, 'Problematic Space', *Race Today* (June/July 1987) 27.

Chambers, Eddie, 'Three Songs on Pain, Light and Time', *Art Monthly* No. 200 (October 1996) 65–66.

Chambers, Eddie, 'Trophies of Empire', *Art Monthly*, no. 162 (December/January 1992) 13–15.

Chambers, Eddie, 'Winner Takes It All', *Frieze,* no. 243 (May 2024) 20–21.

Chambers, Eddie, *Black Artists in British Art: A History since the 1950s* (London: I.B. Tauris, 2014)

Chambers, Eddie, Claudette Johnson, Eric Pemberton, Wenda Leslie, Keith Piper, Donald Rodney and Janet Vernon, *The Pan-Afrikan Connection* (exh. cat.) (Nottingham: The Midland Group, 1983)

Chambers, Eddie, Claudette Johnson, Wenda Leslie, Keith Piper, Donald Rodney and Janet Vernon, *The Pan-Afrikan Connection: An Exhibition of Work by Young Black Artists* (exh. cat.) (Coventry: Herbert Art Gallery, 1983)

Cheddie, Janice 'Looking for Eldorado: Donald Rodney's Early Sketchbooks', *Mousse,* issue 85 (Fall 2023) 57–61.

Clark, Robert 'Truth, Dare, Double Dare', The Guardian (27 June 1995)

Coles, Pippa, Matthew Higgs and Jacqui Poncelet, *The British Art Show 5* (exh. cat.) (London: Haywood Gallery Publishing, 2000)

Cooper, Emmanuel, 'On Black Art', *Time Out* (1–8 February 1989)

Corner, Lena, 'A Body of Work', *The Big Issue,* no. 179 (29 April – 5 May 1996)

Correia, Alice (ed.) *What Is Black Art?: Writings on African, Asian and Caribbean Art in Britain, 1981–1989* (UK: Penguin Books, 2022)

Correia, Alice, 'Self-Portraiture and Representations of Blackness in the Work of Donald Rodney', *Nka Journal of Contemporary African Art,* issue 45 (November 2019) 74–86.

Currah, Mark, 'Donald Rodney: Chisenhale' *City Limits,* no. 384 (9–16 February 1989)

Das, Jareh, 'Illness as Metaphor: Donald Rodney's X-Ray Photographs', *Nka Journal of Contemporary African Art,* issue 45 (November 2019) 88–98.

Das, Jareh, Carolyn Lazard and Robert Leckie, 'In Conversation: Things Arrive Together as Suffused and Inseparable', *Mousse,* issue 85 (Fall 2023) 49–54.

Doy, Gen, *Black Visual Culture: Modernity & Post Modernity* (London: I.B. Tauris, 2000)

Edge, Sarah, *Breaths: Art, Health and Empowerment: Donald Rodney, Mary Duffy, Rosy Martin* (exh. cat.) (Rochdale: Rochdale Art Gallery, 1991)

Farr, Ragnar, *Mirage: Enigmas of Race, Difference and Desire* (exh. cat.) (London: Institute of Contemporary Arts & Institute of International Visual Arts, 1995)

Finn Kelcey, Rose, Donald Rodney, Ivan Unwin and Graham Young, *The Suitcase Show* (exh. cat.) (London: Film and Video Umbrella, 1988)

Finn-Kelcey, Rose, Guy Brett and Donald Rodney, *Truth, Dare, Double-Dare* (exh. cat.) (Birmingham: Ikon Gallery, 1994)

Furse, John, TSWA Four Cities Project, *Art Monthly*, No. 140 (October 1990) 14–15.

Gartside, Mike 'Trophies of Empire', *Venue Magazine* (18 December 1992) n.p.

Grant, Simon, 'Truth, Dare, Double Dare, *Liveart Magazine,* no. 2 (4 July–4 September 1995) 15–16.

Himid, Lubaina, Donald Rodney and Maud Sulter, *Donald Rodney: Critical* (exh. cat.) (Rochdale: Rochdale Art Gallery, 1990)

Hutchinson, Ishion, 'In the Archive: Donald Rodney's "Splash Crowns"', *Tate Etc.,* issue 43 (Summer 2018)

Hylton, Richard, *Donald Rodney: Art, Race and the Body Politic* (London: Bloomsbury Publishing, 2025)

Hylton, Richard, *Donald Rodney: Doublethink* (London: Autograph ABP, 2003)

Joynes, Christine E., 'Optical Allusions? Exploring the Ambiguity of Biblical Texts in Modern and Contemporary Art' in Ben Quash & Chloë Reddaway (eds), *Theology, Modernity, and the Visual Arts* (Turnhout, Belgium: Brepolis, 2024)

Kent, Sarah, 'Donald Rodney and Keith Piper', *Time Out* (2–9 September 1987)

Kent, Sarah, 'Paint it Black', *Time Out* (17 September 1997)

Kingston, Angela & Elizabeth A. Macgregor (eds.), *Searchlight: Visibility/Surveillance/Regard* (Birmingham: Ikon Gallery, 1989)

Lingwood, James (ed.), *TSWA Four Cities Project: New Work for Different Places* (exh. cat.) (Bristol: TSWA Ltd., 1990)

Marriott, David, *Of Effacement: Blackness and Non-Being* (Stanford, California: Stanford University Press, 2023)

Miller, Peter, 'Donald Rodney and the Cyborg', *PMC Notes*, No. 25 (2023)

Nairne, Sandy, Geoff Dunlop, and John Wyver (eds.) *State of the Art: Ideas & Images in the 1980s* (London: Chatto & Windus in collaboration with Channel 4, 1987)

Owusu, Kwesi 'Donald Rodney: Black Art with a Cutting Edge', *Black Arts in London*, issue 64 (16–31 October 1986)

Owusu, Kwesi, *Black British Culture and Society: A Text Reader* (London: Routledge, 2000)

Phillips, Mike & Geoff Cox, 'Donald Rodney: Autoicon. The Death of an Artist' in Ángela Molina Fernández & Kepa Landa (eds.), *Emergent Futures:*

Art, Interactivity and New Media (Valencia: Alfons el Magnanim, 2000)

Phillips, Mike, 'Present in Absentia', *Tate Etc*, issue 62 (Summer 2024)

Piper, Keith (ed.), *Donald Rodney: In Retrospect* (booklet) (London: Institute of Visual Arts, 2008)

Piper, Keith and Marlene Smith, *The Image Employed: The Use of Narrative in Black Art* (exh. cat.) (Manchester: Cornerhouse, 1987)

Piper, Keith, 'In Search of El Dorado', *Tate Etc.*, issue 57 (Spring 2023) 104–107. (Reprinted in this volume, pp. 10–13)

Porter, Cedric, 'In sickness and in Health', *South London Press* (26 September 1997)

Reid, Tricia, 'Explosive Crisis at Chisenhale', *Caribbean Times* (17–23 February 1989)

Rodney, Donald & South London Gallery (eds.), *9 Night in Eldorado* (exh. cat.) (London: South London Gallery, 1997)

Salter, Gregory, 'Intertwining Histories in Donald Rodney's Untitled ('Cowboy and Indian' After David Hockney's 'We Two Boys Together Clinging', 1961), 1989', *Midlands Art Papers*, issue 2 (2018/19) 1–12.

Sebestyen, Amanda, 'Different Diasporas', *New Statesman & Society* (3 February 1989) 49.

Smith, Roberta 'Interrogating Identity', *The New York Times* (17 May 1991)

Smolik, Noemi, 'Four Cities Project', *Kunstforum International* (January/February 1991)

Sokolowski, Thomas W. (ed.), *Interrogating Identity* (exh. cat.) (New York, N.Y.: Grey Art Gallery and Study Center)

Solanke, Adeola, 'Crisis', *Art Monthly*, no.124 (March 1989)

Symons, Diane, 'In the House of My Father: Fragments of Body and Time', in Sonia Boyce (ed.), *PAPER: Returning to the Blk Art Group*, issue 1 (October 2012) n.p. (Reprinted in this volume, pp. 152–158)

Tawadros, Gilane, *The Sphinx Contemplating Napoleon: Global Perspectives on Contemporary Art and Difference* (London: Bloomsbury Visual Arts, 2020)

Tooby, Michael and Nigel Walsh (eds.), *Depicting History for Today* (exh. cat.) (Sheffield & Leeds: Sheffield Arts Department & Leeds City Art Gallery, 1987)

Triscott, Nicola (ed.), *Body Visual* (exh. cat.) (London: Barnican Art Gallery & Arts Catalyst Publications, 1996)

Unger, Miles, 'Interrogating Identity', *Art New England* (December/January 1991)

List of Works

How the West was Won
1982
Acrylic paint on canvas
120 × 121.5 cm
Tate: Presented by the
Donald Rodney Estate 2007

The House that Jack Built
1987
Mixed media
183 × 183 cm
Sheffield Museums

Britannia Hospital 2
1988
Oil pastel on X-ray
122 × 244 cm
Sheffield Museums
Displayed at Spike Island
and Whitechapel Gallery

Britannia Hospital 3
1988
Oil pastel on X-ray
183 × 447 cm
Sheffield Museums
Displayed at Spike
Island and Nottingham
Contemporary

Preparatory drawings for
Soweto/Guernica
1988
Ink on six paper sheets
(34.5 × 145.8 cm); ink on
five paper sheets (20.5 ×
147.5 cm); photocopy on
four acetate sheets (29.8 ×
165.9 cm)
Wolverhampton Art
Gallery

Untitled ('Cowboy and Indian'
after David Hockney's 'We
Two Boys Together Clinging',
1961)
1989
Charcoal on paper
156.5 × 120.9 cm
Wolverhampton Art
Gallery

Black Markets Prints
(Untitled, Black Sapphire)
1990
Digital giclee print on paper
59.4 × 84.1 cm
The Donald Rodney Estate

Black Markets Prints
(Untitled, Mandingo)
1990
Digital giclee print on paper
59.4 × 84.1 cm
The Donald Rodney Estate

Self Portrait: Black Men
Public Enemy
1990
Lightboxes with Duratrans
prints
190.5 × 121.9 cm
Arts Council Collection,
Southbank Centre, London

Visceral Canker
1990
Perspex, wood, silicon
tubing, gold leaf, plastic
bags and electrical pump
4 panels: 122 × 91 cm; 155
× 91 cm; 122 × 91 cm; 122 ×
91 cm
Tate: Presented by Tate
Members 2009

Untitled
c. 1991
Eight oil pastel drawings on
X-rays
Each approx. 30 × 20 cm
The Donald Rodney Estate

Cataract
1991
Projection with 240 slides
to fit 3 projectors
Dimensions variable
The Donald Rodney Estate

John Barnes
1991
Duratrans print on
aluminium framed lightbox
with fluorescent tube lights
107 × 80.8 × 16.7 cm
The British Council
Collection

Mexico Olympics
1991
Duratrans print on
aluminium framed lightbox
with fluorescent tube lights
107 × 80.8 × 16.7 cm
The British Council
Collection

Doublethink
1992
Trophies with engraved
texts (Glass cabinet, larger
trophies and engraved
captions with Eddie
Chambers)
Dimensions variable
The Donald Rodney Estate

Untitled
1994
Mixed media and magazine
cuttings on paper
38.5 × 31 cm
UK Government Art
Collection

Untitled
1994
Paper, mixed media,
magazines
44 × 36 cm
The Donald Rodney Estate

Preparatory photographs
for *Flesh of My Flesh*
c. 1996
Twelve colour photographs
on paper
The Donald Rodney Estate

Flesh of My Flesh
1996
Colour photograph on
aluminium
three panels: 139 × 92 cm;
10 × 92 cm; 110 × 92 cm
South London Gallery
collection, managed by
Southwark Council as
part of the Southwark Art
Collection

Bible
1979–96
printed paper
15 × 10 × 3 cm
The Donald Rodney Estate
Displayed at Whitechapel
Gallery

Arts Council (Collection)
1984–86
1997
Plaster cast
22 × 2 × 1 cm
The Donald Rodney Estate
Displayed at Whitechapel
Gallery

Black Comedy 1
1997
Vinyl and paint on acrylic
sheet
99.3 × 126.3 cm
Tate: Presented by the
executors of the Donald
Rodney Estate 2021

Black Comedy 2
1997
Vinyl and paint on acrylic
sheet
91.4 × 109.1 cm
Tate: Presented by the
executors of the Donald
Rodney Estate 2021

Camouflage
1997
Textile
300 × 862 cm
The Donald Rodney Estate
Displayed at Whitechapel
Gallery

In the House of My Father
1997
Photograph
123 × 153 cm
Arts Council Collection,
Southbank Centre,
London

My Catechism
1997
20 plaster casts
each: 30 × 22 × 5 cm
Tate: Purchased 2005

My Mother. My Father.
My Sister. My Brother
1997
Human skin and pins
2 × 3 × 2 cm
Courtesy The Estate of
Donald Rodney. On long
term loan to Amgueddfa
Cymru – Museum Wales
Displayed at Spike
Island and Nottingham
Contemporary

Psalms
1997
Motorised wheelchair,
laptop, 8 sensors and video
camera
93 × 65 × 110 cm
Tate: Purchased with
funds provided by Tate
International Council 2021

Pygmalion
1997
Animatronic sculpture,
wood and textile
145 × 79.5 × 79.5 cm
Lent by Birmingham
Museums Trust on behalf
of Birmingham City
Council

Autoicon
1997–2000
CD-ROM, digitally
transferred
Dimensions variable
The Donald Rodney Estate

Sketchbooks
1982–98
Sketchbook nos. 9, 18, 23,
24, 26, 28, 30, 36, 38, 41
from series of 48
Each: 21.5 × 15 cm
Tate Archive: purchased
from Diane Symons, on
behalf of the Executors
of the Estate of Donald
Rodney

Black Audio Film
Collective
Three Songs on Pain, Time
and Light
1995
Colour SD video with
stereo sound
25 mins
Courtesy of Smoking Dogs
Films and Lisson Gallery

List of Works

Reproduction Credits

All images © The Donald Rodney Estate

Rasheed Araeen courtesy of Grosvenor Gallery. Image: Sharjah Art Foundation. Photo: Danko Stjepanovic p. 28

The Donald Rodney Estate pp. 29, 66–71, 72 (below), 73, 75–81, 85–87, 92–93, 96–97, 99–102, 104–111, 115–116, 118–119, 139, 163, 193–194, 195 (above), 196 (below), 197 (above), 198–199

The Donald Rodney Estate. Photo: David Lewis p. 21

The Donald Rodney Estate. Photo: Diane Symons back cover

The Donald Rodney Estate. Photo: Vivienne Reiss p. 197 (below)

The Donald Rodney Estate. Photo: Eddie Chambers p. 62

© Jo Spence Memorial Archive, The Image Centre p. 42

The Museum of Modern Art, New York/Scala, Florence p. 59

Keith Piper pp. 11, 148

Photo Schalkwijk/Art Resource/Scala, Florence pp. 55, 60

Arts Council Collection, Southbank Centre, London © David Hockney. Photo: Prudence Cuming Associates p. 142

© UCL Educational Media p. 162

Photo © Tate pp. 65, 120–128, 133

Nottingham Contemporary. Photo: Frederic Griffiths pp. 72 (above), 88–89, 196 (above)

Nottingham Contemporary. Photo: Lewis Ronald pp. 74, 90–91, 94–95, 103, 112–114

Spike Island, Bristol. Photo: Lisa Whiting p. 117

© UK Government Art Collection p. 98

Reproduction by permission of Wolverhampton Art Gallery p. 82–83

All texts reproduced by kind permission of the authors and publishers

© 2018, The Regents of the University of California. Published by the University of California Press pp. 14–25

© 2019, Nka Publications. All rights reserved pp. 26–37

Taylor & Francis and Copyright Clearance Center pp. 50–64

Mousse Magazine & Publishing pp. 129–136, pp. 174–182

© Estate of Maud Sulter. All rights reserved, DACS 2024 pp. 189–191

***Donald Rodney: Visceral Canker* has been generously supported by:**

Weston Loan Programme with Art Fund
Henry Moore Foundation
Paul Mellon Centre for Studies in British Art
Pilgrim Trust

Art Fund_

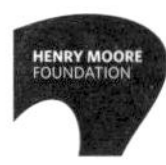

Garfield Weston
FOUNDATION

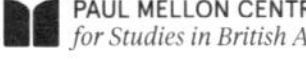

HENRY MOORE
FOUNDATION

PAUL MELLON CENTRE
for Studies in British Art

Pilgrim
Trust

Fine Art Insurance Partner

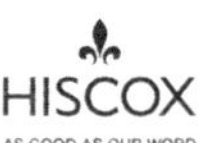

HISCOX
AS GOOD AS OUR WORD

Special thanks to:
Judy Aitken, Sepake Angiama, Richard Birkett, Siobhán Britton, Carolyn Charles, Paula Cooper, Geoff Cox, Emma Dexter, Peter Dunn, Eliza Gluckman, Naomi Greaves, Lubaina Himid, Richard Hylton, Kaitlene Koranteng, Elizabeth Lindley, Matthew Lindop, Clare Marlow, Trevor Mathison, Rita Matos, Emma McMullen, Mousse Magazine & Publishing, Emily Oldfield, Alona Pardo, Mike Phillips, Keith Piper, Vivienne Reiss, Ian Sergeant, Polly Staple, Gary Stewart, Diane Symons, Sam Thorne and Salma Tuqan

Whitechapel Gallery would like to thank its supporters, whose generosity enables the Gallery to realise its pioneering programmes:

Major Donors and Supporters
Arts Council England Catalyst Endowment Fund
Sir Frank Bowling
Bloomberg Philanthropies
D. Daskalopoulos Collection
Ford Foundation
Foyle Foundation
Freelands Foundation
Collezione Maramotti
Max Mara
Paul Mellon Centre for Studies in British Art
The Rose Foundation
Terra Foundation for American Art
Michael and Nina Zilkha
and those who wish to remain anonymous

Exhibitions Programme
A/POLITICAL
Toluwani Adejuyigbe
Ayo Adeyinka
Aldgate Connect BID
Cockayne – Grants
    for the Arts
Collezione Maramotti
Hauser & Wirth
Henry Moore Foundation
Hiscox
Max Mara
Bimpe Nkontchou
Oba Nsugbe
Paul Mellon Centre for
    Studies in British Art
Richard Saltoun Gallery
TrAIN Research Centre
    at University of the
    Arts London
The Whitechapel Gallery
    Commissioning Council
The Whitechapel Gallery
    Patrons
and those who wish to
    remain anonymous

**Participation & Public
Programmes**
The 29th May 1961
    Charitable Trust
Aldgate Connect BID
Big Give
Capital Group
Kurt Forrest Foundation
Phillips
Tower Hamlets Arts
    & Music Education
    Service (THAMES)
The London Borough of
    Tower Hamlets
Glenn Sujo
Stanley Picker Trust
The Whitechapel Gallery
    Education Council

**Whitechapel Gallery
Corporate Patrons and
Members**
Alma
Bloomberg Philanthropies
Frasers Property UK
Gazelli Art House
Lisson Gallery
Phillips

**Whitechapel Gallery
Corporate Supporters**
Aldgate Connect BID
Bloomberg Philanthropies
Champagne Pommery
Crozier Fine Arts
Fredrigoni
Hiscox (Fine Art Insurance
    Partner)
Max Mara
Collezione Maramotti
Omni Colour
    (Signage Partner)
Phillips

**Whitechapel Gallery
Commissioning Council**
Dorota Audemars
Erin Bell
Émilie De Pauw
Irene Panagopoulos
Nicole Saikalis Bay

**Whitechapel Gallery
Education Council**
Julie and Debashis Dey
Alex Sainsbury

**Whitechapel Gallery
Global Circle**
Faisal Tamer and
    Sara Alireza
and those who wish to
    remain anonymous

**Whitechapel Gallery
Director's Circle**
Erin Bell and
    Michael Cohen
Pilar Corrias
Julie and Debashis Dey
Bimpe Nkontchou
Anthea Peers
Thatcher and
    Jill Thompson
and those who wish to
    remain anonymous

**Whitechapel Gallery
Curator's Circle**
Annette Anthony
Bella Kesoyan
Adrian and Jennifer
    O'Carroll
Oba Nsugbe
Audrey Wallrock
and those who wish to
    remain anonymous

**Whitechapel Gallery
Patrons**
Malgosia Alterman
Cedric Bardawil
Sadie Coles HQ
Francesca Consigli
Sarah Elson
Joanna and Alan Gemes
Mark Harris
Pippy Houldsworth
Marie Krauss
Frank Krikhaar
Kate MacGarry
Dr. Vali Mahlouji
Mary E McNicholas
Heike Moras
Maureen Paley
Dominic Palfreyman
Darryl de Prez and
    Victoria Thomas
Maria-Cruz Rashidian
Marina Roncarolo
Marina Ruiz-Colomer
Alex Sainsbury and
    Elinor Jansz
Cherrill and Ian Scheer
Veronica Schwabach
Elisabeth von Schwarzkopf
Amar Singh
Karen and Mark Smith
Bina and Philippe von
    Stauffenberg
Christoph and
    Marion Trestler
and those who wish to
    remain anonymous

We remain grateful for
the ongoing support of
Whitechapel Gallery
Members.

Whitechapel Gallery is
proud to be a National
Portfolio Organisation of
Arts Council England.

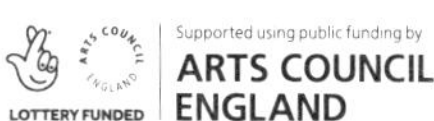

Published on the occasion of the exhibition
Donald Rodney: Visceral Canker

Spike Island, Bristol
25 May – 8 September 2024

Nottingham Contemporary
27 September 2024 – 5 January 2025

Whitechapel Gallery, London
12 February – 4 May 2025

Exhibition
Donald Rodney: Visceral Canker is curated by
Robert Leckie (Director, Gasworks) and
Nicole Yip (Director, Spike Island).

Spike Island
Director: Nicole Yip
Curator: Carmen Juliá
Curatorial Assistant: Diana Lage
Senior Technician: Olivia Jones
Senior AV Technician: Oliver Sutherland

Nottingham Contemporary
Director: Salma Tuqan
Chief Curator: Ali Roche
Curator of Exhibitions: Katie Simpson
Assistant Curator of Exhibitions:
    Niall Farrelly
Gallery Technical Manager: David Thomas
Technician (AV): Jim Brouwer

Whitechapel Gallery
Director: Gilane Tawadros
Head of Exhibitions: Leila Hasham
Curator: Cameron Foote
Curatorial Assistant: Carolina Jozami
Gallery Technical Manager: Luke Edwards
Technical Production Manager:
    Sam Williams

First published 2025 by Whitechapel
Gallery in collaboration with Spike Island
and Nottingham Contemporary

Publication
Editors: Nicole Yip, Robert Leckie,
    Gilane Tawadros and Cameron Foote
Copy Editor: Hannah Young
Publications Coordinator: Joel Cosson
Designed by Mark El-khatib
Printed by Graphius, Belgium

ISBN: 978-0-85488-325-7

A catalogue record for this book is available
from the British Library.

Whitechapel Gallery
77-82 Whitechapel High Street
London E1 7QX
whitechapelgallery.org

Distributed outside the
United States and Canada by:
Thames & Hudson
181a High Holborn
London WC1V 7QX
Tel: +44 (0)20 7845 5000
sales@thameshudson.co.uk

Distributed in the
United States and Canada by:
Artbook / D.A.P.
75 Broad Street, Suite 630
New York, NY 10004
Tel: +1 (212) 627 199

Spike Island   Nottingham Contemporary   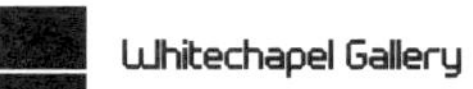 Whitechapel Gallery